THE BOMBAY ARTILLERY
LIST OF OFFICERS

OFFICER BOMBAY HORSE ARTILLERY, 1846.

SAID TO BE LIEUT. AND RIDING-MASTER JAMES RANDALL ON A CHARGER, THE
PROPERTY OF CAPTAIN A. W. ST. CLAIR.

(Reproduced by permission from Ackerman's " Costumes of the Indian Army.")

THE

BOMBAY ARTILLERY

LIST OF OFFICERS

WHO HAVE SERVED IN

THE REGIMENT OF BOMBAY ARTILLERY

FROM ITS FORMATION IN 1749 TO AMALGAMATION WITH
THE ROYAL ARTILLERY, WITH DATES OF FIRST COMMISSIONS,
PROMOTIONS, CASUALTIES, ALSO APPOINTMENTS HELD,
WAR SERVICES, HONOURS, AND REWARDS

LIST OF MEDICAL AND VETERINARY OFFICERS OF THE
BOMBAY ARMY POSTED TO THE BOMBAY ARTILLERY,
OR WHO SERVED IN THE FIELD WITH THE REGIMENT;
ALSO LISTS OF RIDING-MASTERS, QUARTER-MASTERS,
AND MEN COMMISSIONED FOR DUTY IN DEPARTMENTS

*A FEW REMARKS ON THE EARLY DAYS OF THE
REGIMENT, GIVING CHANGES IN DESIGNATION,
AND WAR SERVICE OF TROOPS AND COMPANIES*

COMPILED BY

COLONEL F. W. M. SPRING
RETIRED PAY ROYAL ARTILLERY

The Naval & Military Press Ltd

❖

Reproduced by kind permission of the Central Library,
Royal Military Academy, Sandhurst

Published by

The Naval & Military Press Ltd

Unit 10, Ridgewood Industrial Park,

Uckfield, East Sussex,

TN22 5QE England

Tel: +44 (0) 1825 749494

Fax: +44 (0) 1825 765701

www.naval-military-press.com

© The Naval & Military Press Ltd 2005

INTRODUCTION.

ON seeing Major Leslie's list of Madras Artillery Officers, I addressed the Secretary R.A. Institution, inquiring if the publication of a list of Bombay Artillery Officers was contemplated, offering to do my best to compile a list, if not already in hand, and thus, with General Stubbs's history of the Bengal Artillery, complete the records of the three Indian Corps. My offer was gratefully accepted by the Committee of the R.A. Institution, and the following compilation is the result of research among the records of the India Office.

I regret existing records do not permit the services of the original companies being made more complete; but what has been elicited regarding the early days of the Regiment, will, I trust, be found to contain much of interest to the officers of the Royal Regiment of Artillery, and to relatives of deceased officers of the Bombay Artillery.

My thanks are due to the Secretary of State for India, for access to the records; and to officers of all departments of the India Office, for their invariable courtesy and aid; to the Government of Bombay; the Committee of the R.A. Institution and its Secretary, Major A. C. T. Boileau, R.A.; to Colonel E. S. Standbridge, R.A., Inspector-General of Ordnance, Southern Circle, India; also to officers and others who have helped with information or documents, especially General H. Le Cocq, Colonel Commandant R.A., Major-General T. C. Crowe, Colonels T. N. Holberton and E. S. Torriano, retired R.A.

F. W. M. SPRING.

CONTENTS.

———●◦●———

PART I.

PART II.

PART III.

PART IV.

PART V.

PART VI.

PART VII.

PART VIII.

LIST OF ILLUSTRATIONS.

ABBREVIATIONS.

b. Born.
d. Died.
ret. Retired.
res. Resigned.
R.M.A. Royal Military Academy, Woolwich.
Addis. Military Seminary, Addiscombe.
g. General.
l.g. Lieutenant-General.
m.g. Major-General.
u.s.l. Unemployed supernumerary list.
commdt. Commandant of Bombay Artillery.
col. commdt. Colonel Commandant R.A.
c. Colonel.
brev.- Brevet of.
l.c. commdt. Lieut.-Colonel Commandant.
l.c. Lieut.-Colonel.
m. Major.
cap. Captain.
cap.-l. Captain-Lieutenant.
l. Lieutenant.
lfw. Lieutenant Fireworker.
ante-d. Ante-dated.
C.I.C. Commander-in-Chief.
A.D.C. Aide-de-Camp to the Queen.
a.d.c. Aide-de-Camp.
I.G.O. Inspector General of Ordnance.
G.P. Agent for Gunpowder and Superintendent of Factory.
G.C. Agent for Gun-Carriage and Superintendent of Factory.
Ordce. Ordnance Department.
adjt. Adjutant.
qtrmt. Quartermaster.
intpt. Interpreter.
Goldze. Golundauze.
[R] Reward for distinguished and meritorious Service.
M. Medal.
cl. Clasp.

Batt. Battalion.
A.A.G. Assistant Adjutant-General.
D.A.QM.G. Deputy-Assistant-Quartermaster-General.
G.O. General Officer.
C.R.A. Commanding R.A.
O.C. Officer Commanding.
C.M. Court-Martial.

NOTE.—The numbers after officers' names refer, for officers of the Bombay Artillery, to the List at pp. 67–114; to Kane's List, 4th edition, for officers of the Royal Artillery; to Major-General F. W. Stubbs's List (published in 1892), for officers of the Bengal Artillery; and to Major J. H. Leslie's List (published in 1901), for officers of the Madras Artillery.

THE
EARLY DAYS OF THE REGIMENT.

THE BOMBAY ARTILLERY.

PART I.

THE EARLY DAYS OF THE REGIMENT.

THE old regimental Records say that, prior to the year 1748, the Bombay Artillery existed only as a part of the Bombay Regiment (2nd Battalion Royal Dublin Fusiliers), to the several companies of which a small detail was assigned, and the whole denominated the "Gun-room Crew." The first muster-roll found is dated York Fort, 1 December, 1708, and is as follows :—

Gunner, Peter Warren.
Gunner's mate, Daniel Daniel.
Assistants, Thomas French.
   ,,   Anthony Madras.
   ,,   Newree Cawn Lascar.
Cooper, Peter Masson.

Cooper, Itaman padree.
Carpenter, Thomas Field.
Chief Guardian of Staves, James Clarck.
Sub-Guardian, William Robinson.

1710. The Gunner is also styled "Gentleman of Arms."
1714. Gunner, Thomas Morgan.
1715. Gunner, Thomas Page.
1716. In January, 1716, Captain George Vane, Engineer, heads the roll, promoted to Major, October, 1718, and disappears.
1718. Gunner, Matthew Wood.
1724. Master-Gunner, P. Passwater.
1726. Master-Gunner, William Saunderson.
1729. Master-Gunner, W. Saunderson, styled "Captain of the Artillery."
1733. Master-Gunner and Captain of the Artillery, Thomas Mace.
1745. Master-Gunner, Isaac Ainsworth.
1746. Master-Gunner, Hugh Cameron (1).
1748. In June, 1748, the Honourable Court of Directors of the East India Company sent out the following instructions for the formation of a company of Artillery :—

REGULATIONS FOR THE FORMING, DISCIPLINING, AND GOVERNING A
COMPANY OF ARTILLERY AT BOMBAY, AND FOR THE BETTER
MANAGING, AND KEEPING IN GOOD ORDER, THE ORDNANCE, SMALL
ARMS, AND MILITARY STORES, TOOLS, UTENSILS, AND OTHER HABILI-
MENTS OF WAR.

As it is intended to abolish the offices of Gunners, Mates, Quarter-
Gunners, and Gun-room Crew, and to substitute in lieu of them a regular
Company of Artillery for the better defence of our Settlements in time of
danger, and for the training of a regular and disciplined Corps for the
Ordnance Service, we do hereby order, for the more easy attaining this
end, that the following Regulations be strictly followed and observed :—

1st. That the said Company of Artillery do consist of one Second Captain,
one Captain Lieutenant and Director of the Laboratory, one First
Lieutenant Fireworker, one Second Lieutenant Fireworker, one
Ensign Fireworker, four Sergeants Bombardiers, four Corporal Bombardiers, two Drummers, and one hundred Gunners.

2nd. That the formation of this Company of Artillery shall be set about as
soon as can be after receipt of this ; but as we hope to engage Major
John Goodyere (R.A. 37), now Chief Officer of the Train, under the
Honourable Admiral Boscawen, to reside abroad in our service, on
the same conditions and in the same rank we have engaged Majors
Mosman and Lawrence, and as we intend him to command the
Military at Bombay, according to the Military Regulations newly
made, the formation of the Company of Artillery is to be suspended
till the arrival of the said Major ; and in the mean time the officers
Atkinson (2) and Madox (3) are to be employed in training, teaching,
and disciplining such as may by the Governor, and the first of these
officers, be thought fit men, according to these Regulations for the
Ordnance Service ; but on the arrival of Major Goodyere, he, with
the approbation of the Governor, shall direct the formation of the
Company of Artillery in the manner most suitable to the Service ;
and in case Major Goodyere should not accept of the proposal made
to him by us, or should not arrive at Bombay in the next season
after his acceptance of our proposals, the Governor is to appoint
the next capable Military Officer who shall be in our service at the
time it is known that Major Goodyere either refuses to come into
our service, or that the time for his arrival at Bombay is elapsed, to
form the said Company of Artillery, with his approbation, according to these Regulations, and to act as Captain thereof, as well as
Commander of all the other Military Companies, till the arrival of
Major Goodyere, or till the Court of Directors order otherwise.

3rd. The officers and others already engaged for the service of the Artillery
are to be placed immediately in the several ranks they are engaged
for, in which they are to continue till promoted, unless, by com-
mitting any crimes or offence, they shall be broke by the judgment
of a Court Martial, or dismissed by order of the Court of Directors.

4th. That such of those belonging to the Gun-room as have behaved well, and can give proof of being qualified to serve in the Artillery, be admitted into this Company, in such rank as on trial by the Governor, Major, or next Officer of the Artillery may judge them fit for.

5th. In case any of the Officers, or others belonging to the Company of Artillery in his Majesty's Service under the command of Admiral Boscawen, should obtain leave to stay in the East Indies, in order to enter into the service of the Company, they shall be admitted into such vacant employments as the Governor and Major may judge them qualified for; but as it is intended the Second Captain is to be an Engineer, no one is to be admitted into that rank who hath not a competent knowledge and experience in that profession; it is therefore intended to keep that post open till a person so qualified is named by the Court of Directors.

6th. In order to complete the Company of Artillery as soon as possible, a sufficient number of young, healthy, able-bodied, and most sober men from among the Soldiers, or others belonging to the other Companies, are to be taught the exercise of the Artillery, among whom it is recommended to have as many as possible who have been bred to the occupation of smiths, carpenters, or some other trade or business which may be of use in the service of the Artillery, as also such as can read and write, and seem to have the best capacity to learn the several parts of duty proper for the Ordnance Service; and as soon as they shall have made a sufficient progress in the Artillery exercise, they shall be discharged from the Companies they belong to and entered into the Company of Artillery, and promoted in it according to their merit; and that there may be always a supply of men proper to recruit the Company of Artillery, the Major is to take care that a sufficient number of men, qualified as above as much as possible, be continually instructed in the Artillery discipline for that purpose, our intention being that the Company of Artillery be at all times complete; and in case any person admitted into the Company of Artillery misbehave, so as not to be fit to continue in it, he shall, on the judgment of a Court Martial, be obliged to serve the remainder of his time in the Company he was taken from.

7th. So soon as the Company of Artillery consists of a sufficient number of Officers and Gunners to do the duty of the Gunner and the Gun-room Crew (which, it is strongly recommended, may be as soon as possible), the offices of Gunner and of all belonging to the Gun-room are to be abolished.

8th. The Officers of the Company of Artillery are to take care to teach all persons belonging to the same Company in the practice of Gunnery in general, as the manner of serving and firing all sorts of pieces of Artillery, whether designed for the throwing of shot, shells, stones, grenades, carcasses, or other fireworks. They are to teach them the use and construction of all the instruments used for pointing or levelling great guns or mortars, and to exercise them at convenient times in the hitting marks, whether point-blank, or at any degree of elevation, together with quick firing, for which a proper quantity of ammunition is to be allowed ; they are likewise to instruct them in the making of gabions and fascines, with the manner to use them, in making batteries or breastworks, as also the manner of making instruments, whether of defence or approaches ; and they are likewise to teach them the manner to mount or dismount cannon, or mortar, and to remove them from place to place, at which they are to be exercised at proper times, but so as not to over-fatigue them, or give them disgust to the service ; but the knowledge of this exercise is necessary, as in time of danger no other assistance can be got to this work.

9th. The Artillery Company is to be taught and perfected in the Military exercise of small arms in all its parts, in the same manner as the other Companies are taught, and is to be reviewed in common with the rest of the Garrison towards the end of each month; they shall likewise go through a general exercise of Artillery once in each month, at which the Governor or some of the Council, and the Major or Officer Commanding the Companies, shall be present ; and twice, at least, in every year they shall perform a solemn exercise to fire at marks, and throw shells in presence of the Governor, or Second, and the Major, and to encourage such who perform the best, the Council may order suitable premiums.

10th. The Company of Artillery is to do garrison duty in common, and in proportion with the other Troops, and so many Officers and Gunners are to mount daily as may perform the duty on the platforms and bastions, as was done by the Gun-room Crew heretofore ; and in all respects the Company of Artillery is to be employed as is practised in His Majesty's Garrisons of Gibraltar and Minorca.

11th. No deserter from any nation whatever is to be entertained in the Company of Artillery, not even a British subject who may have once deserted from His Majesty, or the Company's service, although he may have been pardoned for his desertion, nor any Roman Catholic ; and if any persons belonging to the Company of Artillery marry a Roman Catholic, after marriage such person shall be immediately dismissed from the Company of Artillery, and be obliged to serve the remainder of his time in one of the other Companies, or be removed to some other of the Company's settlements to serve it out there, if the Council think fit.

12th. The Major, with the approbation of the Governor, shall regulate the clothing for the Artillery, which is to be of Blue Cloth, out of the Company's warehouses, with Red Cuffs and Facings, and Brass Buttons, with a Cap or Hat which shall be provided by the Major, and paid for by the Company, in the same manner as ordered in the 22nd and 23rd Articles of the Military Regulations ; and the said Company shall be armed in the manner most suitable to the climate, and the nature of their service.

13th. The Company of Artillery is to be paid in the manner by the Military Paymaster, as directed by the 17th, 18th, and 19th Articles of the Military Regulations.

14th. In case of the death of any person belonging to the Company of Artillery, the effects of the deceased are to be taken care of as directed in the 25th Article of the Military Regulations.

15th. The Commission, Non-Commission Officers, and Gunners belonging to the Company of Artillery, are to be promoted, broke, punished, or confined, according to the several Regulations made for the Military in the Company's Service at Bombay, with this distinction, that where an Officer or Gunner belonging to the Artillery is to be tried, so many of the Officers belonging to the Artillery as conveniently can, shall be of the Court Martial; and in all tours of duty, the Officers of the Companies and of the Artillery Company are to roll together, according to their rank and seniority, so far as is consistent with the nature of their different services, and are to have the same Military honours done them. As those who serve in the Artillery may be promoted in the other Companies in case of vacancies, so may those who serve in the other Companies be promoted to vacancies in the Artillery Company, but not unless they have made themselves completely masters of the business and service of the Artillery in all its branches, and give good proofs of their knowledge and experience therein to the satisfaction of the Governor and Major, or Officer Commanding the Companies.

16th. All the posts where cannons or mortars are mounted, or intended to be mounted, shall be visited once in every week, or oftener, by one of the Commission Officers belonging to the Company of Artillery, who is carefully to inspect the Artillery at that part, that the Ordnance, with their carriages, and other appurtenances, be kept in the best order, and if he observe any damage, decay, waste, or embezzlement therein, whether from neglect, the injury of weather, or other causes, he is to make immediate report in writing to the Major, who is to acquaint the Governor therewith, that such damage or waste may be forthwith remedied, and means used to prevent the like for the future. He is at the same time carefully to observe if there be any damage or decay in any of the fortifications or works, and to make report thereof in like manner through the Major to the Governor, that they may be forthwith repaired.

17th. The above Regulations are to be strictly complied with in every Article, and made public in such manner that no one may be ignorant of their contents, so far as he is concerned therein. And as it may be proper to make further Regulations for the Company of Artillery at Bombay than can at present be foreseen, more especially with relation to Detachments sent to the subordinate Garrisons or on parties, it is hereby left to the discretion of the Governor and Council, with the advice of the Major, or Officer Commanding the Companies, to make such further regulations, which they may, from time to time, amend or alter for the good of the

Service, provided such further regulations, alterations, or amendments be not contrary to, and consistent with, the above Regulations.

18th. It is ordered that the Company of Artillery in the East India Company's service consist as follows :—

To reside where the Company's Service may require.

		£	s.	d.
1 First Captain and Chief Engineer ... ... at		200	0	0 per annum

To reside at the Chief Settlements or its Subordinates.

	£	s.	d.	
1 Second Captain and Second Engineer	150	0	0	per annum
1 Captain Lieutenant and Director of the Laboratory	100	0	0	,,
1 First Lieutenant Fireworker	75	0	0	,,
1 Second ,, ,, ...	60	0	0	,,
1 Ensign ,, ,, ...	50	0	0	,,
4 Sergeants Bombardiers ... ... at	0	2	0	per day each
4 Corporals ... ... ,,	0	1	6	,,
100 Gunners ... ... ,,	0	1	0	,,
2 Drummers ... ... ,,	0	1	0	,,

115 Men, exclusive of the Chief Engineer

London, the 17th June, 1748.

1749. Master-Gunner Hugh Cameron (1) was promoted to be the First Captain and Chief Engineer of the Company (1/1, now 86 R.G.A.), and heads the list of Bombay Artillery officers.

1750. On Captain H. Cameron's transfer to the Infantry, October, 1750, Major William Mackenzie became First Captain and Chief Engineer, retaining command of his company of Infantry; and drawing no pay in the Artillery pay-roll, he has therefore not been included in the List. Major Mackenzie also commanded the troops at Bombay, had a seat in Council, was Clerk of the Works and Master of Arms. He commanded the Company of Artillery until 1752, when Captain James de Funck (6) succeeded him, specially engaged for the post, which had apparently been kept open. *Vide* Para. 5 of the Regulations.

1751. In October, 1751, 30 men of the Train went with a force commanded by Captain Lane against Surat. The attempt was unsuccessful, and the force returned to Bombay, May, 1752.

1754. In May, 1754, 300 Topasses sailed for Madras with a force commanded by Captain Forbes, which joined the army under Major Lawrence. The records say the Bombay detachment was present at the battle of the French Rocks with the French, 16 August, 1754; and in 1755, at the capture of Madura and fortified pagoda of Coilgoody, under Lieut.-Colonel Heron; and at the attack by Colleries on 23 May, when the baggage was plundered, and all loot taken was lost. The detachment returned to Bombay, 10 November, 1755. Officers traceable as having been with this force, Lieut. J. W.

Molitore (8), G. Dagon (45), then serving in the ranks of Captain Ziegler's Swiss company of Infantry.

In December, 1754, a detail of Artillery accompanied a force commanded by Captain H. Cameron (1), which occupied Bancote.

1755. Two more companies were raised between January and December (1/2 and 2/1, now 81 and 15 R.F.A.).

1756. Artillery officers at this time were detailed for duty on bomb-ketches and vessels of the H.E.I. Company's service. Two officers, Lieut. S. Young (11) and Lieut. N. B. Burr (14), are shown as being on board the ships under Admiral Watson that conveyed to Gheriah, in February, 1756, the force commanded by Colonel Clive, which effected the capture of that stronghold and complete destruction of the Mahratta fleet. The Artillery was commanded by Captain-Lieut. Jacob Tovey (R.A. 120).

On the 29 October, 1756, a detachment of Artillery embarked for Bengal. The detachment was composed of men of all three Companies (1/1, now 86 R.G.A., 1/2, now 81 R.F.A., and 2/1, now 15 R.F.A.). The officers were Captain-Lieut. J. Edgerton (26), Lieuts. J. W. Molitore (8), J. Kinch (22), and A. Turner (28).

1757. This detail arrived at Calcutta early in March, 1757. The records say it was present at the capture of Chandernagore, under Colonel Clive, 22 March, 1757, a detachment being left to garrison the place. A return of troops serving under Colonel Clive, dated Camp Chinsurah, 7 April, 1757, shows 1 captain-lieutenant, 3 lieutenants and 58 N.C.O.'s and men of the Bombay Artillery present, the names of the officers corresponding with those found in the records and rolls of the Regiment as serving in Bengal. The records also state that a detachment of the Regiment was present at the battle of Plassey under Colonel Clive, 23 June, 1757 ; and in Colonel Malleson's "Decisive Battles of India," a Captain Molitore, of the Bombay Detachment (8), is one of the officers stated to have been summoned to the Council of War before the battle. Captain Molitore was killed at the storm and capture of Masulipatam, 7 April, 1759. In a general return of troops serving under Colonel Clive, dated 3 August, 1759, 1 captain-lieutenant, 1 lieutenant, 40 N.C.O.'s and men of the Bombay Artillery are shown as on the expedition to Moorshedabad. No names are given, but the captain-lieutenant must have been J. Edgerton (26). Lieut. J. Kinch (22) was transferred to the Bengal Artillery (5), and was killed at or near Patna in 1763. The surviving N.C.O.'s and men who proceeded to Bengal were transferred to the Bengal service in September, 1758.

1759. On the 12 February, 1759, the Artillery branch of the Service, which, as far as related to the officers, had hitherto been blended with the Infantry, was separated therefrom, and the officers made a distinct corps.

In February, 1759, a force of 850 Artillery and Infantry, under command of Captain Richard Maitland (R.A. 74) was sent against Surat, and took it by storm on 5 March. The Artillery was Captain Maitland's Company of R.A., but six Bombay officers went with the expedition. Captain L. F. de Gloss (12) was the Engineer, and constructed the approaches, and was left in command of the garrison. Lieuts. W. B. Burr (14), A. Werner (24), E. Hamilton (25), J. Peppard (42) wounded, and E. Smithers (44), are shown as on board the vessels which sailed.

In 1759 the 3rd Company appears to have been reduced.

1763. In October, 1763, a company of Artillery under Captain C. Pemble (33) accompanied two companies of the Bombay Regiment to Bengal. On arrival at Calcutta the following year, the Bengal Government not requiring its services, the Artillery was embarked on board the *York* for Madras, on which coast the records say it was employed until the close of the year, having meantime taken part in the sieges of Madura and Pallamcottah. The only officer traceable as having served in Madras at this time is Lieut.-Fireworker J. Nugent (54). Captain C. Pemble (33), however, remained in Bengal, and having obtained from that Government the brevet commission of Major, was invested with the command of the two companies of the Bombay Regiment of European Infantry. At the battle of Buxar, under Major Hector Munro, 23 March, 1764, he commanded the 2nd line, and was recommended to the Court of Directors for his bravery and good conduct. He also commanded a force sent against Chunar, December, 1764.

1765. On the 22 March, 1765, the third company was re-formed.

1768. Captain L. Nilson (19) was present at the capture of Mangalore, and several officers are shown as on service, probably the same.

1768. On the 6 March, 1768, a fourth company (2/2, now 90 R.G.A.) was raised, and a Battalion formed with one lieutenant-colonel and one major, each holding a company, and in receipt of emoluments from clothing, a third lieutenant being attached to each of their companies.

1771. In January, 1771, a force under Colonel Gordon was sent to reduce the strongholds of the Coolies of Surat. On the 2 February it stormed and took Toolajie Fort after an obstinate resistance. On the 30 April an action was fought under command of Lieut.-Colonel Cay, and the enemy repulsed. On the 7 May Broach was besieged, but siege raised on 19th of the same month. Officers traceable as being with this expedition, Captain L. Nilson (19), Lieut. R. Nicholson (86), Lieut.-Fireworker J. Bellas (97).

1772. Captain L. Nilson (19) and Lieut.-Fireworker J. Bellas (97) were present at the siege and capture of Broach, where General Wedderburn, C.I.C., was killed.

1774. In December, 1774, a force under General Gordon besieged and took Tannah. Captain L. Nilson (19) was the Engineer. Major T. Lee (76) commanded the Artillery; other officers traced as present, Lieuts. J. Nugent (54), W. Brickell (66), Lieut.-Fireworker J. Bellas (97). In the same month, Lieut.-Colonel T. Keating (65) commanded a detachment which took Versova and Karanjah, Lieut. W. Brickell

(66) (specially mentioned) and Lieut.-Fireworker J. Bellas (97) with him.

775. In 1775, Lieut.-Colonel T. Keating (65) commanded the Army ordered to support Ragonath Rao Peishwa. A company of Artillery, commanded by Lieut. J. S. Torriano (80), accompanied the force, and was present at the battles of Hossamlu, Daboun, Hydrabad, and Arras. Lieut.-Fireworker J. Bellas (97) was a.d.c. to Lieut.-Colonel Keating (65). No other officers traceable.

The duties of an Engineer Corps had hitherto been carried out by the Artillery officers, but on the 21 July, 1775, the corps of Bombay Engineers was established, and the following officers were transferred to it :—

    (19) Captain L. Nilson, promoted to Major.
    (55)   ,,   D. Spaeth.
    (73) Lieut. J. McNeill.
    (74)   ,,   C. Turner.
    (86)   ,,   R. Nicholson.

1779. Lieut.-Colonel G. Dagon (45) commanded the Artillery with Colonel Egerton's force above the Ghauts, Lieut.-Fireworker J. Bailie (122) being his a.d.c. Other officers traceable as being with the force, Captain S. Bowles (62) wounded, Lieut. R. Noyes (103), Lieut. T. H. Makon (105) killed, Lieut. St. L. Thomas (107) killed. The Army having marched through the Deccan, ascended the Bhore Ghat without opposition, but at Tulligaum was opposed by so superior a force it had to retire to Wurgaum, where, after having repulsed reiterated attacks for three days, a treaty of capitulation was made with the enemy—a treaty which was not ratified by the Bombay Government, and which received the pointed disapprobation of the Honourable Company.

1780. A company of Artillery, commanded by Captain J. S. Torriano (80), joined the Army under General Goddard, which arrived at Surat from Bengal. The Artillery of the Army was commanded by Lieut.-Colonel W. A. Bailie (Bengal Arty. 33), and Lieut.-Fireworker J. Bailie (122) was his a.d.c. The operations included capture of Ahmedabad, February, 1780, Bassein, December, 1780, and Arnaul, January, 1781, forcing of the Bhore Ghat, and retreat to Panwell. Captain D. Spaeth (55) was Engineer at the siege of Ahmedabad, and died of his wounds, and Lieut. H. Long (115) was wounded.

1783. Captain J. S. Torriano (80) commanded Artillery under General Matthews, which took Onore on 1 January, 1783. Several officers took part in the subsequent operations at Anantpoor and Bednore. At the disaster at Bednore, Captain J. Jackson (101), Lieuts. C. W. M. West (132), L. Olivier (137), R. Bell (145), T. Walton (147), A. Torriano (148), J. Griffith (149), were taken prisoners by Tippoo. Captain Jackson (101) and Lieut. Olivier (137) were supposed to have been poisoned. The remainder were released at the peace, and rejoined. Captain J. S. Torriano (80) commanded the garrison of Onore during the siege and blockade, which together lasted from 14 May, 1783, to 27 March, 1784. In spite of orders from the Bednore Committee to capitulate, Captain Torriano (80), in the face of very great difficulties for want of supplies, defended the position against an army of 10,000 men, with a garrison which, at the commencement of the siege, only numbered 743 men, 42 of whom were Europeans. He held the place until peace was established, the garrison being reduced to 238 persons when landed at Bombay on the 18 April, 1784. Lieuts. J. Courtoy (119) and Jeremiah Hawkes (121), wounded, are mentioned as being in Onore with him.

1783. In March, 1783, Captain J. Bellas (97) commanded Artillery at the taking of Mangalore, Lieut. J. Thompson (118) also present. The latter was also at Mangalore when it was besieged by Tippoo, and was wounded.

Lieut. Seton (142) is mentioned as being on board H.E.I. Company's vessel *Ranger* in the desperate fight with the Mahratta fleet off Geriah, 8 April, 1783. Lieut. Seton was wounded.

1790. Captain J. Thompson (118) commanded the Artillery, said in Lieut. Moor's narrative to have consisted of one European and two native companies of Artillery, which formed part of the force under Captain Little that left Bombay in May, 1790, to co-operate with the Mahrattas' and the Nizam's armies. The operations included the siege and capture of the fort of Darwar, under Colonel Frederick

1791. in February and March, 1791, capture of Hooly Honore and Simoga, December, 1791. The other officers with the Artillery of this force were Lieuts. W. Ince (155) and C. W. M. West (132), the latter having thus an opportunity of revisiting under happier circumstances the scenes of his confinement, and weary marches, whilst a prisoner of Tippoo in 1783.

1790. Four companies commanded by Major R. Jones (98) took part in the Mysore War and the siege of Seringapatam under Lord Cornwallis. Officers who certainly served in this war were Captain J. Bailie (122), Lieuts. W. Hall (130), R. Bell (145), A. Torriano (148), J. Griffith (149), S. Raester (150), W. Ince (155), S. Carter (156), Lieut.-Fireworkers J. Creasy (169), J. Eyles (171), A. G. Fisher (174), Joshua Hawkes (178), and several others are shown as on service, probably the Mysore war.

1792. In February, 1792, Captain-Lieuts. S. Carter (156), R. Blackall (165), and Lieut. J. Eyles (171) were present at the capture of Cannanore.

1796. A fifth company (3/1, now 30 R.F.A.) was raised on 24 May, 1796.

At the capture of Colombo, December, 1796, Captain J. Griffith (149), Captain-Lieut. S. Carter (156), Lieuts. J. Eyles (171), G. Warden (176), were present; and Lieuts. J. Eyles (171) and Joshua Hawkes (178) at the taking of Point de Galle in the same month.

1797. A sixth company (3/2, now 31 R.F.A.) was raised on 13 October, 1797.

1799. The 3rd Company (2/1, now 15 R.F.A.), Captain J. Bailie (122), the 4th Company (2/2, now 90 R.G.A.), Captain A. Torriano (148), the 5th Company (3/1, now 30 R.F.A.), Captain-Lieut. J. Eyles (171), the whole commanded by Major G. A. Lawman (102), took part in the Mysore War, were at the battle of Saidashur under General Stuart, 6 March, 1799, Lieut. J. Lighton wounded; and were present at the siege and fall of Seringapatam under General Harris. Captain A. Torriano (148) of the 4th Company, and Lieut. W. Macredie (177) of the 5th Company, were killed on the same day, 18 April, 1799. Other officers who certainly served in this war, Major J. Thompson (118), Captain J. Griffith (149), Captain-Lieuts. S. Carter (156), J. Comyn (170), J. Eyles (171), Lieuts. D. Urquhart (172), A. G. Fisher (174), H. Hessman (175), G. Warden (176), G. B. Bellasis (180), C. J. Bond (182), H. A. Shewcraft (183), but several others shown as on service were probably employed in Mysore.

1800. Captain-Lieut. J. Eyles (171) was at the reduction of Mangalore, capture and recapture of Jemaulabad in 1800 ; Major J. Thompson (118) and Lieut. G. Warden (176) at first capture of Jemaulabad.

1801–1802. The 1st Company (1/1, now 86 R.G.A.), Captain G. Powell (158), and the 2nd Company (now 81 R.F.A.), Captain-Lieut. W. Smith (173), formed part of Major-General Baird's army in Egypt. Other officers, Lieuts. G. Warden (176), C. J. Bond (182), and T. Morse (187), taken prisoner, and sent home to be exchanged.

1802. A seventh company (4/1, now 91 R.G.A.) raised on 16 March, 1802.

1803. The 3rd Company (2/1, now 15 R.F.A.), Lieut. R. Whish (190), was at the battle of Assaye; and as Lieut. R. Whish (190) was also at the battle of Argaum and taking of Gawilghur, it is probable that the 3rd Company was there also. The 5th Company (3/1, now 30 R.F.A.) was at the battle of Assaye, Lieut. T. Morse (187). Other officers who are traced as engaged in the operations in the Deccan and Guzerat, which included the taking of Ahmednugger, and Jaulna, Sunkheira in Kattywar, July, 1802, siege and capture of Broach under General Woodington, August, 1803, and capture of Baroda : Captain W. Ince (155), G. Powell (158), Captain-Lieuts. J. Eyles (171), A. G. Fisher (174), Lieuts. H. A. Shewcraft (183), H. W. Sealy (185), C. Hodgson (186), E. S. Clifton (189), R. Macintosh (192).

1807. By G.O., 25 June, 1807, it was ordered: " That in future when a vacancy occurs in the command of a Battalion of Artillery, the senior Lieut.-Colonel succeeding to such command shall not in consequence be promoted to the rank of Colonel, but shall be called Lieut.-Colonel Commandant of the Battalion, until by General Brevet Promotion in His Majesty's Army, he becomes entitled to be promoted to the rank of Colonel by the date of his Commission as Lieut.-Colonel in the Company's service." Under this order the following Lieut.-Colonels were promoted to Lieut.-Colonel

Commandant instead of Colonel : H. Hessman (175), 19 June, 1820 ; G. B. Bellasis (180), 1 May, 1824 ; C. Hodgson (186), 30 September, 1825 ; R. Whish (190), 23 September, 1826 ; F. H. Pierce (191), 28 September, 1827.

1809. In consequence of the great want of Artillery officers, the Government of Bombay transferred nine officers from the Infantry and gave them commissions in the Artillery. Their names will be found in the supplementary list on p. 114. These appointments were not approved of by the Court of Directors, and were cancelled in 1810.

First Addiscombe cadets, D. Hogarth (208), A. Manson (209), T. Stevenson (210), reported qualified on 29 December, 1809.

Captain F. H. Pierce (191) commanded Artillery at the capture of Mallia, 7 July, 1809 ; other officers present, Captain G. B. Bellasis (180), Lieuts. E. Hardy (194), L. C. Russell (198), J. Moor (200).

Captain C. J. Bond (182) commanded Artillery, and Captain H. W. Sealy (185) and Lieut. W. H. Sealy (196) accompanied the force under Colonel Lionel Smith to the Persian Gulf, September, 1809. Lieut. W. H. Sealy was drowned on 15 September, immediately after starting, through the foundering of the bomb-ketch *Stromboli.* The force occupied Rus-al-khyma, Luft, and Schinauss.

Captain R. Macintosh (192), with a detail of Artillery, formed part of the force under Lieut.-Colonel Keating, H.M. 56th Regiment which, in September, 1809, took possession of the Isle of Rodriguez, and reduced the Isle of Bourbon. He was also present with the force under General R. Abercrombie, at the second assault and occupation of Bourbon in July, 1810, and at the capture of Mauritius, December, 1810.

1810. Gun-Carriage Agency established. Captain L. C. Russell (198) First Agent, 8 October, 1810.

1811. Captain E. Hardy (194) commanded Artillery at the taking of Chya, 13 April, 1811. Others present, Lieuts. J. G. Griffith (206), A. Manson (209), severely wounded.

1st Troop formed, 11 November, 1811.

1812. Captain C. J. Bond (182) commanded Artillery at the capture of Nowanuggur Kattywar, 24 February, 1812. Others present : Captain E. Hardy (194), Lieuts. J. G. Griffith (206), E. Wyndowe (207), W. K. Lester (213).

1817. Rank of Lieut.-Fireworker abolished, and 2nd Lieutenant substituted.

1817-1819. The Bombay Artillery was actively engaged throughout the Pindari and Mahratta war, in the Deccan and in Guzerat. The 1st Troop, Captain F. H. Pierce (191), served throughout with the 4th Division under General Lionel Smith, but with the exception of the 6th Company (3/2, now 31st Battery R.F.A.), Lieut. J. Laurie (228), which was at the battle of Kirkee, and rendered important service, no record of companies engaged seems to exist. Lieut.-Colonel H. Hessman (175) and Major G. B. Bellasis (180) held commands of Artillery in the Deccan, and with the 4th Division. Other officers who are known to have been engaged in the operations :

Major C. J. Bond (182), Major H. W. Sealy (185), Captain-Lieuts. A. Campbell (199), R. Thew (201), W. G. White (202), J. G. Griffith (206), A. Manson (209), Lieuts. T. Stevenson (210), W. K. Lester (213), J. Barton (214), F. Schuler (216), W. Hutchinson (217), R. Foster (218), T. L. Groundwater (219), W. Miller (220), E. H. Willock (221), G. W. Gibson (226), W. H. Foy (230), J. W. Watson (231), J. Johnson (234), J. A. Davies (235), C. D. Blachford (237), H. L. Osborne (239), G. R. Lyons (240), M. Law (241), M. C. Decluzeau (243), W. Jacob (244).

1818. Rank of Captain-Lieutenant abolished 1 September, 1818.

1819. Appointment of Brigade-Major of the Artillery established 22 April, 1819. First Brigade-Major, Captain E. Hardy (194).

Lieut.-Colonel C. J. Bond (182) commanded Artillery serving under Sir W. G. Keir in the Persian Gulf, December, 1819, and Lieut. W. Morley (242) commanded the Artillery of the detachment which attacked and occupied Zaya. The force was then broken up, but Lieuts. W. Morley (242) and F. J. Otto (249) appear to have remained ; the latter was killed on 9 November, 1820, when the force under Captain Thompson, H.M. 17th Dragoons, sustained a defeat at Beni-boo-ali.

1820. On 1 January, 1820, the 2nd Troop and three companies of Foot Artillery were raised, the Foot Artillery being formed into two battalions of five companies ; one company then formed, afterwards 4/2, is now 55 R.F.A.

The 1st Troop, Captain T. Stevenson (210), and 5th Company 2nd Battalion (reduced in 1824), Captain J. W. Watson (231), went to the Persian Gulf under Sir Lionel Smith in 1820, and were at Beni-boo-ali on 2 March, 1821.

Lieut. W. Jacob (244), with a detachment of Artillery, was, at the capture of Mocha, December, 1820, severely wounded.

1822. Depôt of Instruction established at Matoonga, 1 August, 1822. First Director, Captain W. Miller (220).

1824. On 1 March, 1824, the 3rd and 4th Troops were raised, and two companies of Foot Artillery, 5/1 and 5/2, were reduced.

The 2nd Troop, Captain W. G. White (202), was at the siege and capture of Kittoor, near Dharwar, in December, 1824. Some Foot Artillery was also present, but the particular company is not traceable. Other officers with the troop were, Lieuts. C. D. Blachford (237), F. D. Watkins (245), T. J. Portardent (260). Lieuts. M. F. Willoughby (263), H. W. Hardie (273), and R. Warden (280) were also present.

SUBSEQUENT CHANGES IN ORGANIZATION.

1826. Golundauze Battalion formed on 28 March, 1826, of five companies.

1827. Increased to eight companies 28 September, 1827.

1829. G.O. 93 of 5 May, 1829, directed the granting of rank of Regimental Colonel to every Lieut.-Colonel Commandant on the expiration of one month from the date of the order, and that in future every officer was to be promoted to the rank of Colonel regimentally from the date on which he succeeded to the command of a corps. Under this order the following were made Regimental Colonels from 5 June, 1829 : Lieut.-Colonels Commandant H. Hessman (175), C. Hodgson (186), R. Whish (190), F. H. Pierce (191).

1829. Head Quarters of the Foot Artillery moved from Matoonga to Ahmednuggur.

1843. Golundauze increased to ten companies 1 July, 1843.

1846. Golundauze increased to twelve companies 28 March, 1846, and formed into the 3rd and 4th Battalions.

1853. Rank of Lieut.-Colonel Commandant revived.   Lieut.-Colonels promoted to that rank, J. W. Watson (231), 20 July, 1853, J. Leeson (248), 28 March, 1853, J. Sinclair (251), 10 November, 1854 ; the two last being subsequently made Regimental Colonel from same dates.

1857. Reserve Artillery of four companies raised, which now are 70 and 71 R.F.A., and 90 and 88 R.G.A.

1858. The 3rd and 5th Companies of the 4th Battalion mutinied.

On 27 August, 1858, the rank of Major was abolished, all Majors being promoted to Lieut.-Colonels from date of Major's commission. The rank of Second Captain was introduced, and the grade of Second Lieutenant abolished, all Second Lieutenants being promoted to Lieutenant from date of first commission as Second Lieutenants.

1860. Head Quarters of the Regiment and Foot Artillery established at Kirkee.

1861. The Reserve Artillery was designated 3rd Battalion (European) and the Native Artillery the 4th Battalion (Native) of six companies.

Between 1861 and 1870 the Native Artillery was reduced, except the original 1st Company 4th Battalion, which is still in existence as the Quetta Mountain Battery. In 1875 the Jacobabad Mountain Train, manned by men of Jacob's Rifles, was converted into No. 2 Mountain Battery, and its services are added to those of the Native Artillery.

1862. On the amalgamation with the Royal Artillery the Colonels of the Regiment were promoted to Colonel Commandant Royal Artillery from date of Regimental Colonels commissions, two being subsequently absorbed.

The Horse Brigade became the 4th Brigade R.H.A., changed in 1864 to E. Brigade R.H.A., and ceased to exist as a Brigade in 1871.

The 1st, 2nd, and 3rd Battalions formed the 18th and 21st Brigades R.A., and ceased to exist as Brigades in 1877.

1872. The rank of Major was re-established on 5 July, 1872, all First Captains being promoted to that rank, Second Captains becoming Captains.

1877. Rank of Regimental Colonel abolished, for Lieut.-Colonels promoted to that rank after some date in 1877, the last officer promoted to Regimental Colonel being T. N. Holberton (441).

STAFF APPOINTMENTS AND COLONELS.

PART II.

STAFF APPOINTMENTS AND COLONELS.

OFFICERS IN THE LIST WHO HAVE COMMANDED THE FORCES
IN BOMBAY.

No. in list.			
33	Lieut.-Colonel	C. Pemble	12 Feb. 1768
19	Brig.-General	Lorens Nilson	1784–1788
97	Major-General	J. Bellasis	21 May 1807–11 Feb. 1808
98	Major-General	R. Jones	12 Feb. 1808–16 Oct. 1809
122	Major-General	J. Bailie	7 June–9 Oct. 1819

COMMANDANTS OF THE BOMBAY ARTILLERY.

No. in list.				
33	Captain	C. Pemble		1762
65	Captain	T. Keating	Feb.	1764
76	Major	T. Lee	27 Aug.	1768–2 May 1777
45	Lieut.-Colonel	G. Dagon	8 Jan.	1779
54	Lieut.-Colonel	J. Nugent	31 Dec.	1789
98	Lieut.-Colonel	R. Jones	23 Oct.	1792
97	Colonel	J. Bellasis	8 Jan.	1796
122	Lieut.-Colonel	J. Bailie	21 Sept.	1804
98	Major-General	R. Jones	12 Feb.	1808
122	Colonel	J. Bailie	16 Oct.	1809
158	Major	G. Powell	7 Dec.	1811
173	Captain	W. Smith	9 Jan.	1812
149	Colonel	J. Griffith	23 Oct.	1812
122	Major-General	J. Bailie	13 May	1818
175	Lieut.-Colonel	H. Hessman	24 May	1822
186	Lieut.-Colonel	C. Hodgson	10 Dec.	1825
191	Lieut.-Colonel	F. H. Pierce	19 Apr.	1826
190	Lieut.-Col.-Comdt.	R. Whish	17 May	1827
191	Lieut.-Colonel	F. H. Pierce	31 July	1832
193	Colonel	S. R. Strover	8 Jan.	1833
198	Colonel	L. C. Russell	5 Feb.	1834
206	Lieut.-Colonel	J. G. Griffith	1 Feb.	1836
209	Colonel	A. Manson	16 Feb.	1846
216	Lieut.-Colonel	F. Schuler	19 Feb.	1849
222	Lieut.-Colonel	F. P. Lester	15 May	1850
258	Colonel	A. Rowland	25 Mar.	1856
266	Colonel	C. Lucas	29 May	1861–19 Aug. 1862

BRIGADE-MAJORS.

G.O. 22 April, 1819. Extract from Courts' Letter dated 14 Oct. 1818: "We are of opinion that the reasons given by the Commander-in-Chief for appointing a Brigade-Major to the Corps of Artillery at your Presidency are deserving of attention, and we accordingly authorize you to appoint a Brigade-Major to the Corps of Artillery with the allowances fixed for Brigade-Majors."

No. in list.			
194	E. Hardy	28 Apr.	1819
220	W. Miller	1 Apr.	1820
230	W. H. Foy	1 Nov.	1822
268	T. E. Cotgrave	19 Dec.	1825
244	W. Jacob	26 June	1829
268	T. E. Cotgrave	2 Jan.	1830
261	W. M. Coghlan	12 Dec.	1834
295	J. M. Glasse	19 Apr.	1846
378	H. Wallace	29 Apr.	1857
411	T. M. Harris	22 Oct.	1861 ; also to
	Inspector-General of Arty.	to Oct.	1862
411	T. M. Harris	Oct.	1862, acting A.A.G., R.A.

ASSISTANT-ADJUTANT-GENERALS, R.A., BOMBAY.

No. in list.			
346	W. D. Aitken	24 Feb.	1863
378	H. Wallace	26 July	1864
389	D. G. Anderson	4 Aug.	1869
411	T. M. Harris	7 Sept.	1872
413	T. J. Maclachlan	7 Nov.	1877
441	T. N. Holberton	18 Jan.	1879
474	G. W. Borrodaile	18 Jan.	1884
485	P. H. Greig	18 Jan.	1889–22 Apr. 1894

COLONELS BEFORE THE AMALGAMATION AND LIEUTENANT-COLONELS COMMANDANT.

No. in list.		Lieutenant-Colonel Commandant.	Colonel.	
97	J. Bellasis	—	8 Jan. 1796	First Colonel
98	R. Jones	—	12 Feb. 1808	
			v. J. Bellasis d.	
122	J. Bailie	—	7 Sept. 1812	
			v. R. Jones ret.	
149	J. Griffith	—	1 Sept. 1818	
			augmentation	
175	H. Hessman	19 June 1820	5 June 1829	
		v. J. Griffith d.		
180	G. B. Bellasis	1 May 1824	—	
		augmentation		
186	C. Hodgson	30 Sept. 1825	5 June 1829	
		v. G. B. Bellasis d.		
190	R. Whish	23 Sept. 1826	5 June 1829	
		v. J. Bailie d.		
191	F. H. Pierce	28 Sept. 1827	5 June 1829	
		augmentation		
193	S. R. Strover	—	1 Jan. 1833	
			v. F. H. Pierce d.	
194	E. Hardy	—	28 May 1833	
			v. H. Hessman d.	
198	L. C. Russell	—	26 Dec. 1833	
			v. E. Hardy ret.	
206	J. G. Griffith	—	3 July 1845	
			augmentation	
209	A. Manson	—	16 Apr. 1849	
			v. C. Hodgson d.	
216	F. Schuler	—	28 Apr. 1851	
			v. L. C. Russell d.	
222	F. P. Lester	—	23 Feb. 1852	
			v. A. Manson d.	
231	J. W. Watson	20 Jan. 1853	—	
		v. S. R. Strover d.		
248	J. S. Leeson	28 Mar. 1853	28 Mar. 1853	
		v. J. W. Watson ret.		
251	J. Sinclair	10 Nov. 1854	10 Nov. 1854	
		v. R. Whish d.		
258	A. Rowland	—	4 July 1858	
			v. F. P. Lester d.	
261	W. M. Coghlan	—	8 May 1859	
			v. J. S. Leeson d.	

COLONELS COMMANDANT ROYAL ARTILLERY AND SUCCESSION
TO COLONELS' ALLOWANCES.

No. in list.		Colonels' allowances.	Colonel-Commandant.	
206	J. G. Griffith	—	3 July 1845	d. 31 July 1872 step absorbed
216	F. Schuler	—	28 Apr. 1851	
251	J. Sinclair	—	10 Nov. 1854	d. 28 May 1861 step absorbed
258	A. Rowland	—	4 July 1858	
261	W. M. Coghlan	—	8 May 1859	
266	C. Lucas	29 May 1861 *v.* J. Sinclair	—	
267	H. W. Trevelyan	1 Aug. 1872 *v.* J. G. Griffith	21 July 1874 *v.* F. Schuler	
294	H. Forster	12 June 1873 *v.* C. Lucas	—	
331	G. P. Sealy	21 July 1874 *v.* F. Schuler	1 Sept. 1876 *v.* H. W. Trevelyan	
338	A. B. Kemball	21 Oct. 1875 *v.* H. Forster	30 June 1878 *v.* A. Rowland	
346	W. D. Aitken	1 Sept. 1876 *v.* H. W. Trevelyan	27 Nov. 1885 *v.* W. M. Coghlan	
347	C. B. Fuller	30 June 1878 *v.* A. Rowland	12 Nov. 1892 *v.* G. P. Sealy	
402	A. A. Bayly	27 Nov. 1885 *v.* W. M. Coghlan	19 Nov. 1897 *v.* W. D. Aitken	
435	H. Le Cocq	12 Nov. 1892 *v.* G. P. Sealy	12 Aug. 1900 *v.* A. A. Bayly	
505	F. J. Mortimer	19 Nov. 1897 *v.* W. D. Aitken	—	

INSPECTORS-GENERAL OF ORDNANCE.

G.O. 659, 28 Aug. 1856: "The superintendence and control of the Ordnance Department of this Presidency are to be transferred from the Military Board to an officer to be designated Inspector-General of Ordnance and Magazines, on whom are to be devolved all the duties connected with the Ordnance Department, hitherto performed by the Military Board, excepting those of Audit, which are to be confided to the Auditor-General. Major-General F. P. Lester to be Inspector-General of Ordnance and Magazines, Lieut. A. A. Bayly to be Ordnance Assistant to the Military Auditor-General."

No. in list.			
222	F. P. Lester	28 Aug.	1856
263	M. F. Willoughby	14 Apr.	1857
275	J. Grant	27 Aug.	1859
295	J. M. Glasse	2 Apr.	1860
315	J. B. Woosnam	20 Oct.	1862
349	E. Wray	10 Mar.	1863
346	W. D. Aitken	26 July	1864
348	J. Worgan	26 July	1873
356	W. S. Hatch	26 July	1878
402	A. A. Bayly	2 Mar.	1881
502	F. W. M. Spring	6 Apr.	1886–5 Oct. 1893

AGENTS FOR GUNPOWDER.

The manufacture of gunpowder was being carried on in Bombay in very early days, as Captain and Chief Engineer L. F. De Gloss (12) was brought to notice for improvements in the method of manufacture in 1759. On 9 and 19 Jan. 1786, great explosions took place at Mazagon (cause unknown); the buildings were entirely destroyed, and 56 lives lost. Repairs and improvements cost Rs.1.20.805. The first agents were medical officers, Captain Manson, the first Artillery officer, being appointed in 1821.

No. in list.				
(med.)	—	Mr. Galley	about	1790
	—	Mr. Hollanby	about	1794
	—	Mr. Carnac	about	1795
(med.)	9	Helenus Scott	1797 –	1798
	—	Dr. Keir	about	1814
	—	Dr. Inverarity	about	1817
(med.)	24	Dougall Christie	1818 –	1821
	209	A. Manson	24 Dec.	1821
	206	J. G. Griffith	9 June	1827
	214	J. Barton	1 Oct.	1827
	210	T. Stevenson	19 May	1829
	244	W. Jacob	28 Jan.	1834
	246	J. Lloyd	16 Dec.	1844
	261	W. M. Coghlan	15 June	1846
	263	M. F. Willoughby	20 Mar.	1848
	278	E. A. Farquharson	28 Oct.	1852
	315	J. B. Woosnam	6 Sept.	1855
	369	B. K. Finnimore	27 Aug.	1859
	349	E. Wray	6 July	1860
	356	W. S. Hatch	20 Oct.	1862
	387	T. T. Haggard	10 Mar.	1863; styled

Superintendent Gunpowder Factory 1874, and during his term of office the works were transferred to Kirkee

	402	A. A. Bayly	9 Sept.	1877
	512	F. J. Caldecott	2 Mar.	1881–Oct. 1894

AGENTS FOR GUN-CARRIAGES.

G.O. 8 Oct. 1810: "The Honble. Court of Directors, having authorized establishment of a Gun-Carriage Manufactory at the Presidency, and having directed that an officer of Artillery be appointed to the charge thereof, Lieut. L. Russell to be Agent in that Department."

No. in list.			
198	L. C. Russell	8 Oct.	1810
208	D. Hogarth	22 Jan.	1816
192	R. Macintosh	1 May	1816
201	R. Thew	23 May	1821
209	A. Manson	9 June	1827
230	W. H. Foy	8 Jan.	1834
222	F. P. Lester	7 June	1838
231	J. W. Watson	1 Mar.	1839
252	E. Stanton	2 Apr.	1841
275	J. Grant	1 Feb.	1848
295	J. M. Glasse	14 Apr.	1857
348	J. Worgan	27 Aug.	1859
356	W. S. Hatch	10 Mar.	1863; styled
	Superintendent Gun-Carriage Factory 1874		
467	H. W. Stockley	1 Oct.	1878
506	T. Walker	1 Nov.	1888-11 Mar. 1891

DIRECTORS OF THE DEPÔT OF INSTRUCTION.

G.O. 1 Aug. 1822: "The Honble. the Governor in Council having established an institution at the Head Quarters of the Regiment of Artillery, for the purpose of perfecting the professional education of the younger Officers of Artillery as they join; and of imparting to the Non-Commissioned Officers, and a portion of selected private Soldiers, a degree of instruction in the theoretical parts of their profession, is pleased to appoint Captain Miller to the situation of 'Director of the Artillery Depôt of Instruction.'" The Head Quarters were then at Matoonga.

No. in list.			
220	W. Miller	30 July	1822

Depôt removed to Ashmednuggur, Dec. 1820.

231	J. W. Watson	16 Dec.	1831
280	R. Warden	18 Mar.	1833

Depôt abolished in 1834.
Re-established in 1846.

314	T. Gaisford	4 Sept.	1846
330	J. Pottinger	3 Jan.	1852
356	W. S. Hatch	21 Dec.	1861

THE
HORSE BRIGADE.

PART III.

THE HORSE BRIGADE.

COMMANDANTS HORSE BRIGADE.

Brigade formed G.O. 18 Nov. 1811.

No in list.			
181	James Lighton	18 Nov.	1811
191	F. H. Pierce	16 Apr.	1813
192	R. Macintosh	23 May	1821–31 Jan. 1826
198	L. C. Russell (temporarily)	May	1826
198	L. C. Russell (permanent)	June	1828
210	T. Stevenson	4 Feb.	1834
243	M. C. Decluzeau	11 Apr.	1840
248	J. Leeson		1849
258	A. Rowland	11 July	1855
272	W. T. Whitlie	25 Mar.	1856
304	S. Turnbull	Jan.	1857
294	H. Forster	23 Jan.	1858

ADJUTANTS, HORSE BRIGADE.

No. in list.	1st Troop.			No. in list.	2nd Troop.		
208	D. Hogarth	15 June	1811	240	G. R. Lyons	1 May	1820
206	J. G. Griffith	24 May	1815	237	C. D. Blachford	22 Oct.	1822
221	E. H. Willock	25 Jan.	1817	245	F. D. Watkins	22 July	1825
234	J. Johnson	1 Jan.	1820	260	F. J. Pontardent	25 Jan.	1827
240	G. R. Lyons	22 Oct.	1822	258	A. Rowland	21 Feb.	1829
253	J. H. M. Martin	1 Nov.	1824	265	W. Brett	26 Feb.	1833
298	W. A. St. Clair	10 Aug.	1834	272	W. T. Whitlie	8 Sept.	1837
290	H. W. Brett	13 Oct.	1835				

No.	3rd Troop.			No.	4th Troop.		
253	J. H. M. Martin	7 June	1824	248	J. Leeson	7 June	1824
256	J. T. Leslie	1 Nov.	1824	265	W. Brett	20 Apr.	1830
262	N. Lechmere	18 Apr.	1833	271	J. Stamford	9 Jan.	1832
294	H. Forster	21 May	1834	298	W. A. St. Clair	3 Oct.	1835

G.O. 225 of 1839 : " Adjutants and Quartermasters of Troops of Horse Artillery at Bombay will be abolished as vacancies occur, and a Brigade-Adjutant and Quartermaster in one person appointed."

BRIGADE-ADJUTANTS.

No. in list.			
294	H. Forster	8 May	1840
298	W. A. St. Clair	7 Nov.	1840
322	T. C. Pownoll	1 Feb.	1844
349	E. Wray	16 Jan.	1849
378	H. Wallace	17 Dec.	1852
393	T. B. Gibbard	29 Apr.	1857
413	T. J. Maclachlan	13 May	1859 (afterwards of 4th Brigade R.H.A.)
425	W. Denis de Vitre	18 Feb.	1863 (4th Brigade R.H.A.)
435	H. Le Cocq	15 May	1864 (E Brigade R.H.A.)
447	W. W. Woodward	16 Mar.	1866 (E Brigade R.H.A.)
467	H. W. Stockley	1 Jan.	1867 (E Brigade R.H.A.)
506	T. Walker	12 May	1871 (E Brigade R.H.A. to
		26 June	1871 when Brigade ceased to exist)

1ST TROOP.

1811. Formed at Seroor in December. Of a draft of 103 men taken from the Bombay Regiment (2nd. Batt. Royal Dublin Fusiliers), 40 were posted to the Horse Arty. and 63 men to the Foot Arty. to replace a similar draft therefrom for the Horse. First commander, Cap. J. Lighton (181).

1814–1818. MAHRATTA WAR. Throughout the operations with the 4th Division. Capture of Poona 16 Nov. 1817; battle of Ashtee 20 Feb. 1818. Commander, Cap. F. H. Pierce (191). Gen. Stubbs, in his " History of the Bengal Arty.," vol. ii. p. 116, writes : " The former (*i.e.* H.A.) of the Bombay Corps, admirably horsed, as it always has been, which belonged to the 4th Division under Gen. Sir Lionel Smith, covered 2250 miles in seven months, 'a movement,' says Col. Blacker, whose statements are not rashly made, ' of which there is probably no example in the world.' "

1820–1821. ARABIA. Beni-boo-ali 2 Mar. 1821. Commander, T. Stevenson (210). Authorized to bear " Beni-boo-ali " on the appointments.

1840–1843. SIND and AFGHANISTAN. Left Poona 20 Oct. 1840 for Kurrachee. Marched *viâ* Shikarpore, Kujjuck, Dadur, Bolan pass to Quetta, and back to Shikarpore; again to Quetta, Candahar, Khelat-i-Ghilzie, Ghuzni, Cabul, Jellalabad Khyber pass, Peshawar, Ferozepore to Roree, Hydrabad, and Kurrachee, returning to Poona 6 Jan. 1844, a period of 3 years and 3 months, during which it covered in marches 3552 miles. Engagements : Kujjuck 20 Feb. 1841, Lieut. R. Creed killed; Hykulzie 28 Mar. and 28 Apr. 1842; Gohain 30 Aug.; Ghuzni 5 and 6 Sept.; Beni-Badam and Maidan 13 and 14 Sept. ; Huft Kotal 15 Oct. 1842 ; march from Roree and skirmish 22 Mar. 1843; Hydrabad 24 Mar. 1843, Lieut. J. C. Smith killed. Commander, Cap. J. T. Leslie (256).

G.G O. 11 Apr. 1843. Designated 1st or Leslie's Troop, and authorized to bear the Eagle on appointments for ever; also " Hyderabad."

1857–1858. MUTINY, CENTRAL INDIA. Rathghur 26 Jan. 1858; Barodia 30 Jan., 2 guns; relief of Sangor 3 Feb.; Garrakhota 11 Feb.; forcing of Muddenpore pass ; general action of the Betwa 1 Apr. ; siege and capture of Jhansi 3 Apr., Lieut.-Col. S. Turnbull (304) killed ; capture of Koonch 5 May ; affair of Gallowlee 15 May; capture of Calpee 22 May; Morar 16 June; capture of Gwalior 20 June, and pursuit of Tantia Topee, defeating him at Jowrah Alipore 20 June 1858, taking all his guns. Commanders, Lieut.-Col. S. Turnbull (304) and Cap. J. G. Lightfoot (350). *Lond. Gaz.*, 18 Apr. 1859, Report by Sir Hugh Rose, dated Poona 13 Oct. 1858, regarding the capture of Gwalior: " In making special mention of Cap. Lightfoot for his good services this day, I beg to state how much I am indebted to the officers and men of the 1st or Eagle Troop Bombay Horse Arty. for their excellent and gallant conduct throughout the campaign. In my actions I made very liberal use of the Troop in pouring an unexpected or flank fire into the enemy. On all these occasions the 1st Troop was worthy of its former fame, and proved that no arm of the service is more dangerous to its foes than fleet Arty."

1862. Designated A Battery 4th Brigade R.H.A.
1864.   ,,   A ,, E   ,,   ,,
1871.   ,,   C ,, D   ,,   ,,
1877.   ,,   H ,, B   ,,   ,,
1890.   ,,   N ,, R.H.A.

OFFICERS WHO HAVE SERVED IN THE 1st TROOP.

No. in list.	Captains and Majors Commanding.	No. in list.	Captain-Lieutenants, 2nd Captains, and Captains.	No. in list.	2nd Lieutenants and Lieutenants.
181	J. Lighton	191	F. H. Pierce	206	J. G. Griffith
191	F. H. Pierce	210	T. Stevenson	208	D. Hogarth
192	R. Macintosh	213	W. K. Lester	212	W. W. Quartly
210	T. Stevenson	221	E. H. Willock	192	R. Macintosh
256	J. T. Leslie	234	J. Johnson	221	E. H. Willock
272	W. T. Whitlie	216	F. Schuler	194	E. Hardy
294	H. Forster	417	T. C. Crowe	226	G. W. Gibson
315	J. B. Woosnam	416	R. Pittman	202	W. G. White
304	S. Turnbull	447	W. W. Woodward	234	J. Johnson
350	J. G. Lightfoot	467	H. W. Stockley	213	W. K. Lester
381	G. G. Brown	474	G. W. Borrodaile	231	J. W. Watson
411	T. M. Harris	481	E. G. Battiscombe	240	G. R. Lyons
447	W. W. Woodward	*229*	*J. Cocke*	247	J. Athill
				253	J. H. M. Martin
				248	J. S. Leeson
				252	E. Stanton
				266	C. Lucas
				256	J. T. Leslie
				265	W. Brett
				322	T. C. Pownoll
				311	R. Creed (attached from 2nd Batt.)
				342	R. B. Brett
				354	J. C. Smith
				306	A. F. Rowan
				347	C. B. Fuller
				362	D. Gaye
				381	G. G. Brown
				386	J. C. Hailes
				393	T. B. Gibbard
				425	W. de Vitre

No. in (med.) list.	Assistant Surgeons.			No. in list.	2nd Lieutenants and Lieutenants.
37	D. Craw			411	T. M. Harris
52	W. F. M. Cockerill			440	C. P. Roberts
69	M. A. Rauclaud			417	T. C. Crowe
74	A. H. Leith			416	R. Pittman
77	J. Cramond			466	C. E. Basevi
80	J. J. Atkinson			464	J. T. Leishman
81	R. T. C. Baxter			491	R. Lemesurier
84	W. L. Cameron			483	H. F. Gibb
89	J. Turner			485	P. H. Greig
116	J. Lumsdaine			506	T. Walker
121	D. Simpson			514	F. Lodge

229 C. Blood

426 G. Twiss

2ND TROOP.

1 Jan. 1820. Formed at Seroor by a division of 1st Troop and drafts from the Foot Arty. To replace the latter, recourse was again had to the Bombay Regt. (2nd Batt. Royal Dublin Fusiliers), from which a draft of " unexceptionable men" was taken. First commander, Cap. W. G. White (202).

Dec. 1824. Siege and capture of Kittoor. Commander, Cap. W. G. White (202).

1857–1859. MUTINY. Rajpootana; capture of Awah Jan. 1858; Kotah 30 Mar.; battle of the Bunnass 14 Aug. 1858; pursuit of the rebels till 17 Feb. 1859. Commander, Cap. J. G. Petrie (351).

1862. Designated B Battery 4th Brigade R.H.A.
1864.   „   B „ E „ „
1871.   „   E „ D „ „
1877.   „   K „ B „ „

1 Apr. 1881. Broken up and men distributed to R.H.A. Brigades.

1900. Y Battery R.H.A. raised.

1901. By Army Order 112, H.M. the King was graciously pleased to approve of Y Battery R.H.A. being considered as reformed from the 2nd Troop Bombay Horse Artillery, to perpetuate its memory and carry on its traditions.

Please add to List of 2nd Lieutenants and Lieutenants on p. 30.

437 | J. H. M. Martin.

OFFICERS WHO HAVE SERVED IN THE 2ND TROOP.

No. in list.	Captains and Majors Commanding.	No. in list.	Captain-Lieutenants, 2nd Captains, and Captains.	No. in list.	2nd Lieutenants and Lieutenants.
202	W. G. White	221	E. H. Willock	237	C. D. Blachford
221	E. H. Willock	219	T. L. Groundwater	240	G. R. Lyons
258	A. Rowland	423	J. H. P. Malcolmson	241	M. Law
298	W. A. St. Clair	425	W. Denis de Vitre	245	F. D. Watkins
315	J. B. Woosnam	441	T. N. Holberton	248	J. S. Leeson
304	S. Turnbull	436	A. R. Hoskins	251	J. Sinclair
351	J. G. Petrie	465	C. P. Theobald	222	T. P. Lester
352	J. D. Woollcombe	473	W. J. Finch	260	F. J. Pontardent
366	H. M. Douglas	485	P. H. Greig	262	N. Lechmere
399	A. Blunt			258	A. Rowland
426	G. Twiss			265	W. Brett
435	H. Le Cocq			286	T. W. Hicks
				306	A. F. Rowan
				322	T. C. Pownoll
				344	J. R. Hawkins
				360	G. R. Douglas
				358	J. T. Keir
				346	W. D. Aitken
				342	R. B. Brett
				350	J. G. Lightfoot
				376	W. Cameron
				379	G. Rennie
				382	F. Conybeare
				390	J. Shekleton
				383	D. J. Kinloch
				409	J. H. Reid
				411	T. M. Harris
				423	J. H. P. Malcolmson
				399	A. Blunt
				428	T. Swanson
				433	F. Hemming
				460	J. Vibart
				447	W. W. Woodward
				455	H. C. B. Tanner
				482	T. H. Ouchterlony
				461	H. T. Vachell
				479	A. T. Wallace
				465	C. P. Theobald
				473	W. J. Finch
				475	E. T. Pottinger
				497	H. Stevenson
				499	C. E. Hanbury
				512	F. J. Caldecott
				515	H. C. Seton

No. in (med.) list.	Assistant Surgeons.
50	J. Bird
52	W. F. M. Cockerill
56	S. Love
64	A. Gibson
65	A. Arnott
73	F. W. Watkins
76	W. Parsons
85	R. J. Russell
89	John Turner
96	J. H. Wilmot
109	W. C. Brown
117	J. Cruickshank
119	C. W. Fettes

The Horse Brigade.

3RD TROOP.

1 Mar. 1824. Formed at Poona. First commander, Cap. F. Schuler (216).

1838–1840. SIND and AFGHANISTAN. Left Poona 18 Sept. 1838; landed in Sind at Bominicote; marched *viâ* Tatta, Kotree, Larkhana, Gundava, Dadur, Bolan pass to Quetta, Candahar, Khelat-i-Ghilzie, Ghuznee, Cabul; back to Ghuznee, Quetta, through Bolan pass to Sukkur and Kurrachee; 177 marches, covering 2194 miles. Engagements: Ghuznee 23 July 1839; Khelat, 2 guns, Lieut. H. Forster (294), 13 Nov. 1839. Commander, J. H. M. Martin (253).

1848–1849. PUNJAUB. Siege and capture of Mooltan, Jan.; battle of Goojerat 21 Feb. 1849, and pursuit under Sir W. Gilbert to Rawulpindi. Commander, Cap. C. Blood (279).

1856–1857. PERSIA. Reshire, Bushire, Khooshab, Mohumra. Commander, Major E. S. Blake (318).

1857–1859. MUTINY, CENTRAL INDIA. Marched from Kurrachee 14 Dec. 1857 to Hydrabad and Roree, then across the desert to Nuseerabad, was continuously in the field for 16 months, going into cantonments at Nuseerabad 21 May 1859. Total distance marched, 2626 miles. Engagements: Capture of Kotah 30 Mar. 1858; pursuit of Kotah garrison, 4 guns, 1–11 Apr.; expedition to Pardowa 6 May; recapture of Chandaree 27 May; Kotah-ki Serai 17 June; action heights before Gwalior 18 June; action before and capture of Gwalior 19 June; pursuit of Gwalior garrison, 2 guns, Lieut. T. M. Harris, 20 June; capture of Powree 21 Aug.; pursuit of Maun Sing, and action at Beejapoor, 2 guns, Lieut. A. R. Hoskins (436); pursuit of Tantia Topee, and action at Sindwala, 4 guns; action on 25 Oct.; action at Koondraie 14 Nov. 1858. Commander, Lieut.-Col. E. S. Blake (318).

1862. Designated C Battery 4th Brigade R.H.A.
1864. „ C „ E „ „
1871. „ G „ C „ „
1873. „ G „ D „ „
1875. „ D „ E „ „
1877. „ D „ C „ „
1882. „ K „ B „ „
1889. „ Q „ R.H.A.

1899–1901. SOUTH AFRICA. Embarked at Southampton 19 Dec. 1899. Served in Cape Colony, Orange River Colony, Transvaal, and Natal. Battery entitled to clasps for Relief of Kimberley, Paardeberg, Driefontein, Johannesburg, Diamond Hill, Wittebergen. Longest march in one day, 56 miles. Engagements and actions: Waterval 12th, Modder River 13th, Klip Drift 15th, Dronfield 16th Feb. 1900; Poplar Grove 7th, Abrahams Kraal 10th, Bloemfontein 12th and 13th, Sannas Post 31 Mar. 1900 (4 V.C.'s and 3 D.C.M.'s); Kraalfontein 1st, Houtnek 2nd, Welkom Farm 4th, Winburg 5th, Zand River 10th, Lindley 17th, Rhenoster 20th, Heilbron 22nd, Doornkop 27th May 1900; Diamond Hill 11th and 12th, Heidelberg 23rd June 1900; near Bethlehem 16th, Palmietfontein 19th, Vredefort 24th, Stinkhoutboom 27th July 1900; Lindique 5th, Elandsfontein 14th Aug. 1900; Witkopjes 26th Sept. 1900; Hex River 2nd, Kosterfontein 30th Nov. 1900; Rooiport 3rd, Krooin River 7th, Koorn Kloof 23rd Dec. 1900; Kaalfontein 12th, Wilge River 29th Jan. 1901; Haasfontein 1st, Witbank 2nd, Yxaruarkfontein 3rd, Bethel 5th, Mooiplaats 7th, Kraalfontein 16th, Deelkraal 20th Feb. 1901; Buffelsdoorn 5th, Piet Retief 8th, Roosport 18th, Jacksfontein 21st Mar. 1901; Verkocht 5th, Vaal River 7th, near Vaal River 9th, Platt Kop 12th, Paardefontein 15th, Vaalbank 16th, Bethel 20th, Spion Kop 22nd, Bethel 23rd, Spur Kop 23rd, Winkelpock 24th, South Bethel 24th, Mooifontein 25th, Pretorius Vlei 26th, Witbank

D

28th, Wilgefontein 31st May 1901; Kaffir Spruit 3rd, Welgeledgen 4th, Spitzkop 6th, Kaalfontein 8th and 9th, Dwarsolei 10th, Shikock 14th, Elandsberg Nek 15th, Rooipoort 29th June 1901; Kaffir Spruit 8th, Wolmaranstad 23rd, Rustfontein 26th July 1901; Geduld 6th, Nooitgedacht 7th, Quaggafontein 9th and 14th, Mullars River, Union Dale, 23rd, Doorn River, Oudtshoorn, 24th, Welgedacht, Oudtshoorn, 26th Aug. 1901; Waterval near Riversdale 2nd, Lemans Hoek, South Ladismith, 6th, Zand Drift, Burg River, 21st Oct. 1901; Zward Bosh Kraal 8th, Zuurfontein 14 Nov. 1901. Embarked for England at Cape Town 7 Dec. 1901. Commanders: to 20 Jan. 1901, Major E. J. Phipps Hornby (R.A. 3795); to 9 Apr. 1901, Cap. A. M. Kennard (R.A. 4475); from 9 Apr. 1901, Major G. Humphreys (R.A. 4301).

1902. 13 Jan. F.M. Lord Roberts presented to the Battery a piece of plate, consisting of a solid silver statuette, being a miniature replica of the statue of Armed Science in the R.A. Officers' Mess, Woolwich, subscribed for by the officers who had formerly served in the Battery.

OFFICERS WHO HAVE SERVED IN THE 3RD TROOP.

No. in list.	Captains and Majors Commanding.	No. in list.	Captain-Lieutenants, 2nd Captains, and Captains.	No. in list.	2nd Lieutenants and Lieutenants.
216	F. Schuler	411	T. M. Harris	294	H. Forster
253	J. H. M. Martin	425	W. Denis de Vitre	332	W. C. Say
279	C. Blood	435	H. Le Cocq	338	A. B. Kemball
265	W. Brett	440	C. P. Roberts	311	R. Creed
272	W. T. Whitlie	456	A. Carey	315	J. B. Woosnam
318	E. S. Blake	483	H. T. Gibb	361	D. McDougall
357	H. L. Gibbard			363	W. Stevenson
390	J. Shekleton			373	R. H. Keatinge
413	T. J. Maclachlan			399	A. Blunt
				407	C. E. H. Cotes
				350	J. G. Lightfoot (attached)
				390	J. Shekleton (attached)
				382	F. Conybeare
				413	T. J. Maclachlan
				414	T. W. Grahame
				423	J. H. P. Malcolmson
				393	T. B. Gibbard (attached)

No. in (med.) list.	Assistant Surgeons.			No. in list.	2nd Lieutenants
				435	H. Le Cocq
				436	A. R. Hoskins
70	J. B. Daly			441	T. N. Holberton
73	F. W. Watkins			411	T. M. Harris
78	C. F. Collier			467	H. W. Stockley
82	E. Impey			486	W. H. Sandham
85	R. J. Russell			470	W. W. Benson
90	J. T. Shekleton			481	E. G. Battiscombe
96	J. H. Wilmot			496	M. A. Chaldecott
111	R. C. McConnell (attached)			493	J. B. Walker
				498	C. H. Campbell
117	J. Cruickshank			514	F. Lodge

425 G. Twiss.

425 W. de Vitre

4TH TROOP.

1 Mar. 1824. Formed at Poona. First commander, Cap. T. L. Groundwater (219).

1827. Field Service Southern Mahratta country. Commander, Cap. T. L. Groundwater (219).

1838–1841. SIND and AFGHANISTAN. With the exception of Apr. to Oct. 1840, spent at Deesa, the Troop was in the field for 3 years. Left Poona Nov. 1838, embarked for Sind, landed at Bominicote, marched *viâ* Tatta, Kotree, Gundava, Dadur, Bolan pass to Quetta, Candahar, Ghuznee, Cabul; back to Ghuznee, Quetta, and Kurrachee, then through run of Cutch to Deesa. Engagements : Ghuznee 23 July, Cabul 7 Aug. 1839. Commander, Cap. T. E. Cotgrave (268). Starting from Deesa Oct. 1840, it marched *viâ* run of Cutch to Hydrabad, Kujjuck, Dadur, Bolan pass to Quetta, and eventually returned *viâ* Khelat, Kurrachee, and run of Cutch to Deesa. Commander, Cap. J. S. Leeson (248). Distance marched, about 4100 miles.

1856–1857. PERSIA. Commander, Cap. G. P. Sealy (331).

1857 and 1859. MUTINY. Kolapoor 1857, 2 guns, 2nd Lieut. T. N. Holberton (441). Ahmednuggur flying column; left Ahmednuggur 5 Nov. 1858, returned 27 Mar. 1859, having marched nearly 1300 miles. Commander, Cap. D. Gaye (362).

1862. Designated D Battery 4th Brigade R.H.A.

1864.	,,	D	,,	E	,,	,,
1871.	,,	H	,,	C	,,	,,
1872.	,,	H	,,	D	,,	,,
1875.	,,	E	,,	E	,,	,,
1877.	,,	E	,,	C	,,	,,
1882.	,,	N	,,	A	,,	,,

1882. EGYPT. Kassassin, 2 guns, Lieut. F. E. A. Hunter (R.A. 3550); Tel-el-Kebir. Commander, Major G. W. Borrodaile (474).

Feb. 1884. Reduced.

1900. Z Battery R.H.A. raised.

1901. By Army Order 112, H.M. the King was graciously pleased to approve of Z Battery R.H.A being considered as reformed from the 4th Troop Bombay Horse Artillery, to perpetuate its memory and carry on its traditions.

OFFICERS WHO HAVE SERVED WITH THE 4TH TROOP.

No. in list.	Captains and Majors Commanding.	No. in list.	Captain-Lieutenants, 2nd Captains, and Captains.	No. in list.	2nd Lieutenants and Lieutenants.
219	T. L. Groundwater	413	T. J. Maclachlan	248	J. S. Leeson
248	J. S. Leeson	411	T. M. Harris	261	W. M. Coghlan
268	T. E. Cotgrave	441	T. N. Holberton	271	H. Stamford
322	T. C. Pownoll	453	J. Tasker	280	R. Warden
331	G. P. Sealy	461	H. T. Vachell	290	H. W. Brett
362	D. Gaye	465	C. P. Theobald	268	T. E. Cotgrave
378	H. Wallace			298	W. A. St. Clair
393	T. B. Gibbard			300	R. C. Wormald
425	W. Denis de Vitre			309	J. Jacob
441	T. N. Holberton			349	E. Wray
474	G. W. Borrodaile			352	J. D. Woollcombe
				364	A. C. Romer
				378	H. Wallace
				389	D. G. Anderson
				397	C. Nasmyth
				344	J. R. Hawkins
				390	J. Shekleton
				407	C. E. H. Cotes
				425	W. de Vitre
				426	G. Twiss
				441	T. N. Holberton
				453	J. Tasker
				478	J. H. Lloyd
				482	T. H. Ouchterlony
				455	H. C. B. Tanner
No. in (med.) list.	Assistant Surgeons.			474	G. W. Borrodaile
77	J. Cramond			473	W. J. Finch
81	R. T. C. Baxter			466	C. E. Basevi
84	W. L. Cameron			470	W. W. Benson
96	J. H. Wilmot			498	C. H. Campbell
118	J. F. Straker			492	W. Ward
				505	F. J. Mortimer

Page 37—

OFFICERS WHO SERVED WITH THE HORSE BRIGADE, BUT DO NOT APPEAR TO HAVE BEEN POSTED TO ANY PARTICULAR TROOP, OR WHOSE TROOPS ARE NOT TRACEABLE.

This list is approximate only.

As Captain (198) L. C. Russell.
As Subaltern (263) M. F. Willoughby.
,, (267) H. W. Trevelyan.
,, (272) W. T. Whitlie.
,, (278) G. A. Farquharson.
,, (287) J. E. S. Waring.
,, (292) T. Tarleton.
,, (310) W. Kirkpatrick.
,, (317) R. W. Chichester.
,, (319) E. Welland.
,, (431) T. B. Heathorn with 3rd Troop.

THE
FOOT ARTILLERY.

PART IV.

THE FOOT ARTILLERY.

ADJUTANTS, FOOT ARTILLERY.

No. in list.			No. in list.		
28	A. Turner	1759	171	J. Eyles	1794
25	E. Hamilton	1760	176	G. Warden	6 Nov. 1795
42	J. Peppard	Oct. 1762	173	W. Smith	11 Mar. 1800
53	J. Millet	Apr. 1763	182	C. J. Bond	3 June 1800
50	W. Wilder	Nov. 1764	174	A. G. Fisher	1 July 1802
68	E. Curfy	Dec. 1765	193	S. R. Strover	10 Mar. 1805
79	J. Hassall	Oct. 1768	192	R. Macintosh	22 Jan. 1809
96	J. Wilkinson	Oct. 1772	208	D. Hogarth	3 May 1811
152	A. C. Bellas	Sept. 1784	210	T. Stevenson	6 Dec. 1811
153	W. Piper	Nov. 1789			to 1816

Appointment shown vacant in Army Lists 1817 and 1818.

220	W. Miller	May 1818	222	F. P. Lester	1 Mar. 1819 to 1 Dec. 1819

TWO BATTALIONS FORMED 1 JAN. 1820.

1st Battalion.			2nd Battalion.		
240	G. R. Lyons	1 Dec. 1819	230	W. H. Foy	1 Jan. 1820
244	W. Jacob	18 Feb. 1820	243	M. C. Decluzeau	1 Feb. 1822
224	S. J. C. Falconer	1822	268	T. E. Cotgrave	1 Nov. 1822
269	T. Ritherden	11 Nov. 1822	251	J. Sinclair	27 Jan. 1826
251	J. Sinclair	11 Feb. 1823	275	J. Grant	21 Jan. 1828
267	H. W. Trevelyan	1 Dec. 1824	263	M. F. Willoughby	6 Sept. 1830
252	E. Stanton	21 Apr. 1828	275	J. Grant	19 Sept. 1834
274	H. Sutton	15 Nov. 1832	311	R. Creed	4 June 1838
297	B. Bailey	18 Feb. 1833	291	J. S. Unwin	20 Feb. 1841
295	J. M. Glasse	3 Sept. 1833	342	R. B. Brett	3 July 1845
312	H. Creed	13 May 1840	376	W. Cameron	17 June 1846
330	J. Pottinger	1 Mar. 1841	368	A. M. Murray	16 Oct. 1847
351	J. G. Petrie	15 Oct. 1848	376	W. Cameron	6 Feb. 1850
391	C. J. Barton	6 Jan. 1853	387	T. T. Haggard	1 June 1854
426	G. Twiss	26 Aug. 1859	389	D. G. Anderson	24 June 1857
	to	31 Mar. 1861	448	G. F. Worsley	11 July 1859
				to	31 Mar. 1861

RESERVE ARTILLERY, AFTERWARDS 3RD BATTALION.

390	J. Shekleton	7 Nov. 1857	401	R. C. Battiscombe	8 July 1858

18th Brigade R.A.			21st Brigade R.A.		
426	G. Twiss	1 Apr. 1861	448	G. F. Worsley	1 Apr. 1861
424	J. B. Hardy	9 Dec. 1861	482	T. H. Ouchterlony	14 Jan. 1867
451	T. P. Berthon	10 Oct. 1864		to	21 Jan. 1877
471	T. C. Fletcher	16 Nov. 1868			
481	E. G. Battiscombe	28 Jan. 1871			
	to	13 July 1875			

1st COMPANY.

$$\frac{1/1}{86 \ \text{R.G.A.}}$$

1748. Formed on 17 June.

Mar. 1757. CHANDERNAGORE. Detachment.

1801–1802. EGYPT. Cap. G. Powell (158).

1 Jan. 1820. Designated 1st Company 1st Battalion.

G.O. 20 May 1823. Authorized to bear "Egypt" and the Sphinx on appointments.

1824. BURMAH. Ava. Cap. L. C. Russell (198).

1856–1857. PERSIA, with No. 3 L.F. Battery. Reshire, Bushire, Khooshab. Cap. W. S. Hatch (356).

1862. Designated 1st Battery 18th Brigade R.A.

1863.   „   A   „   18th   „   „

1863.   „   1st   „   21st   „   „

1877.   „   5th   „   11th   „   „

1878. AFGHANISTAN. Candahar. Major C. Collingwood (R.A. 2420).

1882. Designated 5th Battery North Irish Division R.A.

1889.   „   5th   „   Southern Division R.A.

1891.   „   1st Company   „   „

1899.   „   1st   „   „   „   R.G.A.

1902.   „   86th   „   R.G.A.

2ND COMPANY.

1/2
Reduced 1865
81 R.F.A. 1901.

1755. Raised.

Mar. 1757. CHANDERNAGORE. Detachment.

1801-1802. EGYPT. Lieut. W. Smith (173).

1820. Designated 1st Company 2nd Battalion.

G.O. 20 May 1823. Authorized to bear "Egypt" and the Sphinx on appointments.

1838-1839. SIND and AFGHANISTAN, with No. 2 Mule Battery. Cap. T. J. Pontardent (260).

1856-1857. Persia Detachment. Mortar Raft Mohumra. Cap. J. Worgan (348).

1857-1858. MUTINY, with No. 2 L.F. Battery. Rajpootana, Awah Jan. 1858, Kotah Mar. 1858, Lieut. S. K. Pechell (457) wounded, and subsequent operations. Guzerat, Chota Oodeypore 1 Dec. 1858, 2 guns, under Lieut. T. B. Heathorn (431), which marched 241 miles in 9 days. Commander, Cap. W. D. Aitken (346).

1862. Designated 1st Battery 21st Brigade R.A.

1862.   ,,   A   ,,   21st   ,,   ,,

1863.   ,,   B   ,,   21st   ,,   ,,

1865. Reduced.

1895. 81st Field Battery R.A. raised.

1899. Designated 81st Battery R.F.A. Won the Adjutant-General's cup for shooting at Okehampton.

1901. By Army Order 112, H.M. the King was graciously pleased to approve of the 81st Battery R.F.A. being considered as reformed from the 1st Company 2nd Battalion Bombay Artillery, to perpetuate its memory and carry on its traditions.

1900-1902. SOUTH AFRICA. Embarked at Liverpool 31 Dec. 1899, arrived at Cape Town 21 Jan. 1900. Railed to Orange River, marched to Modder River to join the VI. Division, and with advance of VI. Division. Was present at all the actions with Cronje's rearguard, Klip Drift, Klip Kraal, etc. Was the first battery in action at Paardeberg 26 Feb., Cap. A. M. Lennox (R.A. 4413) killed. Remained in action, bombarding the laager, until Cronje's surrender 27 Feb. Marched with Lord Roberts on Bloemfontein, actions of Poplar Grove and Driefontein, Lieuts. A. H. N. Devenish (R.A. 4988) and T. E. P. Wickham (R.A. 5521) wounded. Railed to Kaffir River 12 Apr., joining Gen. Pole Carew's Brigade, and stayed there covering line of communications till 22 Apr., when marched back to Bloemfontein. Marched with Gen. Ian Hamilton on Pretoria. Was in engagements Welkam Farm 4 May, Sand River 10 May, Lindley 18 May, Heilbron 21 May, Dornkoop 29 May, Johannesburg 30 May, Pretoria 4 June. Marched from Pretoria 6 June to join Lord Methuen, was engaged with De Wett at Rhenoster Spruit 10 June. Was present at Prinsloo's surrender 30 July 1900 at Fauriesberg, O.R. Colony. Marched to Pretoria 24 Aug., employed on lines of communication till Mar. 1901. Right section, Cap. H. R. Gotto (R.A. 4642), at Wilge River with 7th Fusiliers and a troop of 18th Hussars, attacked by part of Viljoen's force. Section under fire 9½ hours, and eventually drove away the Boers with loss. Battery in Mar. 1902 employed by separate sections with Col. Benson's, Gen. W. Kitchener's, Gen. B. Hamilton's, Col. J. Campbell's, Lieut.-Col. G. G. Simpson's, Lieut.-Col. Ormiston's, and Gen. Spen's columns. Commanders: Major H. A. Chapman (R.A. 3778) to 23 Apr. 1900; Major G. G. Simpson (R.A. 3710) to Nov. 1901; Cap. H. R. Gotto (R.A. 4642) to Mar. 1902; Major G. S. Cleeve (R.A. 4045). Battery entitled to clasps for Paardeberg, Driefontein, Johannesburg, Wittebergen, Relief of Kimberley, 1 D.S.O., 2 D.C.M.'s.

3RD COMPANY. $\dfrac{2/1}{15\ \text{R.F.A.}}$

1755. Raised.

1757. CHANDERNAGORE. Detachment.

1759. Reduced.

22 Mar. 1765. Reformed.

1799. MYSORE WAR. Battle of Sedaishur 6 Mar.; Seringapatam. Cap. J. Bailie (122).

1803. MAHRATTA WAR. Assaye 23 Sept. Lieut. R. Whish (190).

1 Jan. 1820. Designated 2nd Company 1st Battalion.

G.O. 20 May 1823. Authorized to bear "Seringapatam" and "Assaye" on appointments.

1843. SIND. Hydrabad 24 Mar. Cap. M. F. Willoughby (263).

G.G.O.11Apr. 1843. Authorized to bear "Hyderabad" on appointments.

1848–1849. PUNJAUB, with No. 7 L.F. Battery. Mooltan, Lieut. J. B. Woosnam (315); Goojerat 21 Feb. 1849, and pursuit of Sikh Army. Cap. S. Turnbull (304).

1858. Arabia. Sheikh Othman. Lieut. M. W. B. S. Pasley (446).

1862. Designated 2nd Battery 18th Brigade R.A.

1862.   „   B   „   18th   „   „

1863.   „   A   „   18th   „   „

1877.   „   H   „   2nd   „   „

1889.   „   15th Field Battery R.A.

1899.   „   15th Battery R.F.A.

4TH COMPANY.

$$\frac{2/2}{90 \text{ R.G.A.}}$$

6 Mar. 1768. Raised.

      1799. MYSORE WAR. Battle of Sedaishur 6 Mar.; Seringapatam. Cap. A. Torriano (148) killed.

1 Jan. 1820. Designated 2nd Company 2nd Battalion.

G.O. 20 May 1823. Authorized to bear "Seringapatam" on appointments.

    1838–1839. SIND and AFGHANISTAN, with No. 2 Field Battery. Cap. J. Lloyd (246). Ghuznee 23 July 1839.

    1842–1843. SIND, with Camel Battery. Meanee 17 Feb., Hydrabad 24 Mar. 1843. Cap. W. T. Whitlie (272).

G.G.O.11 Apr. 1843. Authorized to bear "Hyderabad" on appointments.

      1862. Designated 3rd Battery 21st Brigade R.A.

      1868. ABYSSINIA, with Mountain Battery. Arogee, Magdala. Lieut.-Col. L. W. Penn (R.A. 2187).

      1877. Designated 7th Battery   11th Brigade R.A.

      1882.   ,,   8th   ,,   London Division R.A.

      1889.   ,,   7th   ,,   Eastern   ,,   ,,

      1891.   ,,   7th Company   ,,   ,,   ,,

      1899.   ,,   7th   ,,   ,,   ,,   R.G.A.

      1902.   ,,   90th   ,,   R.G.A.

5TH COMPANY.

$\dfrac{3/1}{30 \text{ R.F.A.}}$

1796. Raised 24 May.

1799. MYSORE WAR. Battle of Sedaishur, 6 Mar.; Seringapatam. Cap.-Lieut. J. Eyles (171). Lieut. W. Macredie (177) killed.

1803. MAHRATTA WAR. Assaye 23 Sept. Lieut. T. Morse (187).

1 Jan. 1820. Designated 3rd Company 1st Battalion.

1840. SIND. Taking of Manora. Cap. W. Brett (265).

1841-1842. AFGHANISTAN, with L.F. Battery. Left Sukkur Jan. 1841 for Quetta, then through Kojuk pass to Khandahar, arriving 23 Oct. 1841. Battle of Urghundaub 12 Jan. 1842; action 8 Feb.; left Khandahar 9 Aug.; actions at Gohain 28 and 30 Aug.; occupation of Ghuznee 5 and 6 Sept.; actions at Beni-badam and Maidan 14 and 15 Sept.; Istalaf, 2 guns, Lieut. W. S. Terry (337), 30 Sept. 1842; rear-guard in Khyber pass, Lieut. W. S. Terry killed. Commander, Cap. C. Blood (279).

1858. MUTINY, Southern Mahratta Country, Kulludgee Field Force, with No. 1 L.F. Battery. Capture of Shorapore Feb. 1858; and surrender of Jhumkhundee, 2 guns. 2nd Lieut. H. T. Vachell (461).

1862. Designated 3rd Battery 18th Brigade R.A.

1862.   „   C   „   18th   „   „

1863.   „   B   „   18th   „   „

1877.   „   I   „   2nd   „   „

1882. EGYPT. Tel-el-Kebir. Major W. Ward (492).

1889. Designated 30th Field Battery R.A.

1899.   „   30th Battery R.F.A.

6TH COMPANY. $\frac{3/2}{31 \text{ R F.A.}}$

1797. Raised 13 Oct.
1817–1818. MAHRATTA WAR. Battle of Kirkee. Detachment. Lieut. J. Laurie (228).
1 Jan. 1820. Designated 3rd Company 2nd Battalion.
G.O. 20 May 1823. Authorized to bear "Kirkee" on appointments.
1862. Designated B Battery 18th Brigade R.A.
1863.   ,,   C ,, 18th ,, ,,
1877.   ,,   K ,, 2nd ,, ,,
1889.   ,,   31st Field Battery R.A.
1899.   ,,   31st Battery R.F.A.

7TH COMPANY. $\dfrac{4/1}{91 \text{ and } 92 \text{ R.G.A.}}$

1802. Raised 28 Mar.

1 Jan. 1820. Designated 4th Company 1st Battalion.

1839. Capture of Aden. Cap. M. F. Willoughby (263).

1856–1857. PERSIA, with No. 5 L.F. Battery. Reshire, Bushire, Khooshab. Cap. H. L. Gibbard (357).

1862. Designated 4th Battery 18th Brigade R.A.

1862.   ,,   D   ,,   18th   ,,   ,,

1863.   ,,   4th   ,,   21st   ,,   ,,

1865–1866. Arabia. Expedition against Foodlee Arabs. Major J. B. Hardy (424).

1877. Designated 8th Battery 11th Brigade R.A.

1878. AFGHANISTAN. Major H. H. Murray (Bengal 995).

1882. Designated 5th Battery Southern Division R.A.

1885–1887. BURMAH. Major F. M. E. Vibart (R.A. 3215).

1889. Designated 15th Battery Southern Division R.A.

1891.   ,,   15th Company   ,,   ,,   ,,

1899.   ,,   15th   ,,   ,,   ,,   R.G.A.

1899–1902. SOUTH AFRICA. Embarked at Southampton with siege train 9 Dec., arriving at Cape Town 26 Dec. 1899. Right Half Company with four 6″ B.L. Howitzers arrived at Paardeberg 26 Feb. 1900, and went into action immediately. Present at Cronje's surrender 27 Feb. Marched with the Army to Bloemfontein. Commander, Major J. R. H. Allen (R.A. 3577). Left Half Company proceeded in Apr. 1900 from Orange River Station and joined Right Half Company at Bloemfontein. Proceeded on 24 May with four 6″ B.L. Howitzers by rail to Roodeval, and from thence marched to Johannesburg. Was in action before Pretoria, entering with Lord Roberts' Army on 5 June 1900. One section of Left Half Company then went to Wonderboom, and the other to Balmoral. Actions at Wonderboom and Balmoral. From 1 Feb. 1900 Major F. G. Græme (R.A. 3755) in command.

1900. CHINA. Right Half Company embarked at Cape Town on 18 July 1900 for China, to form part of the China Expeditionary Force, arriving at Wei-hai-wei on 3 Aug. Commander, Cap. G. Tyacke (R.A. 4253).

Right Half Company.	*Left Half Company.*
May 1901. Merged with Half Company 15th Western Division R.G.A. with designation of 15th Company Southern Division R.G.A.	Merged with Half Company 15th Western Division R.G.A. with designation of 15th Company Western Division R.G.A.
1902. Designated 91st Company R.G.A.	Designated 92nd Company R.G.A.

7th COMPANY—*continued.*

91*st Company R.G.A.*   92*nd Company R.G.A.*

4TH COMPANY 2ND **BATTALION.** $\frac{4/2}{55 \text{ R.F.A.}}$

1820. Raised 1 Jan.

1844–1845. Southern Mahratta Country. Capture of Punella Dec. 1844; Monohur and Munsuntosh. Major G. Yeadell (250).

1848–1849. PUNJAUB, with No. 5 L.F. Battery. Mooltan. Cap. Brook Bailey (297) killed.

1857–1858. MUTINY, with No. 4 L.F. Battery. Attack on mutineers at Arungabad, and pursuit June 1857. Central India and Rajpootana: siege and capture of Dhar Oct., Lieut. B. Christie (468) severely wounded; Mundesore 22 Nov., Goraria 25 Nov. 1857; relief of Neemuch, siege and capture of Ratghur Jan. 1858, Barodea 30 Jan., 2 guns, Lieut. C. H. Strutt (450); relief of Sangor 3 Feb., Garrakhota 12 Feb., forcing Muddenpore pass 4 Mar., capture of Chandaree 5 Mar., siege and storm of Jhansi Apr. 1858; also detachments were at the battle of the Betwa 1 Apr., Lohari, Koonch 6 May, Muttra and Deopora, Gallowlee 15 May, Calpee 22 May, Morar 16 June, Kotah-ke-Serai 17 June, taking of Gwalior 18 June 1858. Commanders: Cap. J. D. Woollcombe (352) to 22 May 1858; Lieut. C. H. Strutt (450).

1862. Designated 4th Battery 21st Brigade R.A.

1863.   ,,   2nd   ,,   18th   ,,   ,,

1877.   ,,   L   ,,   2nd   ,,   ,,

1889.   ,,   55th Field Battery R.A.

1899.   ,,   55th Battery R.F.A.

5TH COMPANY 1ST BATTALION.

1820. Raised 1 Jan.
1824. Reduced 1 May.

5TH COMPANY 2ND BATTALION.

1820. Raised 1 Jan.
1820–1821. ARABIA. Beni-boo-ali. Cap. J. W. Watson (231).
Authorized to bear " Beni-boo-ali " on appointments.
1824. Reduced 1 May.

1st COMPANY RESERVE ARTILLERY. $\dfrac{1/R}{70 \text{ R.F.A.}}$

1857. Raised Nov.
1861. Designated 1st Company 3rd Battalion.
1862.   ,,   5th Battery 18th Brigade R.A.
1862.   ,,   E   ,,   18th   ,,   ,,
1877.   ,,   M   ,,   2nd   ,,   ,,
1882.   ,,   M   ,,   4th   ,,   ,,
1889.   ,,   70th Field Battery R.A.
1899.   ,,   70th Battery R.F.A.

2ND COMPANY RESERVE ARTILLERY. $\dfrac{2/\text{R}}{71\ \text{R.F.A.}}$

1857. Raised in Nov.

    MUTINY, with No. 18 L.F. Battery. Ratghur 26 Jan., Barodea 30 Jan., Garrakotah 11 Feb., Jhansi 3 Apr. (1/2 Battery, Lieut. P. H. Harcourt), Calpee 22 May, Morar and recapture of Gwalior 20 June 1858. Caps. J. G. Lightfoot (350) and C. B. Fuller (347), and Lieut. P. H. Harcourt (454).

1861. Designated 2nd Company 3rd Battalion.

1862.   „   6th Battery 18th Brigade R.A.

1863.   „   F   „   18th   „   „

1877.   „   N   „   2nd   „   „

1882. EGYPT. Tel-el-Kebir. Lieut.-Col. W. G. Brancker (R.A. 2535).

1889. Designated 71st Field Battery R.A.

1899.   „   71st Battery R.F.A.

3/R
3RD COMPANY RESERVE ARTILLERY.   Reduced 1865

90 R.F.A. 1901.

1857. Raised Nov.

1861. Designated 3rd Company 3rd Battalion.

1862. „   5th Battery 21st Brigade R.A.

1863. „   G „ 18th „ „

1865. Reduced.

1898. 90th Field Battery R.A. raised.

1899. Designated 90th Battery R.F.A.

1901. By Army Order 112, H.M. the King was graciously pleased to approve of the 90th Battery R.F.A. being considered as reformed from the 3rd Company 3rd Battalion Bombay Artillery, to perpetuate its memory and carry on its traditions.

4TH COMPANY RESERVE ARTILLERY. $\dfrac{4/\text{R}}{88\ \text{R.G.A.}}$

1857. Raised Nov.
1861. Designated 4th Company 3rd Battalion.
1862.   „   6th Battery 21st Brigade R.A.
1863.   „   5th   „   21st   „   „
1867–1868. ABYSSINIA, with Mountain Battery. Magdala. Cap. G. Twiss (426).
1877. Designated 9th Battery 11th Brigade R.A.
1882.   „   5th   „   Lancashire Division R.A.
1889.   „   27th „   Southern   „   „
1891.   „   1st(A) Company Southern   „   „
1 Apr. 1894. „   27th   „   „   „
1899.   „   27th   „   „   „   R.G.A.
1902.   „   88th   „   R.G.A.

THE
NATIVE ARTILLERY.

PART V.

THE NATIVE ARTILLERY.

ADJUTANTS, NATIVE ARTILLERY.

No. in list.	GOLUNDAUZE.	
272	W. T. Whitlie	7 Apr. 1826
284	E. P. Prother	5 Feb. 1831
285	G. Hutt	7 Apr. 1833–Oct. 1841
315	J. B. Woosnam	13 Jan. 1842
295	J. M. Glasse.	27 Aug. 1844
331	G. P. Sealy	5 Aug. 1845

Two Battalions formed 2 July 1846.

No. in list.	3rd Battalion.		No. in list.	4th Battalion.	
331	G. P. Sealy	from Golundauze	347	C. B. Fuller	14 Aug. 1846
348	J. Worgan	16 Oct. 1847	363	W. Stevenson	22 Feb. 1850
385	A. R. Mark	23 May 1851	385	A. R. Mark	22 Feb. 1853
382	F. Conybeare	22 Feb. 1853	398	W. H. Saulez	26 July 1858
404	E. S. Beamish	10 May 1855	407	C. E. H. Cotes	7 Dec. 1859
403	J. R. Henderson	29 Oct. 1859			

One Battalion 4th Native 1861.

No in list.		
403	J. R. Henderson	from 3rd Batt.
459	C. E. Newport	19 Oct. 1861

Called Golundauze Battalion 1862.
Reduced 1863.

1st COMPANY. 1/3

1826. Raised 28 Mar.
1838–1839. SIND and AFGHANISTAN. Ghuznee 23 July 1839.
1844–1845. Southern Mahratta Country. Siege and capture of Punella. Lieut. A. Crawford (359).
20 July 1846. Designated 1st Company 3rd Battalion.
1860. Reduced.

2ND COMPANY.   2/4

1826. Raised 28 Mar.
20 July 1846. Designated 2nd Company 4th Battalion.
1847–1849. PUNJAUB. Mooltan. Lieut. J. Hamilton (345).
      1858. MUTINY. Khandeish ; Durba Bowree and Ambapawnee 10
            and 11 Apr. Cap. G. P. Sealy (331) and 2nd Lieut. C. E.
            Basevi (466).
31 May 1860. Designated 3rd Company 4th Battalion.
      1862.   „   2nd   „   Golundauze Battalion.
      1863. Reduced.

3RD COMPANY.   3/3

1826. Raised 28 Mar.
1840–1842. SIND and AFGHANISTAN. Siege of Kahun, detachment.
            Lieut. D. Erskine (325).
      1843. SIND, with Horse and Mule Battery. Meanee 17 Feb.,
            Hydrabad 24 Mar. Cap. G. Hutt (285).
G.G.O. 11 Apr. 1843. Authorized to bear "Hyderabad" on appointments.
20 July 1846. Designated 3rd Company 3rd Battalion.
      1858. MUTINY. Detachment with Rajpootana Field Force.
21 May 1860. Designated 3rd Company 4th Battalion.
      1862.   „   3rd   „   Golundauze Battalion.
      1863.   „   2nd   „   Native Artillery.
      1870. Reduced.

4TH COMPANY.   4/4

1826. Raised 28 Mar.
20 July 1846. Designated 4th Company 4th Battalion.
1856–1857. PERSIA. With Mountain Train. Cap. J. G. Lightfoot (350).
      1858. MUTINY. Khandeish ; Durba Bowree and Ambapawnee
            11 and 12 Apr. Cap. G. P. Sealy (331).
      1868. Designated 3rd Company Golundauze Battalion.
      1863.   „   3rd   „   Native Artillery.
1865–1866. ARABIA. Expedition against Foodlee Arabs. Beer Said.
            Lieut. J. B. Walker (493).
      1870. Reduced.

5TH COMPANY.   5/3

1826. Raised 28 Mar.
1838–1839. Sind Reserve Force.
1840–1841. SIND and AFGHANISTAN. Lieut. H. Giberne (303).
20 July 1846. Designated 5th Company 3rd Battalion.
      1858. Arabia. Sheikh Othman. Lieut. A. J. Billamore (432).
31 May 1860. Designated 5th Company 4th Battalion.
1860–1861. Siege of Dwarka, with No. 12 L.F. Battery. Cap. A.
            Aytoun (377).
30 Sept. 1862. Reduced.

6TH COMPANY.   6/4

1827. Raised 28 Sept.
20 July 1846. Designated 6th Company 4th Battalion.
      1839. Capture of Aden 19 Jan. Lieut. W. Massie (320).
30 Sept. 1862. Reduced.

7TH COMPANY.   2/3

1827. Raised 28 Sept.
20 July 1846. Designated 2nd Company 3rd Battalion.
      1860. Reduced.

8TH COMPANY. 1/4

1827. Raised 28 Sept.

20 July 1846. Designated 1st Company 4th Battalion.

1848–1849. PUNJAUB. Mooltan. Cap. S. Turnbull (304).

1858–1859. MUTINY, with No. 6 L.F. Battery. Ahmednuggur Flying Column. Cap. J. B. Hardy (424).

1862. Designated 1st Company Golundauze Battalion.

1863. „ 1st „ Native Artillery.

1867–1868. ABYSSINIA. Cap. P. D. Marett (396).

1870. Designated No. 1 Mountain Battery.

1884. Zhob Valley Field Force, 4 guns. Cap. A. Keene (R.A. 3555).

1885. Designated No. 5 (Bombay) Mountain Battery.

1885–1887. BURMAH. Cap. A. Keene (R.A. 3555).

1897. PUNJAUB FRONTIER. Operations of the Mohmund Force. Badmanai Pass 23 Sept., Jarobi Glen 25 Sept., Kuda Khel country 27 Sept. 1897. Cap. F. R. McC. de Butts (R.A. 4139).

1897–1898. TIRAH. Advance to Chagru Kotal and Dargai 18 and 20 Oct.; capture of Sampagha pass 29 Oct., Cap. F. R. McC. de Butts killed; capture of Arhanga pass 31 Oct.; affair of 9 Nov. at Saran Sar; advance into Waran and Rajgul valleys; march down Bara valley; affair of Shin Kimar 29 Jan. 1898. Commanders, Cap. F. R. McC. de Butts (R.A. 4139) and Cap. L. C. Gordon (R.A. 4213).

1901. Designated Quetta Mountain Battery.

9TH COMPANY.   4/3

1843. Raised 1 July.
20 July 1846. Designated 4th Company 3rd Battalion.
1858–1859. MUTINY, with No. 8 L.F. Battery. Battle of Sanganeer 8 Aug.,
     Bunass 14 Aug. 1858. Cap. G. G. Brown (381). Nusseerabad
     Field Detachment Jan. 1859. Lieut. J. Shekleton (390).
31 May 1860. Distributed amongst other companies.

10TH COMPANY.   3/4

1843. Raised 1 July.
20 July 1846. Designated 3rd Company 4th Battalion.
1857. Mutinied at Shikarpore.

11TH COMPANY.   6/3

1846. Raised 28 Mar.
20 July 1846. Designated 6th Company 3rd Battalion.
31 May 1860. Distributed amongst other companies.

12TH COMPANY.   5/4

1846. Raised 28 Mar.
20 July 1846. Designated 5th Company 4th Battalion.
1857. Mutinied at Hydrabad Sind.

JACOBABAD MOUNTAIN TRAIN.

1875. Converted into No. 2 Mountain Battery.

1878–1879. AFGHANISTAN. Cap. R. Wace (R.A. 2997).

1885. Designated No. 6 (Bombay) Mountain Battery.

1897. Two guns with escort of Political Officer attacked in Tochi valley. Cap. J. F. Browne (R.A. 4323) and Lieut. H. A. Cruickshank (R.A. 4858) killed.

Tochi Field Force, 4 guns. Cap. O. C. Williamson (R.A. 4194). Lieut.-Col. W. Du Gray's desp. 20 June 1897: "The indomitable spirit of No. 6 (Bombay) Mountain Battery is beyond all praise."

1901. Designated Jullundur Mountain Battery.

LIST OF
BOMBAY ARTILLERY OFFICERS.

PART VI.

LIST OF BOMBAY ARTILLERY OFFICERS.

NOTE.—*Promotions, appointments, employments, and services in other corps, or after retirement, are printed in italics.*

1 **Hugh Cameron.** *Ensign 3rd Company infantry*, 1738, *l. Dec.* 1746. Master gunner Sept. 1748, 1 cap. and chief engr. Arty. 4 Apr. 1749. *Transferred to the infantry Oct.* 1750, *not in rolls for* 1758. *Commanded force which occupied Bancote Dec.* 1754.

2 **William Atkinson.** Specially sent out from England, arrived in the *Doddington* at Bombay 28 Mar. 1749, and commissioned as cap.l. and drctr. laboratory 4 Apr. 1749. Struck off Feb. 1750 on account of ill health.

3 **Creswell Maddox.** Specially sent out from England, arrived in the *Doddington* at Bombay 28 Mar. 1749, and commissioned as lfw. 4 Apr. 1749.

4 **Eric Roling.** From 1st gunner's mate, lfw. 4 Apr. 1749, cap. 17 Oct. 1752.

5 **John Forcebury.** From gunner's mate, lfw. 4 Apr. 1749, 1 l. 17 Oct. 1752.

6 **James de Funck.** *Was a cap. of the Royal Regiment of Swedes in France.* Specially engaged by Sir Luke Schaub to serve the H.E.I. Company for 7 years as 1 cap. and chief engr. of Arty. at Bombay 1752. Was mostly employed on the fortifications and on survey work. In 1757 was superseded as chief engr. by James Mace (31), and afterwards was dismissed by Governor Bourchier for disobedience of Company's orders. *On arrival in England he memorialized the Court of Directors, who granted him 500 guineas as compensation. He appears to have left a good reputation in Bombay, as Niebuhr, the Danish traveller who landed in Bombay from Arabia on 11 Sept. 1763, says, "The Artillery of Bombay is in very good condition owing to the care of a Swede, whom the English sent out in* 1752, *and who brought with him a company of gunners he had raised in Germany."*

7 **Gilbert Carter,** 2 cap. and 2 engr. 17 Oct. 1752, 1 cap. Dec. 1755. d. 13 Apr. 1758.

8 **John Wolfgang Molitore,** 2 l. Nov. 1753, 1 l. Dec. 1755, cap.l. Oct. 1758. Shown as at Madras 1755. Was probably serving with the force under Maj. Lawrence. Embarked for Calcutta 29 Oct. 1756, was probably at siege of Chandernagore Mar. 1757, present at the battle of Plassey under Col. Clive 23 June 1757. Killed at the storm and capture of Masulipatam 7 Apr. 1759.

9 **James Diamond.** From sergt.-bombardier, 3 l. Nov. 1753, 2 l. 28 Jan. 1756, 1 l. Feb. 1759.

10 **Daniel Hide.** From corp.-bombardier, lfw. Mar. 1753.

11 **Stephen Young.** From corp.-bombardier, lfw. Mar. 1753, 1 l. Nov. 1753. Present with the force under Col. Clive at the taking of Geriah Feb. 1756.

12 **Luis Felix de Gloss.** From l. of infantry, 1 l. 20 Aug. 1753, cap.l. 27 Dec. 1757, cap. 13 Apr. 1758, cap. and engr. 6 Feb. 1759, brev.-m. 15 Jan. 1770. Clerk of the works 18 Oct. 1757. Present at the capture of Surat under Cap. R. Maitland (R.A. 74), constructed the approaches, and remained in command of the garrison nearly 3 years, made improvements in manufacture of gunpowder 1759, went to Bengal 1764 when volunteers were called for, employed on survey duty. Went home sick Feb. 1773, and was made brev.-l.c. as a reward for good service.

13 **Richard Galliard.** From 1. of infantry, cap. of the train 15 Nov. 1754.
d. 16 Oct. 1758.

14 **Newton Barton Burr,** b. 1734. From ensign 6th Company infantry, 3 l.
Jan. 1755, 1 l. Dec. 1755, cap.l. 12 Dec. 1758, cap. 2 Mar. 1759, m. 1 Feb.
1769. At taking of Geriah under Col. Clive Feb. 1756, capture of Surat
under Cap. R. Maitland (R.A. 74), on field service Mar. 1765 and Feb. 1768.
d. 7 May 1776.

15 **John McGowan.** From 1. of infantry, cap.l. Dec. 1755.

16 **James Hogg.** From 1st gunner's mate, cap.l. Dec. 1755, cap. Mar. 1758.
d. 11 June 1758.

17 **William Odieu.** From sergt. of infantry, lfw. Dec. 1755. Returned to
infantry as l. Mar. 1758.

18 **Charles Allen,** cap.l. Dec. 1755.

19 **Lorens Nilson,** nephew of James de Funck (6), a Swede. Bombardier cadet
11 Jan. 1753, lfw. Dec. 1755, 2 l. Mar. 1758, 1 l. Oct. 1758, cap.l. 23 May
1759, cap. 11 Jan. 1765. Field service 1754-1755, reduction of Malwan
forts, capture of Mangalore Feb. 1768, field service to the northward,
chief engr. at capture of Broach Nov. 1772. Transferred to Bombay
Engrs. on separation from Arty. as *m.* 2 *Aug.* 1775. *l.c. by special
appointment of Court of Directors Nov.* 1783, *brig.-gen. June* 1784. *Chief
engr. at siege of Tannah Dec.* 1774, *command of garrison and Bombay troops*
1780, *and chief engr.; brig.-gen. and C.I.C. of forces Western India* 1784,
until superseded by Lieut.-Gen. Meadows of H.M. Army 1788, *when he returned
home, and was, according to Phillipart, granted a pension of £1000 a year
Jan.* 1790.

20 **William Reynolds,** lfw. Dec. 1755. Transferred to the infantry Oct. 1758.

20a **Henry Sheldon,** lfw. Dec. 1755. Transferred to infantry Oct. 1758. d.
Feb. 1759.

21 **James Bennett.** From sergt., lfw. Dec. 1755.

22 **John Kinch.** From sergt., lfw. Dec. 1755. Went to Bengal to serve
under Col. Clive 1756. Transferred to Bengal Arty. (5). *Killed at or near
Patna, struck off* 1763.

23 **André Trembley.** From De Zeigler's Swiss Company, lfw. Dec. 1755, 2 l.
Jan. 1756. Sent home sick 1759.

24 **Andrew Werner,** lfw. for fortifications Dec. 1755, 2 l. Oct. 1758, cap.l. Jan.
1760. Taking of Surat Feb. 1759 under Cap. R. Maitland (R.A. 74). d.
22 Mar. 1765.

25 **Edward Hamilton,** lfw. Dec. 1755, 2 l. Feb. 1759, 1 l. Jan. 1760. Capture
of Surat Feb. 1759 under Cap. R. Maitland (R.A. 74). Adjt. 1760. Trans-
ferrred to infantry 1766.

26 **John Edgerton.** From 1. of infantry, cap.l. Nov. 1756. Embarked for
Bengal 29 Oct. 1756 for service under Col. Clive, probably at siege of
Chandernagore Mar. 1757, on expedition to Moorshedabad Aug. 1757 under
Col. Clive. Did not return to Bombay.

27 **Thomas Kidwell.** From ensign in the infantry, 2 l. Jan. 1756. Dismissed
by Governor Bourchier 1758, memorialized Court of Directors, petition
dismissed as he had signed a seditious letter.

28 **Alexander Turner.** From ensign of infantry, 2 l. Nov. 1756, 1 l. Mar. 1758,
cap.l. Feb. 1759. Went to Bengal 1756 to serve under Col. Clive. Adjt.
1759. Allowed to go to England 1760.

29 **John Newman,** lfw. Nov. 1756, 2 l. Apr. 1756.

30 **Daniel Grose,** lfw. Jan. 1756.

31 **James Mace.** From the infantry, cap. and chief engr. 1757, superseding
James de Funck (6), brev.-m. Apr. 1759. d. 22 Aug. 1763 at Bombay.

32 **Stephen Gore.** From the infantry, cap.l. Mar. 1758. d. 1 July 1763 as
cap. of infantry.

33 **Charles Pemble.** From 1. of infantry, cap.l. Mar. 1758, cap. Oct. 1758,
brev.-m. 1765, m. 26 Mar. 1766, l.c. 12 Feb. 1768, c. Jan. 1769. Dretr.
laboratory 1761. Delivered to Government of Bombay remarks about the

Lieut Col. Gasper Degen,
Comdt Art.y 1789.

(From a silhouette in the Bombay Arsenal with autograph.)

transit of Venus 1 Sept. 1761, which were sent to the Court of Directors. Commdt. of the Arty. 1762–63. Embarked for Bengal 12 Oct. 1763, served under Maj. Hector Munro in command of two companies of infantry, commanded 2nd line at battle of Buxar 23 Mar. 1764, with brevet of major, horse shot under him, highly praised desp. *Lond. Gaz.* 18 June 1765, commanded a force sent against Chunar Dec. 1764. Brevet rank made substantive and 5s. a day extra pay allowed, and appointed 2nd in command of the forces at Bombay. C.I.C. of the forces at Bombay 12 Feb. 1768. d. 11 May 1770 at Bombay.

34 **John Moritz Koetteritz,** lfw. Mar. 1758, 1 l. Mar. 1762.

35 **Richard Johnson,** lfw. Mar. 1758. Transferred to the infantry Jan. 1760.

36 **James Gray,** lfw. Mar. 1758.

37 **Alexander Shaw.** From sergt. of infantry, lfw. Mar. 1758. Was in Bengal in 1758, returned to infantry Apr. 1759.

38 **John Westphal,** a German, b. 1734. Enlisted in Germany 15 Jan. 1753, lfw. 11 Jan. 1758, 1 l. Jan. 1760, cap.l. 19 Oct. 1764, cap. Apr. 1773, m. 3 Feb. 1779. Sent with two guns 14 May 1780 to support of Cap. Campbell at Kalyan. MAHRATTA WAR 1779, wounded on 12 Jan. 1779. d. 30 Aug. 1784.

39 **Paul Beuther.** From the infantry, cap.l. Oct. 1758, cap. Feb. 1759. Returned to the infantry Apr. 1759.

40 **Thomas Deane.** From the infantry, cap.l. Feb. 1759. Returned to infantry Jan. 1760.

41 **Henry McKay.** From sergt. of infantry, lfw. 13 Jan. 1759, 2 l. Jan. 1760, 1 l. Oct. 1762. At capture of Surat Feb. 1759 under Cap. R. Maitland (R.A. 74). d. 31 Mar. 1765.

42 **Joseph Peppard,** lfw. Feb. 1759, 2 l. Jan. 1760. At capture of Surat Feb. 1759 under Cap. R. Maitland (R.A. 74), wounded. Adjt. 1762. d. 21 Nov. 1768.

43 **John Davis,** lfw. Feb. 1759. d. 25 Feb. 1759.

44 **Edward Smithers,** lfw. Feb. 1759. At capture of Surat Feb. 1759 under Cap. R. Maitland (R.A. 74).

45 **Gaspar Degen** (sometimes **Dagon**), b. 1725, a German Swiss. *Service began in 1752, ensign in De Zeigler's Swiss Company 10 Nov. 1755, l. 1758. This company went to Madras 1754, and was present at the battle of French Rocks with the French 16 Aug. 1754, also at the taking of Madura and Coilgooddy, returned to Bombay Nov. 1755.* 2 l. 10 Nov. 1755, 1 l. Apr. 1759, cap.l. 22 May 1759, cap. 28 Aug. 1764, brev.-m. Dec. 1790, m. June 1775, l.c. 5 Jan. 1779. On field service 1765, o.c. Arty. and 3rd in command of the army above the Ghats under Col. Egerton 1779, commdt. of Arty. 8 Jan. 1779–31 Dec. 1789. Returned to Europe 31 Dec. 1789.

46 **Charles Gordon,** lfw. Apr. 1759. d. at Tellicherry 18 July 1761, a l. of infantry.

47 **Richard Hewson.** From sergt., lfw. Apr. 1759.

48 **William Godwin,** lfw. Apr. 1759. Transferred to ensign of infantry Oct. 1760.

49 **Thomas Cranstoun,** lfw. Apr. 1759, 3 l. Oct. 1760, 2 l. Oct. 1762.

50 **William Wilder,** b. 1737. lfw. Jan. 1760, 2 l. Oct. 1760, 1 l. Nov. 1764, cap.l. 10 July 1765, cap. 2 Aug. 1764, adjt. 1764. On field service Mar. 1765. d. 3 Feb. 1779.

51 **John Hughes.** From sergt., lfw. Jan. 1760, 2 l. Jan. 1764, 1 l. Nov. 1764, cap.l. Nov. 1767. d. 1 May 1769.

52 **Edward Willson,** lfw. Jan. 1760.

53 **John Millet,** b. 1734. From sergt., lfw. Oct. 1760, adjt. 1763. Discharged 8 Sept. 1763.

54 **John Nugent,** b. 1735. Cadet 26 June 1759, lfw. 18 Apr. 1760, 2 l. Nov. 1764, 1 l. 8 June 1765, cap.l. Dec. 1770, cap. 14 Jan. 1775, brev.-m. 10 Apr. 1784, m. 1 Sept. 1784, l.c. 31 Dec. 1789. In Madras and Bengal 1765, in Persia 1767–68, siege and capture of Tannah Dec. 1774, recommended for commission as cap. Comg. at Tellicherry 1785, commdt. of Arty. 31 Dec. 1789–23

The Bombay Artillery.

Oct. 1792. d. 23 Oct. 1792 at Bombay. Tablet in Bombay Cathedral erected by Edward Russell Howe, Esq.

55 **David Spaeth,** a German, b. 1735. Enlisted in 1758. From sergt., lfw. 21 Oct. 1760, 1 l. 21 Jan. 1765, cap.l. 6 Oct. 1771, cap. Nov. 1774. Posted to Bombay Engrs. on separation from Arty. Aug. 2 1775. *Chief engr. at capture of Dubhoi by Gen. Goddard* 18 *Jan.* 1780, *severely wounded, highly praised. Siege of Ahmedabad, wounded by a sabre in seven places while filling up ditch for passage of Grenadiers.* d. *of his wounds* 13 *Jan.* 1780.

56 **George Goodchild,** b. 1734. Enlisted 11 Mar. 1751, from sergt., lfw. 14 Oct. 1760, 2 l. 10 July 1765, 1 l. Oct. 1768, cap.l. Mar. 1771. In Persia 1767. Sick at the Hot Wells June 1770 (wells near Callian). d. 1772.

57 **John Hurford,** lfw. Mar. 1762. d. 13 Mar. 1764.

58 **Thomas Durnford,** lfw. Mar. 1762, 2 l. Dec. 1765, 1 l. Feb. 1768. On field service Mar. 1765. d. 21 Mar. 1768.

59 **William Threlkeld.** From Arty. cadet, lfw. Oct. 1762.

60 **George Andrew Scheffeir,** a German from the French service. lfw. Apr. 1763, 1 l. Nov. 1767, cap.l. Oct. 1769. Dismissed 18 Sept. 1770.

61 **Thomas Bawdevin,** lfw. Apr. 1763.

62 **Spotswood Bowles,** b. 1744. lfw. Nov. 1764, 2 l. 23 July 1765, 1 l. Oct. 1768, cap.l. 20 Aug. 1772, 2 cap. 20 July 1775, 1 cap. Nov. 1777, adjt. of detachment Nov. 1767. On field service Feb. 1768, with Col. Cockburn's force above the Ghats, wounded 13 Dec. 1779, present at attack by Mahrattas on Col. Brown's convoy 15 Apr. 1781, wounded. d. 1783.

63 **Benjamin Robbins,** lfw. 12 Sept. 1764, 1 l. Oct. 1768. d. at Surat 30 July 1771.

64 **Charles Lewis Deetz.** From Arty. cadet, lfw. Nov. 1764, 2 l. 17 Dec. 1765. d. 23 Sept. 1766.

65 **Thomas Keating,** b. 1734. *Lieut. Thomas Keating petitioned to be employed in the H.E.I. Company's service* 6 *Oct.* 1762, *stated that he had served as an Arty. officer, an officer of Foot, and an asst. engr., particularly at the reduction of Louisburgh* 1756, *at the sieges of Fort Royal in Martinico* 1762, *and at the Havanas* 1762, *and was wounded at all these places.* cap., chief engr., and commdt. of Arty. Feb. 1764, l.c. 19 Feb. 1768. Commanded the force that took Vervosa and Karanjah Dec. 1774, commanded the force sent against the Mahrattas 1775, engagement of Hossamlu 19 Apr. 1775, battle of Daboun, battle of Hydrabad, battle of Arras, first great battle against the Mahrattas (out of 15 British officers 7 were killed and 4 wounded) 18 May 1775. On return to Bombay tried by C.M. for conduct of campaign and honourably acquitted. Went home in 1776. d. in 1780.

66 **William Brickell,** b. 1746. Enlisted 14 July 1763. From bombardier, lfw. 22 June 1765, 2 l. 3 June 1768, 1 l. Feb. 1769, cap.l. 8 Oct. 1771, cap. Dec. 1777. At the taking of Vervosa Dec. 1774, under Col. Thos. Keating (65), who reported thus: "I should not have made the attack last night, but that I found the men in high spirits and eager for it, together with the confidence I placed in the bravery and coolness of Lieut. Brickell, who commanded the party who were first to mount." res. Jan. 1778.

67 **Robert Hyde.** From Arty. cadet, lfw. 6 Dec. 1764.

68 **Edward Curfy.** From Arty. cadet, lfw. 6 Dec. 1764, adjt. 1765.

69 **Edward Bruce,** b. 1735. lfw. 20 July 1765, 2 l. Nov. 1767, 1 l. Mar. 1771. Dismissed by C.M. 26 Jan. 1772.

70 **John James,** lfw. Dec. 1765. d. 16 Apr. 1766.

71 **Thomas Turner.** From sergt., lfw. Dec. 1765. d. 10 May 1767.

72 **Robert Smyth,** lfw. 2 June 1766. Went home Jan. 1774.

73 **James McNeill,** b. 1744. From the marine, lfw. Nov. 1767, 2 l. Feb. 1768, 1 l. 6 Oct. 1771. On field service Feb. 1768. Posted to the Bombay Engrs. on separation from the Arty. 2 Aug. 1775.

74 **Charles Turner,** b. 1744. lfw. Nov. 1767, 2 l. Oct. 1768, 1 l. Mar. 1772. Posted to the Bombay Engrs. on separation from the Arty. 2 Aug. 1775.

75 **John Holebrook,** b. 1732. Enlisted 4 Jan. 1752, lfw. Nov. 1767, 2 l. Feb.

MAJOR J. S. TORRIANO.

(From a miniature in the possession of Colonel C. E. Torriano, retired, R. A.).

1769, 1 l. Mar. 1774, 2 cap. 3 Dec. 1777, 1 cap. Mar. 1781. On field service Feb. 1768, qtrmt. Oct. 1768, invalided on full pay 24 May 1785. d. 3 Dec. 1787.

76 **Thomas Lee**, b. 1737. From lieut. R.A. (356), m. and commdt. of Arty. 27 Aug. 1768–2 May 1777, l.c. 1777, o.c. Arty at siege of Tauna Dec. 1774. d. 2 May 1777 at Bombay.

77 **Lockhart Russell**, b. 1742. cap. 2 Mar. 1768. Transferred to Bengal as an engr. 1771. Went home 27 Jan. 1772.

78 **Thomas Robinson**, b. 1739. l. 19 Feb. 1768, cap.l. 1 Mar. 1768, cap. 10 Sept. 1771. Sick at the Hot Wells near Callian June 1770. d. 18 Sept. 1778.

79 **John Hassall**, b. 1750. lfw. 26 Feb. 1768, 2 l. 1 May 1769, 1 l. Apr. 1773, cap. 4 Dec. 1777. Adjt. Oct. 1768.

80 **John Samuel Torriano**, son of Charles (R.A. 164), brother of Alexander, (148), great uncle of Charles Edward (R.A. 2300), b. 1751. R.M.A. 1768, lfw. 28 Apr. 1768, 3 l. 27 Sept. 1770, 2 l. Oct. 1772, 1 l. Nov. 1773, brev.-cap. 1777, 2 cap. 5 Dec. 1777, 1 cap. 27 Sept. 1778, ante-d. 5 Dec. 1777, brev.-m. 14 Sept. 1784, m. Dec. 1786. Went with a mission to Poona as surveyor and draftsman 1770, at capture of Broach Nov. 1772, surveyor of fortifications at Bombay 1772. o.c. Arty. Surat 1774. Throughout Col. T. Keating's (65) campaign against the Mahrattas 1775, engagement of Hossamlu 19 Apr. 1775, battle of Daboun. Appointed brgd.-m. battle of Hydrabad, battle of Arras 18 May 1775, when he led the Grenadiers to take the enemy's guns, accompanied British ambassador to Poona 1776 in command of 2 companies of Sepoys to make surveys, services asked for by Gen. Goddard to command a company of European Arty. in his force, capture of Bassein Dec. 1780, services asked for by Gen. Meadows to command Arty. of the Bombay army in MYSORE WAR 1782, capture of Rajamondroog and advance to river Mergui, o.c. Arty. capture of Onore Jan. 1783, wounded. Left in command of Onore. His defence of it against an army of 10,000 men is described as being "one of the finest episodes of the war." On Apr. 30 the Bednore Committee ordered the evacuation, which order he refused to obey. The siege lasted from 14 May–25 Aug. 1783, and the blockade from 26 Aug. 1783–27 Mar. 1784, in all ten months. Cap. Torriano again wounded on 26 June. The defence was carried on under the most pressing events arising from famine, sickness, and desertion. The garrison was assisted by H.E.I. Company's ship *Wolfe*, and occasionally received supplies by a Company's cruiser, but the want of provisions was at one time so serious that a number of horses were killed and salted as a last resource, rather than surrender to Tippoo's forces. The gallant garrison was at length relieved by the peace of 1784, and returned to Bombay, reduced from its original strength of 743 men (of whom only 42 were European N.C.O. rank and file) to 238. Desp., Brev.-m. *Lond. Gaz.* 25 Nov. 1783, says, "A. Cap. Torriano, commandant of Onore, forced the Ghats and took possession of the city of Bednore." Same gazette, "Part of the garrison of Bednore escaped to Onore, which is under the command of Cap. Torriano, who, by his resolute and prudent conduct, prevented the panic from infecting his garrison." res. 19 Aug. 1787. *Commanded Kensington Volunteers* 1824. d. 27 Sept. 1825 at South Kensington. Memorial tablet St. Mary Abbot's Church. Name selected for inscription in list of distinguished Artillerymen on panels of Cadets' library R.M.A. 1902.

81 **Patrick Douglas**, b. 1751. lfw. 26 Feb. 1768.

82 **George Harding**, b. 1748. lfw. 26 Feb. 1768, 3 l. 27 Sep. 1770, 1 l. Apr. 1773. Went home sick Aug. 1775.

83 **Charles Pemble**, b. 1752. lfw. Feb. 1768, cap. 10 Apr. 1758.

84 **Samuel Sears**, b. 1751. lfw. 26 Feb. 1768. Transferred to Bengal Arty. (100) 22 Sept. 1770.

85 **James Jackson**, b. 1729. From sergt. of infantry, lfw. 26 Feb. 1768, 2 l. 31 July 1771, 2 cap. 14 Feb. 1779.

86 **Robert Nicholson**, b. 1746. lfw. 6 Aug. 1768, 3 l. 6 Oct. 1771, 1 l. Apr. 1773. Posted to Bombay Engrs. on separation from Arty. 2 Aug. 1775.

87 **George Black,** a Swiss, b. 1752.   From sergt., lfw. 1 Mar. 1769, 1. Oct.
    1772. d. 13 Nov. 1772.
88 **Daniel Thomas Layton,** b. 1752. lfw. 21 Sept. 1770, l. 26 Dec. 1776, 2 cap.
    13 Feb. 1779, 1 cap. Nov. 1782, ante-d. 12 Feb. 1779.   d. 17 May 1786.
89 **Alexander Fitzgerald,** lfw. Dec. 1770.
90 **Stephen Lynch,** b. 1746.   lfw. 1 Oct. 1769.
91 **Thomas Dighton,** b. 1748.   lfw. 1 Oct. 1769, 3 l. 16 Nov. 1772, cap. Mar.
    1779. d. 25 July 1779.
92 **John Hollomby,** b. 1751.   lfw. 1 Oct. 1769, 3 l. 16 Nov. 1772.
93 **David Thomas,** b. 1749.   lfw. 21 Sept. 1770.   d. 12 Oct. 1772.
94 **Gregory Grant,** b. 1743.   lfw. 21 Sept. 1770, l. Nov. 1774.   d. 19 Dec.
    1774 at Anjengo.
95 **James Bellas,** b. 1748.   lfw. Jan. 1771.
96 **John Wilkinson,** b. 1750.   lfw. Mar. 1771, adjt. Oct. 1772.
97 **John Bellas,** father of George Bridges (180), permitted to resume old name
    of **Bellasis** 1 June 1792, b. 1744. Cadet 1768. From the infantry, lfw. Mar.
    1771, l. 21 Oct. 1778, 2 cap. 23 Oct. 1778, cap. Dec. 1786, ante-d. 21 Oct. 1778,
    m. 31 Dec. 1789, res. 3 Nov. 1790, reinstated 1792 with rank of l.c. super-
    numerary 23 Oct. 1792, c. 8 Jan. 1796, the 1st col. in the regt., m.g.
    1 Jan. 1801. Field service to the northward 1774, capture of Versova and
    Karanjah Dec. 1774. a.d.c. to Col. T. Keating (65) in his campaign against
    the Mahrattas 1775, o.c. Arty. at capture of Mangalore 9 Mar. 1783. Drctr.
    laboratory 1789, kpr. fire-engines 1790, commdt. of Arty. 8 Jan. 1796–
    11 Feb. 1808, comg. the Forces Bombay Presidency 21 May 1807–11 Feb.
    1808, and Pres. Military Board.   d. 11 Feb. 1808 at Bombay while
    presiding at the Board.   Memorial in Bombay Cathedral.
98 **Sir Richard Jones,** K.C.B., b. 1754. Cadet 1770, lfw. March 1771, l. 7 Sept.
    1777, 2 cap. 13 Feb. 1779, 1 cap. June 1789, ante-d. 13 Feb. 1779, m. 3 Nov.
    1790, l.c. 23 Oct. 1792, brev.-c. 3 May 1796, m.g. 1 Jan. 1801, c. 12 Feb.
    1808, l.g. 25 Apr. 1808. MYSORE WAR 1790–92, comg. 4 companies Bombay
    Arty. Seringapatam, commdt. of Arty. 23 Oct. 1792–8 Jan. 1796, comg. at
    Surat 1796–1804, comg. Bombay Troops which joined Gen. Lake at 1st
    siege of Bhurtpore 1804–5, g.o. comg. at Surat 1805–8, commdt. of Arty.
    12 Feb. 1808–16 Oct. 1809, C.I.C. at Bombay 12 Feb. 1808–16 Oct. 1809.
    ret. on off reckoning fund 7 Sept. 1812, K.C.B. 3 Feb. 1817. d. 13 Feb. 1835
    at Worthing.
99 **Robert Joams,** lfw. Oct. 1771.
100 **George Robinson,** b. 1748.   From sergt. Enlisted 4 Aug. 1766, lfw.
    18 Nov. 1771.
101 **James Jackson,** b. 1755.   lfw. Mar. 1772, l. June 1775, cap. Mar. 1781.
    Served with Gen. Goddard's force in Guzerat 1781, MYSORE WAR 1783,
    taken prisoner by Tippoo at Bednore Apr. 1783, and never returned,
    supposed to have been poisoned. Struck off 20 May 1785.
102 **George Augustus Lawman,** b. 1751. Cadet 1772, lfw. 4 Mar. 1772, 2 l.
    4 Dec. 1777, 1 l. 14 Dec. 1777, ante-d. 4 Dec. 1777, 2 cap. 21 Feb. 1782, cap.
    21 Feb. 1782, m. 23 Oct. 1792, brev.-l.c. 3 May 1796. Drctr. laboratory 1790.
    MYSORE WAR 1791–92. res. 21 Dec. 1792, but returned to duty from
    England with his rank. o.c. Arty. Malabar Province 1798, MYSORE WAR
    1799, comg. Bombay Arty. Seringapatam. ret. 3 Dec. 1799.   d. Dec. 1803.
103 **Richard Noyes,** b. 1752.   lfw. 20 Aug. 1772, l. Nov. 1777.   d. near Tulli-
    gaum when with Col. Egerton's force 5 Mar. 1779. Was adjt. of Arty. with
    the force.
104 **Walter Dodmead Day,** b. 1752.   lfw. 13 Oct. 1772.   Went home 1774.
105 **James Holdstock Makon,** l. 1779 when on service with Col. Egerton's
    force. Killed 12 Jan. 1779.
106 **James Smith,** b. 1746.   From the infantry, lfw. 14 Nov. 1772, 3 l. Apr.
    1778, ante-d. 7 Dec. 1777. res. and went home 1780.   d. 12 Oct. 1782.
107 **St. Lo. George Thomas,** b. 1747.   From the infantry, lfw. 21 July 1773,
    2 l. Apr. 1778, 1 l. Apr. 1780. On service with Col. Egerton's force, succeeded

R. Noyes (103) as adjt. of Arty. with the force. Killed 10 May 1780 on the same service.

108 **Samuel Maximilian Richerson**, b. 1745. lfw. 15 Feb. 1774.

109 **Samuel Nicholson**, b. 1756. From the infantry, cap.l. Nov. 1774.

110 **John Draper**, b. 1757. From the marine, lfw. 21 July 1775, l. 10 June 1778, cap.l. 2 Nov. 1782, 2 cap. ante-d. 2 Nov. 1782, cap. 16 Sept. 1785, m. 28 Oct. 1792. On field service 1791, probably 2nd MYSORE WAR. d. 23 June 1794.

111 **Anthony Cartridge**, b. 1757. lfw. Mar. 1776.

112 **James Richardson**, lfw. Mar. 1776. On field service Mar. 1776, with Gen. Goddard's force 1780, capture of Bassein Dec. 1780, desp.

113 **Frederick Dagon**, probably a son or near relative of Gaspar (45), as Col. Gaspar Dagon's remarks in his own handwriting are found about Frederick. b. 1756. From the marine, lfw. 24 July 1776, l. 5 Jan. 1779, ante-d. 21 Oct. 1778, cap.l. 4 Dec. 1783, fixed rank, *i.e.* was never to be promoted higher, Transferred temporarily to the Sepoys 1777. d. 11 Mar. 1787 at Bombay.

114 **Michael Eagan**, b. 1756. lfw. 12 Aug. 1777, 2 l. 8 Dec. 1778, l. ante-d. 8 Dec. 1778. Tried by C.M. June 1781. res. 1782.

115 **Henry Long**, b. 1751. Cadet 1776, lfw. 16 Nov. 1777, l. 5 Jan. 1779, 2 cap. 24 May 1785, 1 cap. Nov. 1789, m. 23 June 1794. Struck off for absence 4 July 1796, but returned to duty without prejudice to his rank 7 Feb. 1798. Brev.-l.c. 1 Jan. 1800. Served with Gen. Goddard's force in Guzerat, siege and capture of Ahmedabad Feb. 1780, wounded. d. 17 Oct. 1803 at Bombay.

116 **Alexander Auchinleck**, b. 1757. lfw. 1 Dec. 1777.

117 **Alexander Finlason**, b. 1753. lfw. 1 Dec. 1777.

118 **Jacob Thompson**, b. 1760. Cadet 1776, lfw. Jan. 1778, 2 l. 14 Feb. 1779, 1 l. Nov. 1782, ante-d. 14 Feb. 1779, 2 cap. 24 May 1785, m. 23 June 1794, brev.-l.c. 1 Jan. 1800. MYSORE WAR 1783, present at all the sieges and engagements of that campaign from the siege of Onore to capture of Mangalore. At the latter he was left in command of Arty. to place it in a state of defence, and during the time he was there, Mangalore was besieged by Tippoo Sultan, on which occasion Lieut. Thompson was wounded. MYSORE WAR 1790–92, throughout the campaign comg. Arty. with Cap. Little's force, siege of Dharwar, capture of Simoga and Hooly Honore. Desp. 31 Dec. 1791. o.c. Arty. Malabar 1792. Pres. of Committee of Survey Bombay 1794, pres. of Committee of Examination in Languages 1795. Ordce. in the field 6 Jan. 1799. MYSORE WAR 1799, Seringapatam and capture of Jemaulabad. ret. 17 Dec. 1802. d. about Mar. 1843.

119 **John Courtoy**, b. 1765. Cadet 1776, lfw. 9 Dec. 1777, l. 15 Feb. 1779. MYSORE WAR 1783, siege, capture, and defence of Onore, wounded. d. on service 1783.

120 **Frederick Jones**, b. 1759. Cadet 1776, lfw. 10 Dec. 1777, l. 16 Feb. 1779, 2 cap. 18 May 1786. res. 28 May 1787.

121 **Jeremiah Hawkes**, b. 1759. lfw. 26 Nov. 1777, l. 1 Aug. 1779, cap. 16 May 1787, brev.-m. 5 May 1795, brev.-l.c. 1 Jan. 1800. MYSORE WAR 1783, siege, capture, and defence of Onore. Drctr. laboratory 1792. MYSORE WAR 1790–92, Seringapatam. Ordce. 1794 to death. Drowned while crossing in a palanquin on an arm of the sea near Bombay. The bearers, frightened at the rising tide, dropped the palanquin and ran away. Though a good swimmer Col. Hawkes was overpowered by the tide, 10 Mar. 1800.

122 **John Bailie**, b. 1762. Cadet 1777, lfw. 25 Mar. 1778, l. 10 May 1780, cap. 22 July 1787, brev.-m. 6 May 1795, brev.-l.c. 1 Jan. 1800, m. 1 Oct. 1803, l.c. 21 Sept. 1804, brev.-c. 25 July 1810, c. 7 Sept. 1812, m.g. 4 June 1813, l.g. 27 May 1825. a.d.c. to Lieut.-Col. G. Dagon (45), o.c. Arty. and 3rd in command of army above the Ghats under Col. Egerton 1779, with Gen. Goddard's force in Guzerat, a.d.c. to Lieut.-Col. W. A. Bailie (Bengal Arty. 33), comg. Arty. and a brigade, engagement of Dubhoi 18 Jan. 1780, capture of Ahmedabad 15 Feb. 1780, Bassein 12 Dec. 1780, Arnaul 18 Jan. 1781, forcing of the Bhor Ghaut and subsequent retreat to Panwell, a.d.c. to Col. Charles Frederick comg. a force attached to the Mahratta army,

reduction of Dharwar Mar. 1791. MYSORE WAR 1792, o.c. Arty. with Col. James Balfour's brigade, Seringapatam, o.c. Arty. at siege and surrender of Cochin under Col. Petrie 1795. MYSORE WAR 1799, battle of Sedaishur 6 Mar. 1799, Seringapatam, o.c. Arty. Canara and Malabar 1800, comg. Batt. 1804. Commdt. of Arty. 21 Sept.1804–12 Feb. 1808, again 16 Oct. 1809–7 Dec. 1811, again 13 May 1818–24 May 1822, comg. the Forces Bombay 7 June–9 Oct. 1819.   d. 22 Sept. 1826 in England.

123 Josiah Morgan, b. 1755. lfw. 2 May 1778, l. 27 Aug. 1779. Dismissed by C.M. 29 June 1781.

124 George Knox, b. 1757. lfw. 10 June 1778, l. 2 Oct. 1782, cap. 23 Oct. 1792; res. 14 Apr. 1793, returned to duty with his rank 1796; brev.-m. 1 June 1800, m. 18 Oct. 1803. Field service 1791, probably MYSORE WAR. MYSORE WAR 1799, comg. Cochin 1799–1800, o.c. Arty. Malabar and Canara 1802. d. 13 Sept. 1804, on board *Essex*, passage home.

125 Galbraith Tredennick, b. 1759. lfw. 7 July 1778, 2 l 2 Jan. 1782, l. Apr. 1784, res. 31 Dec. 1789.

126 George Christie, b. 1759. lfw. 21 Oct. 1778; dismissed 19 Nov. 1779, reinstated 8 Feb. 1780 ; l. 2 Nov. 1782. At capture of Bassein Dec. 1780, desp. res. 27 Apr. 1786.

127 James Burbeck, b. 1761. Cadet 1777, lfw. 7 Feb. 1779. Dismissed by C.M. 19 Nov. 1779.

128 Joseph Cooper, b. 1760. lfw. 8 Feb. 1779.

129 John Collet, b. 1760. lfw. 8 Feb. 1779.

130 William Hall, b. 1762. Cadet 1771, lfw. 20 Feb. 1779, 2 l. 2 Nov. 1782, 1 l. Dec. 1786. MYSORE WAR 1791. d. on service at Cannanore 15 Sept. 1791.

131 Charles Naylor, b. 1760. Cadet 1777, lfw. 21 June 1779, l. 7 Nov. 1783. Tried by C.M. Dec. 1781, honourably acquitted. d. 27 Feb. 1787 at Bombay.

132 Charles William West, b. 1762. Cadet 1777, lfw. 2 Aug. 1779, 2 l. 24 May 1785, l. June 1787, cap. 3 Mar. 1793. MYSORE WAR 1783, taken prisoner at Bednore, released at the peace 1784, MYSORE WAR 1790–92 with Cap. Little's detachment, sieges of Dharwar, Simoga, Hooly Honore ; expedition to the northward, Cambay, where he was killed 9 Oct. 1794.

133 John Brown, b. 1764. lfw. 17 Feb. 1780. Dismissed the service 16 Oct. 1780.

134 Thomas Webster, b. 1755. lfw. Apr. 1780. d. 10 July 1780 at Bombay.

135 Robert Kingston, lfw. 24 Apr. 1780.

136 Robert Gregg, cadet 1778, lfw. 1780. d. 21 Sept. 1780.

137 Lewis Olivier, b. 1765. Cadet 1778, lfw. 21 July 1780. MYSORE WAR 1783. Taken prisoner at Bednore, never returned, said to have been poisoned by Tippoo. Struck off 20 May 1785.

138 George Forbes, b. 1751. Enlisted 7 July 1773. From bombardier, lfw. 25 Sept. 1780, 2 l. 2 Nov. 1782. d. 22 Oct. 1790 at Bombay.

139 Henry Nevil, b. 1767. Cadet 1779, lfw. 10 Mar. 1781. d. 1784.

140 George Kingston, b. 1758. lfw. Mar. 1781.

141 James Gordon, b. 1760. Cadet 1777, lfw. Mar. 1781. d. 14 June 1781.

142 David Seton, lfw. 11 Apr. 1781. On board H.E.I. Company's ship *Ranger* (commander, Lieut. Pruen, Indian Navy) in the desperate fight with the Mahratta fleet off Geriah 5 Apr. 1783, wounded; *Lond. Gaz.* 25 Nov. 1783. res. 29 Mar. 1784.

143 Anthony Vandersteen, From sergt., lfw. 19 June 1781. d. 31 Oct. 1782.

144 Harry Wild, lfw. 2 Nov. 1782. d. 1784.

145 Robert Bell, b. 1764. Cadet 1780, lfw. 2 Nov. 1782, l. 26 Apr. 1786, cap. 14 Apr. 1793. MYSORE WAR 1783. Taken prisoner at Bednore by Tippoo, released at the peace 1784. MYSORE WAR 1791. d. 3 Dec. 1793.

146 John Hoy, b. 1762. Cadet 1780, lfw. 2 Nov. 1782, qtrmt. to Batt. 1789. MYSORE WAR 1793. Killed in a duel at the Poondacherrin Ghat 23 Apr. 1791. The Calcutta register of June 1791 says, "A duel has lately taken place at the Poondacherrin Ghat between Lieut. Hoy, Bombay Arty., and an officer

of the 73rd Regt., in which the former was killed the first shot, the ball passing through his lungs, whereof he died the same evening in great agonies. The survivor as well as the seconds of both parties, officers of the 75th Regt., were sent to Bombay on the *Queen,* Indiaman, to take their trials at the ensuing Quarter Sessions."

147 **Thomas Walton,** b. **1768.** Cadet **1780,** lfw. 2 Nov. **1782,** 2 l. 1 Mar. **1787.** MYSORE WAR **1783,** taken prisoner at Bednore by Tippoo, released at the peace **1784.** res. 10 Feb. **1791.**

148 **Alexander Torriano,** son of Charles (R.A. 164), brother of John Samuel (80), great uncle of Charles Edward (R.A. 2300), b. **1767.** Cadet **1780,** lfw. 2 Nov. **1782,** l. 16 Mar. **1787,** cap. 4 Dec. **1793.** MYSORE WAR **1783,** capture of Forts Onore and Anantpoor, taken prisoner at Bednore by Tippoo, released at the peace **1784.** MYSORE WAR **1791.** MYSORE WAR **1799,** Seringapatam. Advancing his gun from under cover, he was struck by a cannon shot on the shoulder, and killed on the spot, 18 Apr. **1799.**

149 **John Griffith,** b. **1763.** Cadet **1781,** lfw. 2 Nov. **1782,** l. 21 July **1787,** cap. 23 June **1794,** brev.-m. 25 Sept. **1803,** m. 21 Sept. **1804,** l.c. 12 Feb. **1808,** brev.-c. 4 June **1811,** c. 1 Sept. **1818.** MYSORE WAR **1783.** A.d.c. to Gen. Mathews, capture of Onore, Anantpoor, taken prisoner at Bednore, and released at peace **1784.** MYSORE WAR **1791,** o.c. Arty. Malabar **1795,** capture of Colombo and Point de Galle Feb. **1796.** Pres. Committee of Survey **1800,** ordce. **1804–6.** Commdt. of Arty. 23 Oct. **1812–13** May **1818.** d. 18 June 1820 at Bombay.

150 **Samuel Raester,** b. **1760.** Cadet **1781,** lfw. 2 Nov. **1782.** d. 25 Mar. **1787** at Tellicherry.

151 **William Abernethy,** b. **1763.** Cadet **1781,** lfw. 2 Nov. **1782,** l. 22 July **1787.** acting drctr. laboratory **1791,** sub-drctr. **1793.** d. 11 Dec. **1793.**

152 **Alexander Cassel Bellas,** b. **1763,** cadet 6 Jan. **1782,** lfw. 21 Nov. **1782,** adjt. Sept. **1784.** Not in **1792** Army List.

153 **William Piper,** b. **1766.** lfw. 7 Nov. **1783,** l. 31 Dec. **1789,** cap. 9 Oct. **1794.** Adjt. to Batt. **1789–94.** d. 10 Oct. **1796.**

154 **Joseph Plaistow,** b. **1762.** Cadet **1782,** lfw. 9 Nov. **1783.** d. 25 Apr. **1789** at Tellicherry.

155 **William Ince,** b. **1765.** Cadet **1782,** lfw. 9 Nov. **1783,** l. 23 Oct. **1790,** cap.l. 8 Jan. **1796,** cap. 8 Sept. **1797,** m. 21 Sept. **1804.** Tried by C.M. 28 June **1786,** suspended from rank, pay, and emoluments for six months. MYSORE WAR **1791,** with Cap. Little's detachment, sieges of Dharwar, Simoga, Hooly Honore. Ordce. **1800–03.** Field service Red Sea **1800,** field service Guzerat **1802–4,** and **1807** as o.c. Arty. and comg. to the northward. d. 28 Sept. **1808** at Surat.

156 **Samuel Carter,** b. **1769.** Cadet **1782,** lfw. 9 Nov. **1783,** l. 10 Feb. **1791,** cap.l. 8 Jan. **1796,** cap. 19 Apr. **1799,** m. 12 Feb. **1808.** MYSORE WAR **1791,** capture of Cannanore Dec. **1792,** of Colombo Feb. **1796,** MYSORE WAR **1799,** Seringapatam, comg. at Cannanore **1804,** o.c. Arty. Goa **1805–6,** comg. at Agoada **1806.** d. 21 Sept. **1810** at Bombay.

157 **Peyton Phibbs,** lfw. 9 Nov. **1783.**

158 **George Powell,** b. **1769.** lfw. 28 Feb. **1784,** l. 22 Apr. **1791,** cap.l. 8 Jan. **1796,** cap. 11 Mar. **1800,** brev.-m. 26 Apr. **1808,** m. 29 Sept. **1808,** l.c. 7 Sept. **1812.** Field service, probably MYSORE WAR **1791.** qtrmt. to Batt. **1792–97,** ordce. **1797.** Field service Red Sea **1800,** Egypt **1801–2.** Ordce. **1803–4.** Field service (Poona **1803.** o.c. Arty. Subsidiary Force, Poona **1804–5,** ordce. **1810.** Commdt. of Arty. 7 Dec. **1811–9** Jan. **1812.** d. 21 June **1814** in England.

159 **George Lee,** cadet **1781,** lfw. **1783.**

160 **William Leyton,** b. **1752.** lfw. **1784.** res. **1784.**

161 **Joseph Twells,** b. **1766.** Cadet **1782.** From the infantry, lfw. 18 May **1786.** d. 7 Sept. **1787.**

162 **George Manuel,** b. **1764.** Cadet 7 Oct. **1784.** From the infantry, lfw. 18 May **1786,** l. 4 June **1791.** res. 3 Mar. **1793.** Name appears in Retired List up to June **1840.**

163 **Thomas Ireland,** b. 1767. Cadet 10 Dec. 1784. From the infantry, lfw.
     1 Mar. 1787. Field service 1791, probably MYSORE WAR. d. 6 Feb. 1793.
164 **Thomas Moore,** b. 1764. From the infantry, lfw. June 1787. d. 22 Nov.
     1787.
165 **Robert Blackall,** b. 1765. Cadet 1782, lfw. 22 July 1787, 2 l. 3 Mar.
     1793, l. Apr. 1795, cap.l. 8 Jan. 1796, cap. 11 Mar. 1802, m. 1808. Capture
     of Cannanore Dec. 1792. Ordce. 18 Dec. 1793–1805. Capture of Colombo
     Feb. 1796. ret. 4 May 1808. d. 14 Mar. 1855 at Colamber Manor, Co.
     Longford. Memorial window in Streete Church, Co. Westmeath.
166 **Benjamin Randall Mason,** b. 1767. Cadet 1782. From 9th Infantry, lfw.
     9 Sept. 1787, 2 l. 3 Mar. 1793, l. Apr. 1795, cap.l. 8 Jan. 1796, cap. 18
     Oct. 1803. Fort adjt., garrison qtrmt., and kpr. of the fire-engines Tannah
     1795–1803. Transferred to Invalid Batt. 27 Apr. 1804. d. 7 Mar. 1808 at
     Bombay.
167 **Thomas Grant,** b. 1767. Cadet 1782, lfw. 20 Jan. 1789. Not in 1792
     Army List.
168 **Charles McLean,** b. 1764. From the infantry, lfw. 27 Apr. 1789, 2 l. 9 Oct.
     1794, l. Apr. 1797, cap.l. 14 Aug. 1800. Capture of Cannanore Dec. 1792.
     d. 14 May 1802 on passage to India.
169 **Thomas Creasy,** b. 26 Oct. 1768. Cadet 1788, lfw. 31 Dec. 1789. d. on
     service, probably MYSORE WAR, 5 May 1792.
170 **John Comyn,** b. 13 Nov. 1771. Cadet 1788, lfw. 31 Dec. 1789, 2 l. 14 Apr.
     1793, l. Apr. 1797, cap.l. 6 Sept. 1797. Field service 1791, probably
     MYSORE WAR. MYSORE WAR 1799, Seringapatam. Ordce. 1797–1800.
     d. 13 Aug. 1800 at Prince of Wales' Island.
171 **James Eyles,** b. 1773. Cadet 1788, lfw. 31 Dec. 1789, 2 l. 4 Dec. 1793, l.
     Apr. 1797, cap.l. 6 Sept. 1797, cap. 28 Apr. 1804, m. 22 Sept. 1810. MYSORE
     WAR 1791–92, capture of Cannanore Dec. 1792, action of 22 Feb. 1792,
     known by the name of the duck fight, Seringapatam. Field service in
     Cochin, adjt. of Batt. 1794, o.c. Arty. Palgautcherry 1795, capture of
     Columbo and Point de Galle Feb. 1796 as adjt. of Arty. Field service
     Cotiote 1797 as o.c. Arty. and ordce. and secretary to o.c. MYSORE WAR
     1799 as adjt. of Arty., Seringapatam, capture of Mangalore, Jemaulabad,
     and recapture of Jemaulabad 1800. Ordce. 1800–2 and 1805–10. Field
     service Guzerat 1805, taken prisoner by Gungaram Cotaree. ret. 6 Feb.
     1812. d. 14 June 1845 at Amersham, Bucks.
172 **David Urquhart,** b. 1771. Cadet 1788, lfw. 23 Oct. 1790, 2 l. 11 Dec. 1793,
     l. 19 Apr. 1797, cap.l. 19 Apr. 1799. Field service 1791, probably MYSORE
     WAR. MYSORE WAR 1799, Seringapatam. d. 9 Nov. 1800 at Calicut.
173 **William Smith,** b. 1772. Cadet 1788, lfw. 23 Oct. 1790, 2 l. 23 June 1794,
     l. Apr. 1797, cap.l. 6 Mar. 1800, cap. 14 Sept. 1804, brev.-m. 1 Jan. 1812,
     m. 7 Feb. 1812, l.c. 22 June 1814. Feld service 1791 and 1799, probably
     MYSORE WARS. Adjt. to Batt. 11 Mar. 1800, qtmrt. to Batt. Aug. 1800,
     and Committee of Survey, Service Red Sea 1800, Egypt 1801–2, ordce.
     1802–16. Commdt. of Arty. 9 Jan. 1812–23 Oct. 1812. d. 2 Feb. 1816 at
     Bombay.
174 **Andrew Gideon Fisher,** b. 1775. Cadet 1790, lfw. 30 Nov. 1791, 2 l. 8 Jan.
     1796, l. 1798, cap.l. 10 Nov. 1800, cap. 21 Sept. 1804. MYSORE WAR 1790–
     92, Seringapatam. MYSORE WAR 1799, Seringapatam. Ordce. 1800, adjt.
     to Batt. 1 July 1802, ordce. 1802–4. MAHRATTA WAR 1803, taking of
     Ahmednuggur and Jalna. ret. 9 Dec. 1807. d. Oct. 1828.
175 **Henry Hessman,** b. 1773. Cadet 1791, lfw. 7 July 1792, 2 l. 8 Jan. 1796, l.
     1798, cap.l. 11 Mar. 1802, cap. 21 Sept. 1804, m. 7 Sept. 1812, l.c. 2 Feb.
     1816, l.c. commdt. 19 June 1820, c. 5 June 1829. Field service Guzerat
     1803–5. Ordce. 1802–5, Poona Subsidiary Force 1807–9, o.c. Arty. Goa
     1809–10, o.c. Arty. on service Guzerat 1816–18, MAHRATTA WAR 1817–
     19, o.c. Arty. Deccan 1819–20, comg. 2nd Batt. 1821, commdt. of Arty. 24
     May 1822–10 Dec. 1825, brigadier comg. at Presidency 1825, Surat Division
     1826. d. 27 May 1833 on passage home.
176 **George Warden,** b. 1775. Cadet 1791, lfw. 5 Feb. 1793, 2 l. 8 Jan. 1796, l.

LIEUT.-COLONEL WILLIAM SMITH, 1816.

(From a miniature in the Bombay Arsenal.)

1800, cap.l. 11 Mar. 1802. Field service against the Coolies under Cap. Little 1794, capture of Colombo Feb. 1796. Adjt. at Colombo 1796, adjt. to Batt. 1795, qtrmt. to Batt. 11 Mar. 1800 and Committee of Survey. MYSORE WAR 1799, battle of Sedaishur 6 Mar. 1799, Seringapatam, Jemaulabad. A.d.c. to President in Council, ordce. 1800–5, Red Sea and Egypt 1801–2, ordce. 1806. Feld service Kattywar 1807. d. 5 Oct. 1807 in the village of Choor-Verah on way to Cambay. Memorial tablet Bombay Cathedral.

177 **William Macredie,** b. 18 Nov. 1772. Appointed cadet in Bombay 12 July 1792, lfw. 6 Feb. 1793, 2 l. 8 Jan. 1796. MYSORE WAR 1799, Seringapatam. Exposing himself to take an account of the ammunition, his head was carried off by a shot from the same gun that killed Cap. A. Torriano (148) 18 Apr. 1799.

178 **Joshua Hawkes,** b. 1 Jan. 1773. Cadet 12 July 1792, lfw. 3 Mar. 1793, 2 l. 8 Jan. 1796, l. 1800, cap.l. 17 May 1802. Field service 1795 as qtrmt. ret. 21 Aug. 1805. d. 9 Oct. 1853 at Chelsea.

179 **Charles Wilder,** b. Apr. 1777. Cadet 1791, lfw. 3 Mar. 1793. d. 4 May 1795.

180 **George Bridges Bellas,** son of John (97), b. 1760. 2 l. *H.M. Marine Forces* 11 Dec. 1782, *half pay* 1783, *and remained on that list till* 1808. Permitted to resume old name of **Bellasis** 1 June 1792. Cadet 1791, lfw. 14 Apr. 1793, l. 6 June 1797. A.d.c. to Gen. Brownrigg 1797. MYSORE WAR 1799, battle of Sedaishur 6 Mar. 1799, Seringapatam, capture of Mangalore and recapture of Jemaulabad 1800. o.c. Arty. Goa 1800, ordce. 1801. Struck off for absence without leave 21 July 1801. Having killed Mr. Arthur Andrew Forbes Mitchell in a duel, he and his second, Cap. Charles William Byne, H.M. 86th Regt., were tried in the Recorder's Court, Bombay, found guilty, and sentenced on 21 July 1801, Lieut. Bellasis to 14 years' and Cap. Byne to 7 years' transportation. On arrival in New South Wales he was pardoned by the Governor, on condition that he should remain in the territory of New South Wales during the term for which he was sentenced, and was appointed, on 16 June 1802, a lieut. of Arty. of the Colonial Forces. Cap. Byne received the King's pardon in June 1802, and Lieut. Bellasis in Dec. 1806. He was "imported" to Bombay, arriving on 27 May 1807, and was then reinstated in his original place in the regt. cap.l 18 Oct. 1803, cap. 10 Dec. 1807, brev.-m. 14 June 1814, m. 22 June 1814, l.c. 1 Sept. 1818, l.c. commdt. 1 May 1824. o.c. Arty. field service Kattywar, capture of Mallia 1809, o.c. Arty. Surat 1809–10, MAHRATTA WAR 1817–18, brigadier comg. Horse and Foot Arty., capture of Poona 16 Nov. 1817, o.c. Arty. Guzerat 1820–21, o.c. Arty. Poona Division 1821–23, comg. 1st Batt. 1823, comg. Poona Brigade 1825. d. 30 Sept. 1825 at Poona. Tomb erected by brother officers.

181 **James Lighton,** b. June 1772. Cadet 1791. From ensign of infantry lfw. 14 Apr. 1793, 2 l. 6 Sept. 1797, l. 1802, cap.l. 18 Oct. 1803, cap. 12 Feb. 1808, brev.-m. 14 June 1814, m. 2 Feb. 1816. MYSORE WAR 1799, battle of Sedaishur 6 Mar. 1799, wounded, Seringapatam, adjt. Arty. Malabar 1800–4, qtrmt. to Batt. 29 Aug. 1804–5, also on Committee of Survey ; engineer surveying forest of Canara 1805, comg. H.B. 18 Nov. 1811–16 Apr. 1813, ordce. 1815. Field service Guzerat 1815. d. 19 Sept. 1816 at Bombay.

182 **Charles John Bond,** b. 1780. Cadet 1794, lfw. 20 Dec. 1796, 2 l. 6 Sept. 1797, l. 1802, cap.l. 28 Apr. 1804, cap. 5 May 1808, m. 20 Sept. 1816, l.c. 1 Sept. 1818. MYSORE WAR 1799, Seringapatam, wounded, 1800 field service Canara, capture of Jemaulabad, adjt. to Batt. 3 June 1800, volunteered for service in the Red Sea and Egypt 1800–1, accompanied the army across the desert from Cossier to Geunah on the Nile, reaching Grand Cairo just as the French troops were about to evacuate the city. Qtrmt. to Batt. 1 June 1802–4, Committee of Survey 1803. Field service in the Deccan 1806, field service Persian Gulf comg. Arty. 1809, field service Kattywar comg. Arty. 1812, capture of Nowannuggur 24 Feb. 1812, desp.; comg. Arty. at attack on Severndroog in conjunction with Cap. Hill, H.M.S. *Tower*, 1816, MAHRATTA WAR 1817–19, comg. Arty. at captures of Pallee, Boorup, Loghur

Essaupoor, Koaree, and Ryghur 9 May 1818, desp.; field service Cutch, capture of Bhooj 25 Mar. 1819, field service Persian Gulf 1819, o.c. Arty. under Sir W. G. Keir, o.c. Arty. Guzerat 1819.   d. 10 Sept. 1820 at Surat.

183 **Hugh Alexander Shewcraft,** b. 1780. Cadet 1794, lfw. 20 Dec. 1796, 2 l. 6 Sept. 1797, l. 1802, cap.l. 14 Sept. 1804. MYSORE WAR 1799 Seringapatam.   d. 3 Oct. 1808 at Bombay.

184 **John William Hewetson,** b. 1758.   Cadet 1795, lfw. 20 Dec. 1796. Transferred to the infantry 1797.   d. 7 Aug. 1799 at Bombay.

185 **Henry William Sealy,** father of George Prince (331), grandfather of Charles William Henry (R.A. 3153), b. 17 May 1783. R.M.A. 1797, lfw. 26 Dec. 1798, l. 16 Oct. 1801, cap.l. 21 Sept. 1804, cap. 29 Sept. 1808, brev.-m. 14 June 1814, m. never, l.c. 1 Sept. 1818.   Feld service to the northward 1802, field service Guzerat 1803, qtrmt. to Batt. 29 Jan. 1807. Ordce. 1809, field service Persian Gulf, o.c. Arty taking of Schinauss Nov. 1809, desp.   On duty Persian Gulf H.E.I. Company's cruiser *Benares* (commander, Charles Sealy) 1811–12.   MAHRATTA WAR 1817–18.   Ordce. 1819, o.c. Arty. Deccan 1820.   d. 13 May 1821 at Seroor.

186 **Christopher Hodgson,** b. 1782.   R.M.A. 1797, lfw. 27 Dec. 1798, l. 18 Oct. 1801, cap.l. 21 Sept. 1804, cap. 22 Sept. 1810, brev.-m. 21 June 1814, m. 1 Sept. 1818, l.c. 19 June 1820, l.c. commdt. 30 Sept. 1825, c. 5 June 1829, m.g. 28 June 1838. Field service Kattywar, taking of fortress of Sunkheira July 1802, thanks of Govt., field service Guzerat 1803–4, qtrmt. to Batt. 1806–7, a.d.c. to governor 1815, ordce. 1816–18, ordce. 1825, o.c. Arty. Poona division 3 Nov. 1825. Commdt. of Arty. 10 Dec. 1825–19 Apr. 1826. d. 16 Apr. 1849 at Tonbridge Wells.

187 **Thomas Morse,** brother of Charles (188), b. 1778. From the infantry, lfw. 21 Sept. 1798, l. 28 Dec. 1798, cap.l. 22 Aug. 1805. Feld service Egypt 1802. A prisoner of war on parole, had leave to proceed to Europe to effect an exchange 18 Feb. 1802. MAHRATTA WAR 1803, Assaye 23 Sept. 1803, qtrmt. to Batt. 1805–6, ordce. 1806–11.   d. 6 Sept. 1811 at Poona.

188 **Charles Morse,** brother of Thomas (187), b. 1779. From the infantry, lfw. 21 Sept. 1798, l. 8 Aug. 1799. Ordce. 1805.   d. 15 Feb. 1806 at Fort Cornwallis, Prince of Wales' Island.

189 **Edward Sergeant Clifton,** b. 5 Apr. 1782. R.M.A. 1797, lfw. 21 Sept. 1798, 2 l. 19 Oct. 1801, l. 1805, cap.l. 12 Feb. 1808, cap. 7 Feb. 1812. Field service to the northward 1802.   d. 30 Nov. 1812 at Bombay.

190 **Richard Whish,** father of Frederick Alexander (444), brother of Sir William Simpson (Bengal Arty. 332). R.M.A. 1800–2, lfw. 14 May 1802, l. 15 May 1802, cap.l. 12 Feb. 1808, cap. 7 Sept. 1812, m. 1 Sept. 1818, l.c. 11 Sept. 1820, l.c. commdt. 23 Sept. 1826, c. 5 June 1829, m.g. 28 June 1828, l.g. 11 Nov. 1851. MAHRATTA WAR 1803, capture of Ahmednuggur, battle of Assaye 23 Sept. and Argaum 29 Sept., storm of Gawilghur 14 Nov. 1803. Brigade major Poona 1807, ordce. 1807–17, comg. 1st Batt. 1821–23, o.c. Arty. Guzerat 1823. Commdt. of Arty. 17 May 1827–31 July 1832, comg. Northern Division Army 1832.   d. 10 Nov. 1854 at Clifton.

191 **Fortunatus Hagley Pierce,** C.B., b. 1784. R.M.A. 1800–2, lfw. 15 May 1802, l. 16 May 1802, cap.l. 5 May 1808, cap. 7 Sept. 1812, m. 1 Sept. 1818, l.c. 14 May 1821, l.c. commdt. 28 Sept. 1827, c. 5 June 1829. In the field with Col. Murray 1804–5, o.c. Arty. capture of Mallia 7 July 1809, attached to troop of Native Cavalry 1811, sent to Broach to superintend formation of brigade of H.A. 30 Nov. 1811, comg. H.B. 16 Apr. 1813–23 May 1821. MAHRATTA WAR 1817–19, battle of Ashtee 20 Feb. 1818. *Lond. Gaz.* 20 Jan. 1821. o.c. Arty. Surat division 24 May 1821. Ordce. 1825. Commdt. of Arty. 24 May 1822–10 Dec. 1825, again 19 Apr. 1826–17 May 1827. C.B. 27 Sept. 1831.   d. 31 Dec. 1832 at Bombay.

192 **Robert Macintosh,** b. 1784. Cadet 1801, lfw. 6 Sept. 1802, l. 7 Sept. 1802, cap.l. 29 Sept. 1808, cap. 22 June 1814, m. 19 June 1820, l.c. 30 Sept. 1825. Field service Guzerat 1803. Barrack master and fort adjt. Goa 1805, adj t. of Batt. 22 Jan. 1809. Captures of Isle de Bourbon Sept. 1809 and July 1810, and Mauritius Dec. 1810. *Lond. Gaz.* 26 Oct. 1810. Ordce. 1811–14,

G.C. 1 May 1816-23 May 1821. Arabia 1820-21, o.c. Arty. Beni-boo-ali. *Lond. Gaz.* 7 Nov. 1821. Comg. H.B. 23 May 1821-31 Jan. 1826. d. 30 May 1826 at Poona. Tomb erected by brother officers.

193 **Samuel Rogers Strover,** b. 1784. R.M.A. 1800-2, lfw. 25 Nov. 1802, l. 26 Nov. 1802, cap.l. 4 Oct. 1808, cap. 2 Feb. 1816, m. 10 Sept. 1820, l.c. 31 May 1826, brev.-c. 18 June 1831, c. 1 Jan. 1833, m.g. 28 Nov. 1841, l.g. 11 Nov. 1851. Adjt. to Batt. 10 Mar. 1805-22 Jan. 1809. Volunteered 1807, and went with expedition against the French in Persia. Ordce. 1813-20. Volunteered 1814, and served with field force in Guzerat, and again in 1816. Taking of Bhuj 26 Mar. 1819. Comg. 2nd Batt. 1820-23, o.c. Arty. Northern Division and garrison of Surat Nov. 1824, comg. at Ahmednuggur Aug. 1832. Commdt. of Arty. 8 Jan. 1833-5 Feb. 1834. d. 20 Jan. 1853 at Bath.

194 **Edmund Hardy,** father of John Braithwaite (424), b. 1785, R.M.A. 1803-4, lfw. 1 May 1804, l. 27 May 1804, cap.l. 22 Sept. 1810, cap. 20 Sept. 1816, m. 14 May 1821, l.c. 23 Sept. 1826, c. 28 May 1833. Qtrmt. to Batt. 16 Sept. 1809. Field service Kattywar 1807-9, capture of Mallia 7 July 1809, o.c. Arty. capture of Chya 13 Apr. 1811, desp.; capture of Nowannuggur 24 Feb. 1812. Compiled a map of Kattywar. Ordce. 1812. MAHRATTA WAR 1817-19, battle of Kirkee 5 Nov. 1817, capture of Singhur, Poorundhur Mar. 1818. Brigade-major of Arty. 28 Apr. 1819-1 Apr. 1820, military sec. to o.c. forces 1819, acting drctr. Depôt of Instruction 1823, ordce. 1826, qtrmt.-gen. of the Army 1827-33. ret. 25 Dec. 1833. d. 28 Mar. 1848 at Clifton.

195 **Justinian Nutt,** b. 1786. R.M.A. 1801, lfw. 1 May 1804. Transferred to Bombay Engrs. 17 Oct. 1804.

196 **William Hinton Sealy,** b. 13 Mar. 1787. R.M.A. 1803-4, lfw. 1 May 1804, l. 27 May 1804. Lost in the foundering of the bomb-ketch *Stromboli* when proceeding on service to the Persian Gulf 15 Sept. 1809.

197 **Thomas Eustace Newcomen,** b. 3 Mar. 1786. R.M.A. 1803-4, lfw. 1 May 1804, l. 27 May 1804. d. 4 Sept. 1805 at Broach.

198 **Lechmere Coore Russell,** C.B., b. 1787. R.M.A. 1803-4, lfw. 1 May 1804, l. 27 May 1804, cap.l. 7 Sept. 1811, cap. 1 Sept. 1818, m. 24 May 1826, l.c. 21 Sept. 1827, brev.-c. 18 June 1831, c. 26 Dec. 1833, m.g. 23 Nov. 1841. Adjt. Fencible Regt. Nov. 1804. Ordce. 1805-10. Embarked with detachment of Arty. on board *Camden,* a 60-gun frigate, to convoy Indiamen of the season to China 1807. Field service Kattywar, capture of Mallia 7 July 1809. G.C. 8 Oct. 1810-22 Jan. 1816. Capture of Bhooj 26 Mar. 1819. Comg. 2nd Batt. 1821, acting drctr. Depôt of Instruction 1823. Burmah 1824-25, Rangoon and Mergwui, comg. Bombay Arty. on board H.E.I. Company's cruiser *Thetis.* Desp. *Lond. Gaz.* 24 Mar. and 20 Apr. 1825. o.c. Arty. Doab Field Force 1827, comg. H.B. May 1826-4 Feb. 1834. Commdt. of Arty. 5 Feb. 1834-31 Jan. 1836. C.B. 20 July 1838 on the Coronation. d. 28 Apr. 1851 at Ashford Hall, Salop.

199 **Andrew Campbell,** b. 30 June 1783. *lfw. Forfar Arty. Militia* 1802. R.M.A. 1803-4, lfw. 1 May 1804, l. 11 June 1804, cap.l. 7 Feb. 1812, cap. 1 Sept. 1818, m. 6 Mar. 1826, l.c. 28 Sept. 1827, brev.-c. 18 June 1831. Field service Guzerat 1815-16. MAHRATTA WAR 1817-19. o.c. Arty. Guzerat 1820. Staff employ qtrmt.-gen.'s Dept. Guzerat 1820-21, ordce. 1822-23, o.c. Arty. Guzerat 1829. Was on board the first steamer that left Bombay for Suez, and thence by overland route to Europe about 1830. ret. 29 Dec. 1831. m.g. 28 Nov. 1854. d. 25 Dec. 1860 at Cheltenham.

200 **John Moor,** b. 14 Jan. 1787. lfw. 14 Sept. 1804, l. 16 Feb. 1806, cap.l. 7 Sept. 1812, cap. 1 Sept. 1818, m. 6 Mar. 1826, l.c. 30 Dec. 1831. Field service Kattywar, capture of Mallia 7 July 1809. Ordce. 1811-19, o.c. Arty. Guzerat 1830, comg. Goldze. Batt. 1833. d. 5 May 1833 at Mahableshwar.

201 **Robert Thew,** b. 18 Apr. 1788. lfw. 4 Mar. 1805, l. 16 Feb. 1806, cap.l. 7 Sept. 1812, cap. 1 Sept. 1818, m. 6 Mar. 1826. Field service Guzerat 1810, o.c. Arty. of H.H. the Peishwa 1815-17. MAHRATTA WAR 1817-19, battle of Kirkee 5 Nov. 1817. *Lond. Gaz.* 18 Apr. 1818. Capture of

Chakun 28 Feb. 1818, Desp. Ordce. 1818-21. G.C. 23 May 1821-9 June 1827. ret. 6 Aug. 1829. d. 10 July 1855 in Kensington.

202 **William Glendower White,** b. 7 Aug. 1790. lfw. 8 Apr. 1808, l. 9 Apr. 1808, cap.l. 22 June 1814, cap. 1 Sept. 1818, m. 28 Sept. 1820, l.c. 1 Jan. 1833. MAHRATTA WAR 1817-18, capture of Poona 16 Nov. 1817, capture of Kittoor Dec. 1824, o.c. Arty. Doab Field Force 1826, o.c. Arty. Northern Division 1833-34. Transferred to corps of Native Invalids 15 May 1834. ret. 8 July 1834. d. 24 Jan. 1863 in England.

203 **James Thomas Taylor,** b. 1785. From Engrs. l. 10 Apr. 1808. Went with expedition for capture of Mauritius 1810. Permitted to resign. Struck off 21 June 1810.

204 **John Gordon,** b. 1790. R.M.A. 1809, lfw. 26 Mar. 1809, l.!27 Mar. 1809. d. 23 Aug. 1809 on board H.M.S. *Vestal* on passage to India.

205 **James Clements Page,** b. 25 Nov. 1791. lfw. 27 Mar. 1809, l. 6 Aug. 1809. d. 31 Dec. 1809 in the Persian Gulf.

206 **Julius George Griffith,** b. 7 Oct. 1792. lfw. 26 May 1810, l. 27 May 1810, cap.l. 2 Feb. 1816, cap. 1 Sept. 1818, m. 28 Sept. 1826, l.c. 6 May 1833, brev.-c. 26 Dec. 1844, c. 3 July 1845, m.g. 20 June 1854, l.g. 4 Feb. 1859, g. 7 Sept. 1860. Col. commdt. from 3 July 1845. Field service Katty-war and Okamundel, capture of Chya 20 Apr. 1811, Poseitra Aug. 1811, Nowannuggur Feb. 1812. Adjt. 1st Troop 24 May 1815-25 Jan. 1817. MAH-RATTA WAR 1814-18, battle of Ashtee 20 Feb. 1818. Desp. and thanks of Govt. Taking of Singurh, Sattara, Poorundhur, Wasoota, and other hill forts, capture of Poona 16 Nov. 1817. Ordce. 1817. G.P. 9 June 1827-1 Oct. 1827, ordce. 1827-35. Commdt. of Arty. 1 Feb. 1836-16 Feb. 1846, brgdr. comg. Mhow Division Army 15 June 1846-24 Aug. 1846. d. 31 July 1872 at Boulogne.

207 **Edwin Wyndowe,** b. 1791. R.M.A. 1806-9, lfw. 2 July 1810, l. 3 July 1810. Field service Kattywar, capture of Nowannuggur 24 Feb. 1812. d. 2 Nov. 1813 in India.

208 **David Hogarth,** b. 25 Oct. 1792. Addis. 1809-10, lfw. 2 July 1810, l. 3 July 1810. Adjt. to Batt. 3 May 1811-15 June 1811, adjt. 1st Troop 15 June 1811-24 May 1815, a.d.c. to Governor 1815, G.C. 22 Jan.-1 May 1816. d. 30 Sept. 1816 at Byculla, Bombay.

209 **Alexander Manson,** C.B., father of Henry Forbes (418), b. 26 Feb. 1793. Addis. 1809-10, lfw. 2 July 1810, l. 3 July 1810, cap.l. 20 Sept. 1816, cap. 1 Sept. 1818, m. 7 Aug. 1829, l.c. 28 May 1833, brev.-c. 26 Dec. 1844, c. 16 Apr. 1849. Qtrmt. to Batt. and Committee of Survey 1811. Capture of Chya 13 Apr. 1811, severely wounded. Ordce. 1811-13. On service against Pah-lunpore and Deesa Oct. 1817, throughout MAHRATTA WAR 1817-19, taking of Asseerghur 8 Apr. 1819, attack on Nuggur Parkur 25 Jan. 1820, o. c. Arty. capture of Dwarka 26 Nov. 1820 (*Lond. Gaz.* 18 May 1821), attack on Meeteallah 1 Feb. 1821, ordce. 1820-21, G.P. 24 Dec. 1821-9 June 1827, G.C. 9 June 1827-8 Jan. 1834, C.B. 27 Sept. 1831, brgd.-g. comg. N.W. Frontier Sind 1838, comg. Batt. 1840, comg. Ahmednuggur 1843, comg. Mhow Division Army 1845, comg. Southern Division Army 1845. Commdt. of Arty. 16 Feb. 1846-19 Feb. 1849. Comg. Poona Division Army 1848, comg. Sind Division Army 1850. Expedition to Roree against Ali Murad 1852. d. 23 Feb. 1852 at Bombay.

210 **Thomas Stevenson,** C.B., father of William (363), Walter James Hodgson (410), Russell Alexander (445), b. 1 Jan. 1792. Addis. 1809-10, lfw. 16 Sept. 1810, l. 17 Sept. 1810, cap. 1 Sept. 1818, m. 30 Dec. 1831, l.c. 26 Dec. 1833. Adjt. Batt. 6 Dec. 1811-16, adjt. Field Service Guzerat 1815, a.d.c. to Governor 1815, MAHRATTA WAR 1817-19, ARABIA, Beni-boo-ali 2 Mar. 1821, G.P. 19 May 1829-28 Jan. 1834, comg. H.B. and Arty. Poona Division 4 Feb. 1834-11 Apr. 1840, Special Committee on equipment Calcutta 1836-37, Sind and Afghanistan 1839, brgd.-g. comg. Arty. Ghuznee 23 July 1839, Khelat 7 Aug. 1839, *Lond. Gaz.* 30 Oct. 1839. C.B. 20 Dec. 1839, order of

Durr-i-Durani Empire 1st class. Brgd.-g. comg. Upper Sind 1840. d. 9 Aug. 1840 at Sukkur.

211 **Peter Breton,** b. 17 Dec. 1792. R.M.A. 1807-10, lfw. 16 Sept. 1810, l. 17 Sept. 1810, cap. 1 Sept. 1818. ret. 7 Mar. 1821. d. 17 July 1862, at Southampton.

212 **William Waller Quartly,** b. 3 Dec. 1792. R.M.A. 1807-10, lfw. 16 Sept. 1810, l. 17 Sept. 1810. Struck off, absent from India beyond prescribed period, 13 Aug. 1817.

213 **William Kidman Lester,** brother of Frederick Parkinson (222), b. 27 Feb. 1793. R.M.A. 1808-10, lfw. 16 Sept. 1810, l. 17 Sept. 1810, cap. 1 Sept. 1818, m. 1 Jan. 1833, l.c. 16 June 1834. Field service Kattywar, Nowannuggur 24 Feb. 1812, MAHRATTA WAR 1817-18, capture of Poona 16 Nov. 1817. Ordce. 1825-33. Was robbed and illtreated by Chinese pirates journeying from Lintin to Macao. Comg. 1st Batt. 1833, comg. Arty. Northern Division 1838. d. 4 June 1838 at Baroda.

214 **James Barton,** father of Charles James (391), grandfather of ~~Richard Lionel (~~R.A. 5256), lfw. 8 June 1811, l. 9 June 1811, cap. 1 Sept. 1818. Brgd.-m. Arty. Deccan 1818, MAHRATTA WAR 1817-18, as brgd.-m. to o.c. Arty., adjt. and qtrmt. Arty. Deccan 1825, G.P. 1 Oct. 1827-19 May 1829. d. 19 May 1829 at Matoonga. Tomb erected by brother officers.

215 **William Bromley Cadogan Stirling,** b. 3 July 1791. Addis. 1809-10. d. 11 May 1811 on board the *Henry Addington* on passage to India.

216 **Frederick Schuler,** b. 28 Mar. 1793. Addis. 1809-10, lfw. 8 June 1811, l. 7 Sept. 1811, cap. 1 Sept. 1818, m. 6 May 1833, l.c. 4 June 1838, brev.-c. 19 Mar. 1849, c. 28 Apr. 1851, m.g. 28 Nov. 1854, c. commdt. from 28 Apr. 1851, l.g. 17 Sept. 1861, g. 11 Dec. 1868. MAHRATTA WAR 1817-18, field service Guzerat 1815. Ordce. 1821, o.c. Arty. Field Force Maheekanta, comg. force that captured Maguna in Guzerat 1824, ordce. 1836-41, o.c. Arty. Sind and Beloochistan 1843, brgd.-g. comg. Arty. of Brigade proceeding northward on service Mar. 1846, comg. in Khandeish 1847. Commdt. of Arty. 19 Feb. 1849-15 May 1850, comg. Southern Division Army 1853, Poona division Army 1854, comg. in Sind 1858. Presented to the regiment a handsome silver centre-piece now at R.A. mess Woolwich. d. 20 July 1874 in London.

217 **William Hutchinson,** b. 1 July 1794. Addis. 1809-10, lfw. 8 June 1811, l. 7 Feb. 1812. Field service Kattywar and Guzerat 1814-15. d. 2 Sept. 1815 in Kattywar on service.

218 **Robert Foster,** b. 18 Dec. 1792. Addis. 1809-10, lfw. 8 June 1811, l. 7 Sept. 1812, cap. 1 Sept. 1818. MAHRATTA WAR 1817, field force Guzerat 1815, ordce. 1820-25. d. 27 May 1825 at Parell, Bombay.

219 **Thomas Lane Groundwater,** b. 23 Mar. 1793. Addis. 1809-10, lfw. 8 June 1811, l. 7 Sept. 1812, cap. 1 Sept. 1818, m. 28 May 1833. Capture of Bhuterangur, also of Ramghur 6 Apr. 1818 (*Lond. Gaz.* 20 Jan. 1821), capture of Rairee 14 Feb. 1819 (*Lond. Gaz.* 27 Aug. 1819), ordce. 1818-19. ret. 20 June 1839. l.c. 28 Nov. 1854. d. 12 Aug. 1870 at Wadhurst, Sussex and Kent.

220 **William Miller,** b. 23 Jan. 1795. Addis. 1809-10, lfw. 8 June 1811, l. 3 Oct. 1813, cap. 1 Sept. 1818, m. 26 Dec. 1833. Qtrmt. to Batt. 1812, afterwards adjt. 1818. MAHRATTA WAR 1817-19, capture of Ryghur 10 May 1818, desp. Ordce. 1817-20, brgd.-m. of Arty. 1 Apr. 1820-1 Nov. 1822. Appointed to superintend alterations and improvements in cantonment of Matoonga 17 Oct. 1821. Drctr. Depôt of Instruction 30 July 1822-16 Dec. 1831, o.c. Arty. Northern Division 1835, Judge Advocate General 1836. d. 14 May 1836 at Mahableshwar.

221 **Edward Hulse Willock,** brother of Frederick (Madras Arty. 287), b. 5 Aug. 1794. Addis. 1809-10, lfw. 8 June 1811, l. 22 June 1814, cap. 1 Sept. 1818, m. 16 June 1834. Adjt. and qtrmt. 1st Troop 25 May 1817-1 Jan. 1820. MAHRATTA WAR 1817-18, capture of Poona 16 Nov. 1817, capture of Singhur 2 Mar. 1818, severely wounded by an explosion destroying captured guns, comg. Golze. Batt. 1834, comg. 1st Batt. 1834, o.c. Arty. Northern

G

Division 1836. Drowned riding his horse across the Saburmati river Ahmedabad, no boat being ready, 8 July 1839.

222 **Frederick Parkinson Lester,** brother of William Kidman (213), b. 5 Feb. 1795. Addis. 1810-11, lfw. 25 Oct. 1811, l. 3 Sept. 1815, cap. 1 Sept. 1818, m. 14 May 1836, l.c. 9 Aug. 1840, brev.-c. 15 Mar. 1851, c. 23 Feb. 1852, m.g. 28 Nov. 1854. Adjt. Batt. 1 Mar. 1819-1 Dec. 1819, employed at Addis. 18 Dec. 1822-25 Mar. 1824, ordce. 1835-36, comg. 1st Batt. 1836, G.C. 7 June 1838-1 Mar. 1839, Sec. Military Board 20 Feb. 1839-27 Mar. 1844, Stipendiary Member Military Board 1844-47. Commdt. of Arty. 15 May 1850-24 Mar. 1856, I.G.O. 28 Aug. 1856-14 Apr. 1857, comg. Southern Division Army 1858. d. 3 July 1858 at Belgaum.

223 **William Henry Rochfort,** b. 1795. Addis. 1810-14, lfw. 25 Oct. 1811, l. 2 Feb. 1816. res. 6 Dec. 1816.

224 **Samuel John Crofts Falconer,** b. 14 Dec. 1793. Addis. 1809-11, lfw. 25 Oct. 1811, l. 1 May 1816, cap. 1 Sept. 1818. Adjt. 1st Batt. 1822, ordce. 1827-35. d. 20 Aug. 1835 at Ahmedabad. Memorial tablet Bombay Cathedral, erected by friends and brother officers.

225 **Thomas D'Oyly,** b. 12 July 1794. Addis. 1809-10, lfw. 25 Oct. 1811. Transferred to Bengal Arty. (437) 7 May 1812.

226 **George Washington Gibson,** b. 12 Feb. 1795. Addis. 1810-11, lfw. 10 July 1812, l. 20 Sept. 1816, cap. 1 Sept. 1818, brev.-m. 10 Jan. 1837, m. 4 June 1838. MAHRATTA WAR 1817-18, capture of Poona 16 Nov. 1817, ordce. 1825-36, served in Upper Sind 1838-39, o.c. Arty. Northern Division 1840, o.c. Arty. Poona Division and 1st Batt. 1843. ret. 7 Jan. 1844. l.c. 28 Nov. 1854. d. 10 Mar. 1872 in Kensington.

227 **Peter Jenkins,** b. 3 Apr. 1794. Addis. 1809-11, lfw. 10 July 1812, d. 21 Aug. 1814 at Bombay.

228 **John Laurie,** b. 25 July 1794. Addis. 1809-11, lfw. 10 July 1812, l. 7 Dec. 1816, cap. 1 Sept. 1818, brev.-m. 10 Jan. 1837, m. 20 Jan. 1839. MAHRATTA WAR 1817-19, battle of Kirkee 5 Nov. 1817 (*Lond. Gaz.* 18 Apr. 1818), taking of Singhur 2nd Mar. 1818, Poorundhur 16 Mar. 1818, Wassoota 7 Apr. 1818, ordce. 1819-37. Transferred to corps of Native Invalids 30 Sept. 1839. ret. 10 Aug. 1842. l.c. 28 Nov. 1854. d. 25 Jan. 1860 in London.

229 **James Cocke,** b. 1793. Addis. 1809-11, lfw. 10 July 1812, l. never, cap. 1 Sept. 1818, brev.-m. 10 Jan. 1837, m. 8 July 1839. Field service Khandeish 1818-21, o.c. Arty. Northern Division 1839. d. 13 Dec. 1839 at Kurrachee.

230 **William Henry Foy,** b. 1794. Addis. 1810-12, lfw. 9 May 1813, l. 1 Sept. 1818, cap. 19 June 1820, brev.-m. 10 Jan. 1837. MAHRATTA WAR 1815-17, field service Guzerat 1816-17, field service Kattywar 1819, capture of Chooria 18 May 1819, wounded; desp. Adjt. and qtrmt. 2nd Batt. 1 Jan. 1820-1 Feb. 1822, brgd.-m. of Arty. 1 Nov. 1822-19 Dec. 1825, G.C. 8 Jan. 1834-38. d. 29 Mar. 1838 on passage to Cape of Good Hope.

231 **John Willis Watson,** b. 13 Nov. 1794. Addis. 1810-12, lfw. 9 May 1813, l. 7 Dec. 1816, cap. 11 Sept. 1820, brev.-m. 10 Jan. 1837, m. 30 Sept. 1839, l.c. 3 July 1845, l.c. commdt. 20 Jan. 1853. Field service Guzerat 1815, capture of Jooria, MAHRATTA WAR 1816-18, capture of Poona 16 Nov. 1817, Sattara 11 Feb. 1818, Singhur 2 Mar. 1818, Poorundhur 16 Mar. 1818, Wassoota 7 Apr. 1818, and other forts, o.c. Arty. siege of Malligaum June 1818, ARABIA, Beni-boo-ali 2 Mar. 1821. Ordce. 1821-25, drctr. Depôt of Instruction 16 Dec. 1831-18 Mar. 1833, Ordce. 1836-39, G.C. 1 Mar. 1839-2 Apr. 1841, Ordce. 1841-53. ret. 28 Mar. 1853. c. 28 Nov. 1854. d. 11 June 1870 in Kensington.

232 **James Rankin Watson,** b. 15 May 1794. Addis. 1811-12, lfw. 9 May 1813. d. 1 Oct. 1814 at Kaira.

233 **Alexander Allardice Auldjo,** b. 15 May 1794. Addis. 1810-12, lfw. 9 May 1813, l. 1 Sept. 1818, cap. 8 Mar. 1821. Field service Guzerat 1816. Transferred to corps of Native Invalids 11 Apr. 1826. d. 11 June 1826 at Mahim.

234 **John Johnson,** b. 1796. Addis. 1809-10, lfw. 3 Oct. 1813, l. 1 Sept. 1818,

cap. 14 May 1821. Field service Guzerat 1816, MAHRATTA WAR 1817-18, adjt. and qtrmt. 1st Troop 1 Jan. 1820-22 Oct. 1822, ARABIA, Beni-boo-ali 2 Mar. 1821. Drowned 29 Jan. 1823 at Surat.

235 **James Alexander Davies**, b. 25 Feb. 1796. Addis. 1811-14, lfw. 22 May 1814, l. 1 Sept. 1818. Field service Guzerat 1815, MAHRATTA WAR 1817-18, adjt. and qtrmt. Arty. Guzerat 1818-20. d. 24 Nov. 1820 at Surat.

236 **Joseph Walker**, b. 12 Apr. 1795. Addis. 1811-14, lfw. 23 Aug. 1814, l. 1 Sept. 1818, cap. 30 Jan. 1823. Field service Kutch 1819. ret. 20 Jan. 1826. d. 13 July 1868 at Melbourne, North, Colony of Victoria.

237 **Charles Dick Blachford**, b. 16 Jan. 1795. Addis. 1810-14, lfw. 2 Oct. 1814, l. 1 Sept. 1818. Field service Guzerat 1816, MAHRATTA WAR 1817-18, capture of Singhur 2 Mar. 1818, Poorundhur 16 Mar. 1818, Wassoota 7 Apr. 1818, adjt. and qtrmt. 2nd Troop 22 Oct. 1822-21 July 1825, capture of Kittoor Dec. 1824. d. 21 July 1825 at Poona. Tomb erected by brother officers.

238 **John James Sibald Jervis**, b. 8 Nov. 1797. Addis. 1812-14, lfw. 27 May 1815, l. 1 Sept. 1818. Ordce. 1819-24. d. 6 Apr. 1824 at Bombay.

239 **Henry Lowry Osborne**, b. 22 July 1797. Addis. 1813-14, lfw. 3 Sept. 1815, l. 1 Sept. 1818. A.d.c. to C.I.C. 1816-17. MAHRATTA WAR 1817-19, ordce. 1817. d. 29 Aug. 1819 at Bombay.

240 **George Rose Lyons**, b. 29 May 1796. Addis. 1812-14, lfw. 2 Feb. 1816, l. 1 Sept. 1818. Adjt. to 1st Batt. 1 Dec. 1819-18 Feb. 1820, adjt. and qtrmt. 2nd Troop 1 May 1820-22 Oct. 1822, and to 1st Troop 22 Oct. 1822-1 Nov. 1824. MAHRATTA WAR 1817-19. d. 14 Dec. 1824 at Surat.

241 **Mathew Law**, b. 28 Nov. 1796. Addis. 1813-16, lfw. 22 Apr. 1816, l. 1 Sept. 1818, cap. 28 Sept. 1827. MAHRATTA WAR 1817-18, comg. detachment of Arty. at capture of Cherokee, highly commended in General Orders, Burmah 1824, ordce. 1826-30, o.c. Arty. Cutch 1833. d. 23 Dec. 1833 at Poona.

242 **William Morley**, b. 23 Mar. 1798. Addis. 1814-16, lfw. 31 May 1816, l. 1 Sept. 1818, cap. 28 Sept. 1827. Field service Southern Concan, capture of Rairee 13 Feb. 1819, o.c. Arty. at capture of Zyah, Persian Gulf, Dec. 1819 (desp. *Lond. Gaz.* 28 Apr. 1821), Arabia 1820 with Cap. Thompson's force, defeated at Beni-boo-ali 9 Nov. 1820. Tried by C.M. for conduct there, sentenced to be admonished on account of peculiar difficulties of his position. ret. 8 Sept. 1837. d. 5 June 1839 at Bombay.

243 **Marcus Claudius Decluzeau**, b. 1 Jan. 1799. Addis. 1814-16, lfw. 27 Sept. 1817, l. 1 Sept. 1818, cap. 28 Sept. 1827, m. 13 Dec. 1839, l.c. 3 July 1845. Field service Southern Concan, capture of Rairee 13 Feb. 1819, adjt. 2nd Batt. 1 Feb. 1822-1 Nov. 1822, adjt. and qtrmt. Arty. Guzerat 1825, brgd.-m. Detail Malwa Field Force 1824, ordce. 1835-39, comg. H.B. 11 Apr. 1840-49. ret. 17 Sept. 1850. d. 30 May 1881 at Baden.

244 **William Jacob**, father of Samuel Swinton (500), b. 21 Sept. 1800. Addis. 1816-17, acting lfw. 29 May 1817, 2 l. 1 Sept. 1818, 1. 1 Sept. 1818, ante-d. 29 Sept. 1817, cap. 28 Sept. 1827, m. 9 Aug. 1840, l.c. 16 Apr. 1849. MAHRATTA WAR 1817-18, taking of forts Loghur, Vezcaaghur, Coaree, Tully, Goosala, and Ryghur, adjt. and qtrmt. 1st Batt. 18 Feb. 1820-21, service in the Red Sea comg. detachment Bombay Arty. with fleet under Cap. Lumley, R.N., H.M.S. *Topaze*, capture of Mocha Dec. 1820, severely wounded (desp. *Lond. Gaz.* 28 Apr. 1821), thanks of Court of Directors. Employed at the recruiting depôt in England 1822-26, member of Special Committee to report on Gunpowder Agency 1827, ordce. 1827, brgd.-m. of Arty. 26 June 1829-2 Jan. 1830, special duty revising ordnance and other establishments consequent on suspension of Military Board 1830, granted Rs. 3000 for his "Telegraphic Dictionary" 1829, ordce. asst. to commdt. 1831-34, G.P. 28 Jan. 1834-16 Dec. 1844, member of Special Committee on Aden defences 1842-43, started the Cap Factory 1844, and by zealous exertions much improved the manufacture of gunpowder, and greatly reduced the cost, thanks of Govt. of Bombay and Court of Directors, Asst. Prof. of Fortification Addis. 2 Jan. 1846-53. ret. 25 June 1849. d. 18 June 1854 at Croydon.

245 **Frederick Dick Watkins**, b. 18 Aug. 1799. Addis. 1816–18, 2 l. 1 Sept. 1818, l. 1 Sept. 1818, cap. 20 Sept. 1827. ARABIA, Beni-boo-ali 2 Mar. 1821, capture of Kittoor Dec. 1824, adjt. and qtrmt. 2nd Troop 22 July 1825–25 Jan. 1827. ret. 2 Apr. 1831. d. 10 Sept. 1879 at Marylebone, London.

246 **John Lloyd**, C.B., father of John Henry (478), b. 18 Nov. 1799. Addis. 1816–18, 2 l. 1 Sept. 1818, l. 1 Sept. 1818, cap. 30 May 1829. Permitted to retire whilst in England 17 June 1834, but returned to duty. brev.-m. 23 July 1839, brev.-l.c. 4 July 1843, m. 7 Jan. 1844, l.c. 25 June 1849. Under Resident Nagpore serving with Auxiliary Force H.H. the Nizam 1819–30, SIND and AFGHANISTAN 1838–39, Ghuznee 23 July, Kabul 7 Aug. 1839, Desp. *Lond. Gaz.* 30 Oct. 1839, brev.-m., o.c. Arty. Sind 1840–42, SIND campaign comg. Arty. Meanee, Hydrabad, brev. of l.c., C.B. 4 July 1843, Desp. *Lond. Gaz.* 11 Apr. and 9 May 1843, o.c. Madras and Bombay Arty. at capture of fortress of Punella 1 Dec. 1824, Desp. Comg. Goldze. Batt. 1844, G.P. 16 Dec. 1844–15 June 1846. ret. 15 Apr. 1850. c. 28 Nov. 1854. *Lieut.-col. comg. Cheshire Volunteer Arty. Administrative Brgd.* 5 *corps.* 20 Oct. 1860. d. 3 Nov. 1862 at Chester, suddenly.

247 **John Athill**, b. 19 June 1800. Addis. 1816–18, 2 l. 1 Sept. 1818, l. 1 Sept. 1818. d. 9 June 1820 at Seroor.

248 **John Sackville Leeson**, b. 2 June 1800. Addis. 1816–18, 2 l. 1 Sept. 1818, l. 1 Sept. 1818, cap. 7 Aug. 1826, m. 3 July 1845, brev.-l.c. 7 June 1849, l.c. 15 Apr. 1850, l.c. commdt. 28 Mar. 1853, c. ante-d. 28 Mar. 1853, c. Army 28 Nov. 1854. Capture of Bhooj 26 Mar. 1819, adjt. and qtrmt. 4th Troop 7 June 1824–20 Apr. 1830, field service against Kolapoor 1827, taking of Akulkote 1830, march from Quetta *via* Khobat and Sonumeanee to Kurrachee in command 4th Troop 1840, thanks of Supreme Govt., PUNJAUB 1848–49, brgd.-g. comg. Bombay Arty. Mooltan, charger killed; Goojerat, pursuit of Shere Sing and Dost Mahomed, M. 2 cl., Desp. *Lond. Gaz.* 7 Mar. and 19 Apr. 1849, comg. H.B. 1849–11 July 1855. d. 7 May 1859 at Paris.

249 **Frank Josiah Otte**, b. 27 Oct. 1801. Addis. 1817–18, 2 l. 26 Sept. 1818, l. 27 Sept. 1818. Arabia 1820. Killed at Cap. Thompson's defeat at Beni-boo-ali 9 Nov. 1820.

250 **George Yeadell**, b. 1 Sept. 1800. Addis. 1817–18, 2 l. 16 Oct. 1818, l. 16 Oct. 1818, cap. 3 Apr. 1831, m. 3 July 1845. Qtrmt. and intpt. 2nd Batt. 2 June 1822, Ordce. 1825, qtrmt. and intpt. 2nd Batt. 1827, capture of fortress of Punella 1 Dec. 1844, o.c. Arty. Aden 1839, o.c. Arty. Northern Division 1846. ret. 15 Jan. 1847. l.c. 28 Nov. 1854. d. 14 Sept. 1875 at Greaves, Lancaster.

251 **James Sinclair**, b. 20 Aug. 1802. Addis. 1817–18, 2 l. 17 Oct. 1818, l. 17 Oct. 1818, cap. 30 Dec. 1831, m. 3 July 1845, l.c. 17 Sept. 1850, l.c. commdt. 10 Nov. 1854, c. ante-d. 10 Nov. 1854, c. Army 28 Nov. 1854. Col. commdt. from 10 Nov. 1854. Adjt. 1st Batt. 11 Feb. 1823–1 Dec. 1824, ARABIA 1820–21, Beni-boo-ali 2 Mar. 1821, adjt. 2nd Batt. 27 Jan. 1826–21 Jan. 1828, executive engr. Baroda 1829, Ordce. 1830, Ordce. asst. to commdt. 1834, auditor Ordce. accounts 1837, Ordce. 1839–42, Ordce. 1844–45, o.c. Arty. Sind 1851–55, expedition to Roree against Ali Murad 1852. d. 28 May 1861 at Dublin.

252 **Edward Stanton**, b. 9 Mar. 1801. Addis. 1817–18, 2 l. 4 July 1819, l. 5 July 1819, cap. 1 Jan. 1833, brev.-m. 9 Nov. 1846, m. 15 Jan. 1847. ARABIA 1820–21, Beni-boo-Ali 2 Mar. 1821, adjt. 1st Batt. 21 Apr. 1828–15 Nov. 1822, Ordce. 1837, Ordce. asst. to commdt. 1838, a.d.c. to Governor 1839, Ordce. 1839, G.C. 2 Apr. 1841–1 Feb. 1848. ret. 4 Feb. 1850. l.c. 28 Nov. 1854. d. 25 Nov. 1875 at Blackheath.

253 **James Henry Murray Martin**, father of James Henry Murray (437), b. 17 June 1801. Addis. 1817–18, 2 l. 5 July 1819, l. 6 July 1819, cap. 6 Aug. 1833. ARABIA 1820–21, Beni-boo-ali 2 Mar. 1821, adjt. and qtrmt. 3rd Troop 7 June 1824–1 Nov. 1824, and of 1st Troop 1 Nov. 1824–10 Aug. 1834, SIND and AFGHANISTAN 1838–39, Ghuznee 23 July 1839, Desp. *Lond. Gaz.* 30 Oct. 1839. ret. 1 Aug. 1846. m. 28 Nov. 1854. d. 19 Apr. 1870 at Ashbourne, Derbyshire.

MAJOR J. T. LESLIE, C.B., 1854.

(From a portrait in possession of Miss Leslie.)

254 **James William Fraser**, b. 26 Sept. 1803. Addis. 1818–20, 2 l. 16 June
1820, l. 17 June 1820, cap. 28 Aug. 1833. Qtrmt. and intpt. 2nd Batt.
1825. ret. 6 Feb. 1834. Not shown in retired list after June 1840.

255 **Thomas Sutton**, brother of Henry (274), b. 1 Sept. 1803. Addis. 1818–20,
2 l. 16 June 1820, l. 17 June 1820. Adjt. and qtrmt. Arty. Surat Division
1824. Tried by C.M. Jan. 1827 for permitting music to be played in his
quarters after ordered to desist; sentenced to lose 7 steps and put below
M. F. Willoughby (263). Supdt. public buildings Rajkote. d. 17 Apr.
1831 at Malligaum.

256 **John Thomas Leslie**, C.B., b. 15 May 1803. Addis. 1818–20, 2 l. 16 June
1820, l. 17 June 1820, cap. 21 Dec. 1833, brev.-m. 28 Dec. 1842, brev.-l.c.
4 July 1843. Field service Guzerat comg. detail of Arty. 1824, adjt. and
qtrmt. 3rd Troop 1 Nov. 1824–18 Apr. 1833, Persian Gulf 1838, SIND and
AFGHANISTAN 1840–42, actions at Kujjuck, Hykulzie, Johain, Ghuznee 5 Aug.
1842, Beni-Badam, Maidan (Desp.), Huft-Kotal, Desp. *Lond. Gaz.* 6 Dec.
1842, M. 1 cl., brev.-m., SIND, Hydrabad, Desp. *Lond. Gaz.* 6 June 1843,
brev.-l.c., M. 1 cl. His Troop designated 1st or Leslie's Troop, and to
bear the eagle on its appointments for ever. G.G.O. 11 Apr. 1843, C.B.
4 July 1843. ret. 20 Sept. 1844. *Recruiting officer Newry* 1847–49, *2nd in
command Warley Depôt* 1849–50, *and commdt.* 1850–61. c. 28 Nov. 1854.
d. 7 June 1868 at St. Leonards. Name selected for inscription in the list
of distinguished Artillerymen on panels of Cadets' Library R.M.A. 1902.

257 **Francis Smith**, b. 1803. Addis. 1819–20, 2 l. 16 June 1820, l. 17 June
1820. Tried by C.M. at Poona June 1824 for having ridden in a violent
and outrageous manner across two officers, intending to provoke them to
a personal quarrel; sentenced to be reprimanded. d. 27 Dec. 1826 at
Surat.

258 **Andrew Rowland**, b. 15 Dec. 1801. Addis. 1819–20, 2 l. 19 Dec. 1820, l.
20 Dec. 1820, cap. 26 Dec. 1833, brev.-m. 9 Nov. 1846, m. 16 Apr. 1849,
l.c. 28 Apr. 1851, c. 4 July 1858, col. commdt. from 4 July 1858, m.g. 6 Jan.
1863, l.g. 1 Aug. 1872, ret. list 1 Oct. 1877, g. 1 Oct. 1877. Adjt. and
qtrmt. 2nd Troop 21 Feb. 1829–26 Feb. 1833, o.c. Arty. Northern Division
1849, o.c. Arty. Poona Division and 1st Batt. 1853, comg. H.B. 11 July
1855–25 Mar. 1856. Commdt. of Arty. 25 Mar. 1856–29 May 1861. d.
29 June 1878 at Horsell, Surrey.

259 **Frederick F. Haslewood**, Addis. 1818–20. res. 12 Dec. 1821 in England.

260 **Francis John Pontardent**, b. 17 Feb. 1804. Addis. 1819–20, 2 l. 19 Dec.
1820, l. 20 Dec. 1820, cap. 7 Feb. 1834. Capture of Kittoor Dec. 1824,
adjt. and qtrmt. 2nd Troop 25 Jan. 1827–21 Feb. 1829, SIND and
AFGHANISTAN 1838–41, brgd.-m. of Arty. Field Force N.W. Frontier
1838, 1st Asst. Political Agent Sind 1842, brgd.-m. of Arty. Southern Mahratta Country 1844–
45, capture of Munsuntosh, wounded. d. 25 June 1845 at Bombay.

261 **Sir William Marcus Coghlan**, K.C.B., grandfather of P. H. Hay-Coghlan
(R.A. 5438), b. 31 May 1804. Addis. 1819–20, 2 l. 19 Dec. 1820, l. 20 Dec.
1820, cap. 16 June 1834, brev.-m. 13 Nov. 1839, m. 25 June 1849, brev.-l.c.
11 Nov. 1851, l.c. 23 Feb. 1852, ante-d. 25 June 1849, brev.-c. 28 Nov.
1854, c. 8 May 1859, col. commdt. from 8 May, 1859, m.g. 14 Apr. 1863, l.g.
6 Oct. 1872, ret. list 1 Oct. 1877, g. 1 Oct. 1877. Doab Field Force 1826–27,
Kolapoor Field Force 1827–28, brgd.-m. of Arty. 12 Dec. 1834–19 Apr.
1846, AFGHANISTAN 1838–40 as brgd.-m. of Arty. Ghuznee 23 July, Kabul
7 Aug., Khelat 13 Nov. 1839, Desp. *Lond. Gaz.* 30 Oct. 1839 and 13 Feb.
1840, M., brev.-m., Sec. Select Committee of Arty. Officers 1842, G.P.
15 June 1846–20 Mar. 1848, comg. 1st Batt. 1849, o.c. Arty. Southern
Division 1854, Political Resident and brigadier comg. Aden 1856, commanded column in Arabia 1858, Sheikh Othman, K.C.B. (civil) 6 June
1864. d. 26 Nov. 1885 at Ramsgate.

262 **Nicholas Lechmere**, b. 1803. Addis. 1819–20, 2 l. 19 Dec. 1820, l. 20 Dec.
1820, cap. 20 Aug. 1835. Adjt. and qtrmt. 3rd Troop 18 Apr. 1833–21 May
1834, brgd.-m. Arty. Doab Field Force Jan. 1826 and of Arty. Poona
Division 1830. d. 19 Dec. 1841 at Karrack, Persian Gulf.

263   **Michael Franklin Willoughby,** C.B., b. 12 Nov. 1803.   Addis. 1818–20,
      2 l. 19 Dec. 1820, l. 20 Dec. 1820, brev.-cap. 19 Dec. 1835, cap. 14 May
      1836, brev.-m. 4 July 1843, m. 4 Feb. 1850, l.c. 20 Jan. 1853, ante-d. 4
      Feb. 1850, brev.-c. 20 Nov. 1854.   o.c. Arty. on service Mahee Kanta 1822–
      23, field service 1824 taking of Godra and Champaneea, capture of Kittoor
      brgd.-m. Madras and Bombay Arty. Dec. 1824, o.c. Arty. operations in
      Kattywar 1825, adjt. 2nd Batt. 6 Sept. 1830–19 Sept. 1834, o.c. Arty. Red
      Sea and capture of Aden 1839, Ordce. 1839–41, fort adjt. Bombay 1841,
      Military Sec. to Governor 1841, SIND 1843, Hydrabad, Desp. *Lond.*
      Gaz. 6 June 1843, M., brev.-m., C.B. 4 July 1843, G.P. 20 Mar. 1848–28
      Oct. 1852, Ordce. 1853–57, I.G.O. 14 Apr. 1857–27 Aug. 1859, Inspector of
      Stores, India Office Store Dept. 1859–70.   ret. 29 Mar. 1860.   m.g. 3 July
      1860.   d. 20 Aug. 1871 in London.

264   **John Sterry Webb,** b. 5 June 1804.   Addis. 1818–20, 2 l. 19 Dec. 1820, l.
      20 Dec. 1820.   d. 20 May 1827 on board *Royal George* passage home.

265   **William Brett,** b. 6 Dec. 1803.   Addis. 1818–20, 2 l. 19 Dec. 1820, l. 20 Dec.
      1820, brev.-cap. 19 Dec. 1835, cap. 8 Sept. 1837, brev.-m. 9 Nov. 1846, m.
      15 Apr. 1850, l.c. 25 Mar. 1853, brev.-c. 18 Feb. 1856.   Adjt. and qtrmt. 4th
      Troop 20 Apr. 1830–9 Jan. 1832, and of 2nd Troop 26 Dec. 1833–8 Sept.
      1837, Sind Reserve Force 1838, service at Akulkote 1840, o.c. Arty. taking
      Manora and Kurrachee 1839, comg. 2nd. Batt. 1854–55.   ret. 3 Jan. 1857.
      m.g. 17 Feb. 1857.   d. 16 June 1858 at Cheltenham.

266   **Charles Lucas,** father of Charles Shaw de Neufville (419), George Doyle
      Albert (422), James Cock de Neufville (463), b. 31 Dec. 1804.   Addis. 1818–
      20, 2 l. 19 Dec. 1820, l. 20 Dec. 1820, brev.-cap. 19 Dec. 1835. cap. 30 Mar.
      1838, brev.-m. 9 Nov. 1846, m. 17 Sept. 1850, brev.-l.c. 20 June 1854. l.c.
      10 Nov. 1854, ante-d. to 17 Sept. 1850, brev.-c. 13 Nov. 1857, c. 18 Feb.
      1861, c.'s allowances 29 May 1861, m.g. 26 Apr. 1866.   Ordce. 1840–54,
      o.c. Arty. Southern Division 1854–55, o.c. Arty. Northern Division 1855–60,
      brgd.-g. comg. Neemuch 1860–61.   Commdt. of Arty. 29 May 1861–19 Aug.
      1862, I.G. of Arty. Bombay 1 Nov. 1862–67.   d. 11 June 1873 in London.

267   **Henry Willoughby Trevelyn,** C.B., b. 26 Jan. 1803.   Addis. 1819–20, 2 l.
      19 Dec. 1820, l. 20 Dec. 1820, brev.-cap. 19 Dec. 1835, cap. 4 June 1838,
      brev.-m. 9 Nov. 1846, m. 28 Apr. 1851, brev.-l.c. 5 Mar. 1859, c. 18 Feb.
      1861, m.g. 25 Mar. 1867, c.'s allowances 1 Aug. 1872, col. commdt. 21 July
      1874.   Adjt. 1st Batt. 1 Dec. 1824–21 Apr. 1828, Asst. Political Agent
      Ajmere 1833, Supdt. Ajmere 1836, Political Agent Kotah 1837,
      2nd Asst. Agent to the Gov. Gen. Rajpootana 1839, 1st Asst. Resident
      Indore 1841, Political Agent Bhopal 1842, Political Agent Mahee Kanta
      1854, Political Agent Cutch 1854, PERSIA 1856–57, o.c. Arty. Reshire,
      Bushire, Khooshab, Desp. *Lond. Gaz.* 30 Jan. 1857 and 11 Aug. 1859, M.
      1 cl., C.B. 21 Jan. 1858.   d. 31 Aug. 1876 at Bath.

268   **Thomas Eaton Cotgrave,** b. 26 Nov. 1803.   *Royal Navy* 1812, *midship-*
      man H.M.S. "Superb," bombardment of Algiers 27 *Aug.* 1816, M. Addis. 1818–
      20, 2 l. 19 Dec. 1820, l. 20 Dec. 1820, brev.-cap. 19 Dec. 1835, cap. 20 Jan.
      1839, brev.-m. 9 Nov. 1846.   Adjt. 2nd Batt. 1 Nov. 1822–27 Jan. 1826,
      brgd.-m. of Arty. 19 Dec. 1825–26 June 1829, brgd.-m. of Arty. Poona
      Division 1829–30, brgd.-m. of Arty. 2 Jan. 1830–12 Dec. 1834, SIND
      and AFGHANISTAN 1838–41, Ghuznee 23 July 1839, Desp. *Lond. Gaz.* 3
      Oct. 1839, Ordce. 1841–42, o.c. Arty. Northern Division 1851.   ret. 15
      Aug. 1852, l.c. 28 Nov. 1854.   d. 30 Nov. 1887 at Banwell, Somerset.

269   **Talbot Ritherden,** b. 27 Oct. 1802.   Addis. 1818–21, 2 l. 18 Apr. 1821, l. 19
      Apr. 1821.   Adjt. 1st Batt. 11 Nov. 1822–11 Feb. 1823.   res. 28 June 1825.
      Orderly and Staff Officer Addis. 1825–51.   d. 23 Dec. 1886.

270   **John Wenham Lewis,** b. 1804.   Addis. 1818–21, 2 l. 18 Apr. 1821, l. 19
      Apr. 1821.   Operations against Asseerghur Apr. 1819, slightly wounded.
      Dismissed by C.M. 23 July 1828.

271   **Henry Stamford,** b. 20 Feb. 1804.   Addis. 1819–21, 2 l. 9 June 1821, l. 10
      June 1821, brev.-cap. 9 June 1836, cap. 8 July 1839, brev.-m. 9 Nov. 1846.
      BURMAH 1824–25, Kolapoor Field Force 1827, adjt. and qtrmt. 4th Troop

9 Jan. 1832-3 Oct. 1835, SIND 1839-44, attempt to relieve Kabul disaster of Nuffoosk 24 Aug. 1840, Ordce. 1841-49. ret. 31 Mar. 1849. l.c. 28 Nov. 1854. d. 3 Nov. 1869 in Kensington.

272 **William Thomas Whitlie**, C.B., b. Jan. 1806. Addis. 1819-21, 2 l. 9 June 1821, l. 10 June 1821, brev.-cap. 9 June 1836, cap. 30 Sept. 1839, brev.-m. 4 July 1843, m. 15 Aug. 1852, brev.-l.c. 20 June 1854, brev.-c. 18 Mar. 1856. Qtrmt. and intpt. 1st Batt. 1822, adjt. Goldze. Batt. 7 Apr. 1826-5 Feb. 1831, Kolapoor Field Force 1827, adjt. and qtrmt. Arty. Northern Division 1831, member of Committee at Calcutta to establish uniformity in Field Arty. equipment 1836-37, intpt. H.B. 1837, adjt. and qtrmt. 2nd Troop 8 Sept. 1837-30 Sept. 1839, SIND 1840-43, Meanee, Hydrabad, expedition against Shere Mahomed June 1843, Desp. M., C.B. 4 July 1843, brev. of m. *Lond. Gaz.* 4 Apr., 9 May, 6 June 1843, comg. 2nd Batt. 1852, comg. 3rd Batt. 1853, Ordce. 1854, comg. H.B. 25 Mar. 1856-Jan. 1857. d. 12 Apr. 1857 on board *Seringapatam* passage home.

273 **Henry Wilkinson Hardie**, b. 2 Jan. 1805. Educated at the Royal Military School, La Fleche, France. Addis. 1820-21, 2 l. 9 June 1821, l. 10 June 1821. Capture of Kittoor Dec. 1824. d. 17 Dec. 1825 at Broach.

274 **Henry Sutton**, brother of Thomas (255), b. 10 Dec. 1804. Addis. 1819-21, 2 l. 9 June 1821, l. 10 June 1821. Adjt. 1st Batt. 15 Nov. 1832-18 Feb. 1833. d. 14 Feb. 1833 at Bombay.

275 **John Grant**, b. 1804. Addis. 1819-21, 2 l. 9 June 1821, l. 10 June 1821, brev.-cap. 9 June 1836, cap. 3 Dec. 1839, brev.-m. 9 Nov. 1846, m. 20 Jan. 1853, brev.-l.c. 20 June 1854, brev.-c. 20 June 1857, l.c. 4 July 1858, ante-d. to 20 Jan. 1853. Adjt. 2nd Batt. 21 Jan. 1828-6 Sept. 1830, Orderly officer Addis. 1832, adjt. 2nd Batt. 19 Sept. 1834-4 June 1838, Ordce. 1838, SIND 1840-41, G.C. 1 Feb. 1848-14 Apr. 1857, Ordce. 1857-59, I.G.O. 27 Aug. 1859-2 Apr. 1860. ret. 10 Apr. 1860. m.g. 3 July 1860. d. 30 Sept. 1861 at Nairn, N.B.

276 **William Morse Webb**, b. 23 Apr. 1803. Addis. 1819-21, 2 l. 9 June 1821, l. 20 June 1821, brev.-cap. 9 June 1836, cap. 9 Aug. 1840. Ordce. 1833-42, Sec. to Select Committee Arty. Officers 1840. d. 27 June 1842 at Bombay.

277 **William Abraham Welland**, brother of Edward (319), b. 1805. Addis. 1819-21, 2 l. 9 June 1821, l. 10 June 1821. d. 16 Oct. 1822 at Bushire.

278 **Edward Anstruther Farquharson**, b. 22 May 1803. Addis. 1819-21, 2 l. 9 June 1821, l. 10 June 1821, brev.-cap. 9 June 1836, cap. 19 Dec. 1841, brev.-m. 9 Nov. 1846, m. 28 Mar. 1853, brev.-l.c. 20 June 1854. Orderly officer Addis. 1828-29, Ordce. 1831-52, Sind Reserve Force 1838, G.P. 28 Oct. 1852-6 Sept. 1855. ret. 12 Sept. 1855. c. 30 Oct. 1855. d. 19 May 1870 at Brighton.

279 **Clements Blood**, b. 20 Apr. 1805. Addis. 1819-21, 2 l. 9 June 1821, l. 10 June 1821, brev.-cap. 9 June 1836, cap. 27 Dec. 1842, brev.-m. 23 Dec. 1842, brev.-l.c. 7 June 1849, brev.-c. 28 Oct. 1854, m. 10 Nov. 1854, l.c. ante-d. to 10 Nov. 1854. Orderly officer Addis. 1829-31, SIND and AFGHANISTAN 1841-42, Kujjuck 20 Feb. 1841 wounded, Khandahar, battle of Urghundaub 12 Jan. 1842, action 8 Feb., Gohain 28 and 30 Aug. (Desp), Ghuznee 5 and 6 Sept., Beni-Badam and Maidan 14 and 15 Sept. 1842 (Desp.), M. 1 cl., brev. of m., Desp. *Lond. Gaz.* 24 Nov. 1842, PUNJAUB 1848-49, Mooltan, Goojerat, M. 1 cl., brev. of l.c., Desp. *Lond. Gaz.* 7 Mar., 19 Apr. 1849, brigadier comg. Khandeish 1855, brigadier comg. Ahmed-nuggur 1856, brigadier comg. at Hydrabad 1858. ret. 12 May 1859. m.g. 12 May 1859. d. 10 Apr. 1869 at Brentford.

280 **Richard Warden**, b. 16 Mar. 1805. Addis. 1820-21, 2 l. 10 June 1821, l. 17 Jan. 1822, brev.-cap. 10 June 1837, cap. 7 May 1844. Asst. to Francis Warden, Esq., 4th Member of Council 1823, capture of Kittoor Dec. 1824, intpt. at Head Quarters 1825, Kolapoor Field Force 1827. Acting drctr. Depôt of Instruction 1833, carried out abolition of Depôt at Ahmednuggur 1834, Ordce. 1830-45, SIND and AFGHANISTAN 1838-39, Ghuznee 23 July 1839. d. 1 June 1845 at Rahmutpoor near Sattara.

281 **Thomas Cleather**, b. 5 May 1808. Addis. 1821-23, 2 l. 6 June 1823, l. 7

June 1823, brev.-cap. 6 June 1837. Qtrmt. and intpt. Goldze., afterwards 3rd Batt. 1826. d. 24 Feb. 1840 at Poona.

282 **Thomas Hamilton Heathcote**, b. 1806. Addis. 1821–23, 2 l. 6 June 1823. d. 8 Dec. 1824 at Matoonga.

283 **John Liddell**, b. 11 May 1805. Addis. 1820–23, 2 l. 6 June 1823, l. 7 Apr. 1824. d. 14 Oct. 1824 near Cape of Good Hope.

284 **Edward Ramsay Prother**, b. 23 May 1806. Addis. 1820–23, 2 l. 6 June 1823, l. 6 May 1826. Qtrmt. and intpt. 1st Batt. 1826, adjt. Goldze. 5 Feb. 1831–7 Apr. 1833. Pensioned on Lord Clive's Fund 10 Oct. 1833. d. 25 June 1874 at Sturminster.

285 **Sir George Hutt**, K.C.B., b. 1 Mar. 1809. Addis. 1823–25, 2 l. 15 Oct. 1825, l. 20 Sept. 1827, brev.-cap. 15 Oct. 1840, cap. 20 Sept. 1844, brev.-m. 21 Sept. 1844, brev.-l.c. 20 June 1854, m. 12 Sept. 1855, brev.-c. 4 July 1858, l.c. ante-d. 12 Sept. 1855. Adjt. Goldze. 7 Apr. 1833–Oct. 1841, adjt. Arty. Sind Reserve Force 1838, SIND 1839–43, Meanee, Hydrabad, expedition against Shere Mahomed June 1843, M., brev.-m., Desp. *Lond. Gaz.* 11 Apr. 1843, C.B. 26 Feb. 1846, Ordce. 1849–52, PERSIA 1856–57, o.c. Arty. 2nd Division Mohumra, o.c. Arty. Sind 1857, Ordce. 1858. ret. 9 Nov. 1858. m.g. 18 Jan. 1859, K.C.B. 21 June 1887. *Sec. Royal Hospital, Chelsea,* 6 Mar. 1865–31 *Dec.* 1886. d. 27 Oct. 1889 at Appley Tower, Ryde.

286 **Thomas William Hicks**, C.B., b. 1808. Addis. 1823–25, 2 l. 16 Dec. 1825, l. 28 Sept. 1827, brev.-cap. 16 Dec. 1840, cap. 1 June 1845, brev.-m. 7 June 1849, brev.-l.c. 28 Oct. 1854, m. 3 Jan. 1857, l.c. ante-d. 3 Jan. 1857. Adjt. and qtrmt. Arty. Northern Division 1835, Ordce. 1846–58, PUNJAUB 1848–49, Mooltan, M. 1 cl., Desp. *Lond. Gaz.* 7 Mar. 1849, MUTINY, o.c. Arty. Central India Field Force Kotah-ke-Serai, specially mentioned, action heights before Gwalior, capture of Gwalior, *Lond. Gaz.* 5 Oct. 1859, 18 Apr. 1859, C.B. 21 Mar. 1859. Sir Hugh Rose reports: " Lieut.-Col. Hicks' very gallant conduct in leading a most gallant charge of the squadron H.M. 8th Hussars at Kotah-ke-Serai through the enemy's camp and battery of field guns, bringing back two of the enemy's field-pieces under a cross fire." ret. 24 Nov. 1858. c. 18 Jan. 1859. d. 9 Oct. 1892 at Plympton.

287 **John Edward Scott Waring**, b. 2 June 1807. Addis. 1824–25, 2 l. 16 Dec. 1825, l. 28 Sept. 1827. d. 20 Apr. 1839 in Yorkshire.

288 **Charles Robert Rowan**, brother of Arthur Francis (306), b. 1809. Addis. 1825–26, 2 l. 16 Dec. 1825, l. 28 Sept. 1827. Qtrmt. Goldze. 1831. d. 2 Oct. 1833 at Belfast.

289 **James Ash**, b. 20 Feb. 1808. Addis. 1825–26, 2 l. 16 June 1826, l. 28 Sept. 1827, brev.-cap. 16 June 1841, cap. 25 June 1845. Ordce. 1830–31, Road and Tank Dept. 1844. Transferred to Invalid Establishment 25 Feb. 1854. ret. 27 Nov. 1858. m. 4 June 1859. d. 11 Nov. 1880 at Balham.

290 **Henry Whalley Brett**, b. 23 Nov. 1808. Addis. 1825–26, 2 l. 15 Dec. 1826, l. 28 Sept. 1827, brev.-cap. 15 Dec. 1841, cap. 3 July 1845. Adjt. and qtrmt. 1st Troop 13 Oct. 1835–42. Ordce. 1842–43, sec. to Select Committee Arty. Officers 1842. Ordce. 1852–54. d. 27 Feb. 1854 at Bombay.

291 **James Sims Unwin**, b. 3 Jan. 1811. Addis. 1825–26, 2 l. 15 Dec. 1826, l. 28 Sept. 1827, brev.-cap. 15 Dec. 1841. Adjt. and qtrmt. 2nd Batt. 20 Feb. 1841–3 July 1845, SIND, Hydrabad 1843, M. d. 1 May 1846 on board *Childe Harold* passage home.

292 **Thomas Tarleton**, b. 9 Oct. 1810. Addis. 1825–26, 2 l. 15 Dec. 1826, l. 28 Sept. 1827. d. 8 May 1832 at Alexandria.

293 **Charles Henry Boyé**, b. 26 Apr. 1808. Addis. 1824–26, 2 l. 15 Dec. 1826, l. 28 Sept. 1827. Transferred to corps of Native Invalids 20 Oct. 1834. *Paymaster of Pensioners Northern Concan* 1836, *of Southern Concan* 1842. *ret.* 25 *Sept.* 1861. d. 26 Nov. 1886 at Sydenham.

294 **Henry Forster**, C.B., b. 24 June 1809. Addis. 1825–27, 2 l. 15 June 1827, l. 28 Sept. 1827, brev.-cap. 15 June 1842, cap. 3 July 1845, brev.-m. 20 June 1854, m. 12 Jan. 1857, l.c. 27 Aug. 1858, ante-d. to 12 Jan. 1857, c. 18 Feb. 1861, m.g. 6 Mar. 1868, c.'s allowances 12 June 1873.} Adjt. 3rd Troop 21

May 1834–8 May 1840, AFGHANISTAN 1839, Ghuznee 23 July, Khelat 13 Nov. 1839 comg. 2 guns, M., Desp. *Lond. Gaz.* 30 Oct. 1839, adjt. and qtrmt. H.B. 8 May 1840–7 Nov. 1840, comg. H.B. Jan. 1857, comg. 4th Brigade R.H.A. and Arty. Poona Division 1862–65, [R] 11 Feb. 1866, brgd.-g. and insp.-g. of Arty. Bombay 1866–70, comg. Northern Division of the Army 1869, C.B. 24 May 1869. d. 20 Oct. 1875 at Tonbridge.

295 **John Maxwell Glasse,** b. 11 July 1810. Addis. 1825–27, 2 l. 15 June 1827, l. 28 Sept. 1827, brev.-cap. 15 June 1842, cap. 3 July 1845, brev.-m. 20 June 1854, m. 4 July 1858, l.c. 27 Aug. 1858, ante-d. to 4 July 1858, c. 18 Feb. 1861. Adjt. 1st Batt. 3 Sept. 1833–13 May 1840, adjt. Goldze. 27 Aug. 1844–5 Aug. 1845, field service Southern Mahratta Country as brgd.-m. of Madras and Bombay Arty. 1844, capture of Forts Monohur and Munsun-tosh, capture of Punella Dec. 1844; brgd.-m. of Arty. 19 Apr. 1846–29 Apr. 1857, G.C. 14 Apr. 1857–27 Aug. 1859, I.G.O. 2 Apr. 1860–20 Oct. 1862. rct. 1 Sept. 1863. m.g. 1 Sept. 1863. d. 15 Apr. 1867 at Earley Hill, Reading.

296 **Gother Kerr Mann,** b. 20 Feb. 1809. Addis. 1825–27, 2 l. 15 June 1827, l. 24 July 1828. Orderly officer Addis. 1831–32. Absent from India over 5 years, so was struck off, but was allowed to retire 5 Sept. 1838 on Lord Clive's Fund on account of ill health. d. 1 Jan. 1899 at Greenwich Lane Cove, Sydney, New South Wales.

297 **Brook Bailey,** b. 13 Jan. 1811. Addis. 1825–27, 2 l. 15 June 1827, l. 20 May 1829, brev.-cap. 15 June 1842, cap. 3 July 1845. Adjt. 1st Batt. 18 Feb. 1833–3 Sept. 1833, engaged in repelling an attack by Arabs on Aden 1840, PUNJAUB 1848, Mooltan, Desp. *Lond. Gaz.* 7 Mar. 1849. d. 8 Jan. 1849 from wound received on 27 Dec. 1848.

298 **William Augustus St. Clair,** son of James Pattison (R.A. 950), b. 18 Oct. 1810. Addis. 1825–27, 2 l. 15 June 1827, l. 28 May 1833, brev.-cap. 15 June 1842, cap. 3 July 1845. Adjt. and qtrmt. 1st Troop 10 Aug. 1832–3 Oct. 1835, and of 4th Troop 3 Oct. 1835–44, AFGHANISTAN 1839–40, Ghuznee 23 July, Kabul 7 Aug. 1839, Kujjuck 20 Feb. 1841, M. ret. 28 Feb. 1851, m. 28 Nov. 1854. *Cap. Royal Sussex Arty. Militia* 10 May 1853, *l.c. commdt.* 2 May 1861. d. 8 Jan. 1879 at Colney Hatch.

299 **James Nicholas Rooke,** b. 16 Mar. 1811. Addis. 1825–27, 2 l. 15 June 1827, l. 2 Oct. 1833. Dismissed by C.M. 21 May 1832, and went to England. Restored to the service by Court of Directors, arrived in Bombay 22 Mar. 1834. res. 6 Nov. 1834.

300 **Robert Croft Wormald,** b. 1810. Addis. 1825–27, 2 l. 15 June 1827, l. 10 Oct. 1833, brev.-cap. 15 June 1842, cap. 3 July 1845, brev.-m. 20 June 1854, l.c. 19 Nov. 1858, brev.-c. 18 Feb. 1861. AFGHANISTAN 1838–40, Ghuznee 23 July, Kabul 7 Aug. 1839, M., adjt. and qtrmt. Arty. Northern Division 1841–45, Ordce. 1851–58, comg. 1st Batt. 1858, o.c. Arty. Southern Division 1859, comg. 2nd Batt. and Arty. Bombay 1861. ret. 1 Sept. 1863. m.g. 1 Sept. 1863. d. 14 Apr. 1897 in Jersey.

301 **Henry Lambert Brabazon,** b. 20 June 1811. Addis. 1825–27, 2 l. 15 June 1827, l. 24 Dec. 1833. d. 27 May 1842 at Singapore.

302 **Alexander Samuel Pemberton,** 2 l. 27 June 1827. d. 21 Sept. 1830 at Macoa.

303 **Henry Giberne,** b. 17 Oct. 1810. Addis. 1825–26, 2 l. 9 Sept. 1827, l. 26 Dec. 1833, brev.-cap. 9 Sept. 1842, cap. 3 July 1845. Operations in Mahee Kanta 1837, supdt. Mahee Kanta Survey 1837–40, SIND 1840–41, Meanee, Hydrabad, M., Ordce. 1843–44. d. 1 Sept. 1848 at Hackney.

304 **Sydney Turnbull,** b. 28 Feb. 1811. Addis. 1826–27, 2 l. 13 Dec. 1827, l. 7 Feb. 1834, brev.-cap. 13 Dec. 1842, cap. 1 May 1846, brev.-m. 7 June 1849, brev.-l.c. 28 Oct. 1854. Line-adjt. Ahmednuggur 1841–42, PUNJAUB 1848–49, Mooltan, Goojerat, M. 2 cl., brev.-m., Desp. *Lond. Gaz.* 27 Mar. and 9 Apr. 1849, MUTINY 1857–58, Ratghur, Barodea, comg. advanced guard, horse shot, relief of Sangor, Garrakhota, forcing of Muddenpore pass, general action of the Betwa, siege and capture of Jhansi, where he was killed 4 Apr. 1858, *Lond. Gaz.* 20 Apr., 11 May, and 17 July 1858. Sir Hugh

Rose reports : " In the despatches I have recorded the excellent service performed by Lieut.-Col. S, Turnbull, particularly in the general action of the Betwa, always exposing himself to the fire of the enemy, in order to choose the best positions for his guns. This devoted officer was as useful to me as commandant of Arty. as captain of a Troop. His premature fall prevents his receiving the reward which was his due."

305 **Charles Berthon**, b. 24 Nov. 1809. Addis. 1826–27, 2 l. 13 Dec. 1827, l. 16 June 1834. ret. 28 Feb. 1837. d. 9 Apr. 1837 at sea on voyage to Tasmania.

306 **Arthur Francis Rowan**, brother of Charles Robert (277), b. 1811. Addis. 1826–27, 2 l. 13 Dec. 1827, l. 7 Nov. 1834, brev.-cap. 13 Dec. 1842. SIND 1843, Hydrabad, M., Ordce. 1845–51. ret. 31 Dec. 1853. m. 28 Nov. 1854. d. 25 Feb. 1875 at Ryde.

307 **Charles Henry Nixon**, b. 5 Mar. 1810. Addis. 1826–27, 2 l. 13 Dec. 1827, l. 21 Nov. 1834. Qtrmt. and intpt. 2nd Batt. 1835. d. 19 Nov. 1837 on board *Atlanta* at sea.

308 **Eldred Pottinger**, C.B., half-brother of John (330), uncle of Eldred Thomas (475), of Brabazon Henry (476), great uncle of Eldred Charles (R.A. 4562), Robert Southey (R.A. 4787), b. 20 Aug. 1811. Addis. 1826–27, 2 l. 13 Dec. 1827, l. 20 Aug. 1835, brev.-cap. 13 Dec. 1842, brev.-m. 23 July 1839. Qtrmt. and intpt. 2nd Batt. 1834–35. With Poona Auxiliary Horse 1835, with Cutch Irregular Horse 1836, allowed by Government to examine the countries and passes west of the Indus ; travelled in the disguise of a native horse-dealer ; was at Herat when it was besieged by the Persians 1838, where, " by his fortitude, ability, and judgment, he honourably sustained the reputation and interests of his country " (*Calcutta Gaz.* 24 Oct. 1838). Brev.-m. 23 July 1839, C.B. 20 Dec. 1839, Durr-i-Durani Order 3rd Class, Political Asst. at Kohistan to the Envoy in Afghanistan 1838, Political Agent Herat 1840, Political Agent Bameean 1840, Political Agent Afghanistan 1841 ; AFGHANISTAN campaign, Khandahar, Kabul, Ghuznee ; wounded at Chareekar 6 Nov. 1841 at the rising of the Kohistanis. Was handed over with other officers as a hostage to Akbar Khan 8 Jan. 1842, and remained a prisoner until 29 Sept. 1842. Taking of Istalaf 30 Sept. 1842. Granted a year's full pay besides wound pension for his services. d. 15 Nov. 1843 at Hong Kong on way home *viâ* China of fever aggravated by his wounds. At his death his stepmother was granted an annuity of £100, and his four half-brothers £20 each. Name selected for inscription in List of distinguished Artillerymen on panels of Cadets' Library R.M.A. 1902.

309 **John Jacob**, C.B., A.D.C., b. 11 Jan. 1812. Addis. 1826–27, 2 l. 11 Jan. 1828, l. 14 May 1836, brev.-cap. 11 Jan. 1843, cap. 15 Jan. 1847, brev.-m. 16 Jan. 1847, brev.-l.c. 20 Nov. 1854, brev.-c. 20 Mar. 1857, l.c. 25 Oct. 1858. Superintending boring experiments Guzerat 1838. With army of the Indus SIND 1839–40, o.c. Arty. expedition against Bhoogtee and Murre tribes. Sind Field Force Cutchee and Beloochistan 1840 ; surveyed a route hitherto deemed impracticable for troops, across the Thur, between Sind and Guzerat May 1840 ; conducted troops proceeding from Guzerat to Sind by this route ; thanks of Govts. of Bombay, India, and Court of Directors ; appointed commdt. Sind Irregular Horse and Asst. Political Agent Sind and Beloochistan 10 Jan. 1842 ; held military and political charge of the frontier during the evacuation of Afghanistan, and protected the march of Gen. England's troops through Cutchee ; in command of Sind Irregular Horse throughout the operations in SIND 1842–43, including expedition to and destruction of Emamghur Dec. 1842, Meanee, Hydrabad, and surrender of Omerkote, hon. a.d.c. to Gov.-Gen. 8 Mar. 1843, *Lond. Gaz.* 6 June 1843 ; commanded force of about 800 men sent against Meer Shere Mahomed June 1843, utterly dispersed the Meer's force of 10,000 men, and took all his guns ; recommended by Gov.-Gen. for brev. of m. and C.B. on promotion to regimental cap., commanded advanced guard of Army under Sir C. Napier in expedition against tribes of Cutchee 1844–45, with Sind Horse, took Shapoor in a night attack Jan. 1845, and formed advanced party of Indus Field Force to Bhawulpore 1846 ; brev. of m. 16 Jan.

MAJOR ELDRED POTTINGER, C.B.
(IN THE DISGUISE OF A NATIVE HORSE-DEALER.)
(*Reproduced from Vincent Eyre's "Military Operations at Cabul."*)

1847, C.B. 10 Sept. 1850; conducted all operations against predatory border tribes 1847-56, commdt. Upper Sind Frontier and Political Supdt. 21 Dec. 1853, Acting Commissioner in Sind 1856, PERSIA 1856-57, in command of cavalry, command of garrison at Bushire, and in command of whole force after departure of Sir James Outram. M., A.D.C. 20 Mar. 1857, brgd.-g., C.I.C. Sind Irregular Horse "for special service" 24 Feb. 1858. d. 5 Dec. 1858 at Jacobabad. Name selected for inscription in list of distinguished Artillerymen on panels of Cadets' Library R.M.A. 1902.

310 **William Kirkpatrick**, b. 9 Mar. 1812. Addis. 1826-27, 2 l. 9 Mar. 1828. d. 11 Aug. 1834 at Sholapoor.

311 **Richard Creed**, twin brother of Henry (312), b. 27 Mar. 1812. Addis. 1826-28, 2 l. 12 Dec. 1828, l. 28 Feb. 1837. Field Force Persian Gulf 1838, adjt. 2nd Batt. 4 June 1838-20 Feb. 1841, attached to 1st Troop for service in SIND 1840-41, led a storming party of dismounted men of 1st Troop at attack on Kujjuck, when he was killed 20 Feb. 1841. Tablet in Westminster Abbey by his brother officers.

312 **Henry Creed**, twin brother of Richard (311), b. 27 Mar. 1812. Addis. 1826-28, 2 l. 12 Dec. 1828, l. 9 Sept. 1837, brev.-cap. 12 June 1843, cap. 1 Sept. 1848. Qtrmt. and paymtr. 1st Batt. 1837, AFGHANISTAN 1839-40, Ghuznee 23 July, Khelat 7 Aug. 1839, asst. qtrmt. gen. Bombay Infantry Division Kabul 7 Nov. 1839, adjt. and qtrmt. 1st Batt. 13 May 1840-1 Mar. 1841. ret. 4 Oct. 1849. *Cap. commdt. 1st Middlesex Arty. Volunteers* 15 *Jan.* 1861, *m.* 14 *Mar.* 1861, *l.c.* 6 *Oct.* 1862; *Administrative Brigade 1st Middlesex and 1st Tower Hamlets Arty. Volunteer Corps, l.c.* 21 *June* 1864-25 *Mar.* 1871. d. 3 Oct. 1877 at Maida Vale, London.

313 **Frederick Ayrton**, b. 20 Mar. 1812. Addis. 1826-28, 2 l. 12 June 1828, l. 19 Nov. 1837, brev.-cap. 12 June 1843. Orderly officer Addis. 1833, superintending experiments boring for water in Colaba 1836, Revenue Survey 1838. ret. 11 Sept. 1843. d. 20 June 1873 in Kensington.

314 **Thomas Gaisford**, b. 14 June 1810. Addis. 1827-28, 2 l. 12 June 1828, l. 30 Mar. 1838, brev.-cap. 12 June 1843, cap. 8 Jan. 1849. Intpt. H.B. 5 Feb. 1831, qtrmt. and intpt. 1st Batt. 1832, survey duty 1837, SIND and AFGHANISTAN 1839-40, Ghuznee 23 July 1839, qtrmt. and intpt. Goldze. 1842, special duty Sholapoor collectorate 1845, drctr. Depôt of Instruction 4 Sept. 1846-3 Jan. 1852. ret. 17 Feb. 1852. d. 26 Sept. 1900 at Ilfracombe.

315 **James Bowen Woosnam**, b. 28 Jan. 1812. Addis. 1827-28, 2 l. 12 Dec. 1828, l. 4 June 1838, brev.-cap. 12 Dec. 1843, cap. 31 Mar. 1849, brev.-m. 20 June 1854, brev.-l.c. 6 Mar. 1858, l.c. 4 Dec. 1858, c. 29 May 1861. Intpt. H.B. 1832, AFGHANISTAN 1838-39, Ghuznee 23 July, Khelat 7 Aug. 1839, M., Desp. *Lond. Gaz.* 13 Feb. 1840, qtrmt. and intpt. Goldze. 1840, adjt. Goldze. 13 Jan. 1842-27 Aug. 1844, line adjt. Ahmednuggur 1843, PUNJAUB a.d.c. to o.c. Bombay Arty. 1848-49, Mooltan, M. 1 cl., Desp. *Lond. Gaz.* 7 Mar. 1849, Ordce. 1850-55, G.P. 6 Sept. 1855-27 Aug. 1859, I.G.O. 20 Oct. 1862-10 Mar. 1863. ret. 13 July 1863. m.g. 13 July 1863. d. 14 Oct. 1877 at Weston-super-Mare.

316 **David James Cannan**, b. 28 Apr. 1812. Addis. 1827-28, 2 l. 12 Dec. 1828. d. 24 Sept. 1834.

317 **Robert William Chichester**, b. 29 Mar. 1811. Addis. 1827-28, 2 l. 25 Apr. 1829. In command of detail of Arty. at capture of Fort Panogurgh 25 Feb. 1836. d. 30 Oct. 1837 at Belgaum.

318 **Edward Samuel Blake**, C.B., b. 2 Mar. 1811. Addis. 1827-29, 2 l. Army 12 June 1829, Regt. 26 Dec. 1833, l. 4 Sept. 1838, brev.-cap. 12 June 1844, cap. 16 Apr. 1849, brev.-m. 28 Nov. 1854, brev.-l.c. 19 Jan. 1858, l.c. 8 May 1859, c. 29 May 1868. Service against Bheels in Guzerat 1837-38, adjt. Arty. Upper Sind Frontier Force 1840-42, PERSIA 1856-57, Bushire, Khooshab, Mohumra, *Lond. Gaz.* 30 Jan. 1857. M. 1 cl., brev.-l.c., MUTINY 1858-59, o.c. Arty. Rajpootana Field Force, Kotah and pursuit of the rebels, recapture of Chandaree, Kotah-ke-Serai, siege and capture of Gwalior, Powree, pursuit of rebels at Kurai and Khundrai, *Lond. Gaz.*

special mention 18 Apr. 1859, C.B. 23 Mar. 1859.   d. 26 June 1862 at Bayswater, London.

319   **Edward Welland,** brother of William Abraham (277), b. 15 Oct. 1811. Addis. 1827-29, 2 l. Army 12 June 1829, Regt. 7 Feb. 1834, l. 30 May 1839. Service in AFGHANISTAN 1842.   d. 27 Dec. 1842 at Sukkur.

320   **Watkin Massie,** b. 1 Nov. 1812.   Addis. 1828-29, 2 l. Army 11 Dec. 1829, Regt. 16 June 1834, l. 20 Apr. 1839. Burmah 1824, capture of Aden 1839. ret. 28 June 1842.   d. 8 July 1881 at Croydon.

321   **George Paxton Kennett,** b. 14 Apr. 1810.   Addis. 1827-29, 2 l. Army 12 June 1829, Regt. 12 Aug. 1834, l. 8 July 1839. SIND and AFGHANISTAN 1842.   res. 25 Aug. 1842.   d. 22 May 1861.

322   **Thomas Cole Pownoll,** b. Dec. 1812.   Addis. 1828-29, 2 l. Army 11 Dec. 1829, Regt. 25 Sept. 1834, l. 30 Sept. 1839, brev.-cap. 11 Dec. 1844, cap. 25 June 1849.   SIND and AFGHANISTAN 1840-42, Hydrabad wounded, adjt. and qtrmt. H.B. 1 Feb. 1844-16 Jan. 1849.   d. 18 July 1852 at Deesa.

323   **George Augustus Pruen,** b. 18 Jan. 1812.   Addis. 1827-29, 2 l. Army 11 Dec. 1829, Regt. 7 Oct. 1834, l. 13 Dec. 1839, brev.-cap. 11 Dec. 1844, cap. 4 Oct. 1849.   SIND and AFGHANISTAN 1838-42, Ghuznee 23 July 1839, action near Kotra Cutch with Nusseer Khan's Army 1 Dec. 1840. ret. 17 Aug. 1851.   d. 22 May 1861 at Clifton.

324   **Charles Robert Dent,** b. 19 May 1814.   Addis. 1828-30, 2 l. Army 11 June 1830, Regt. 7 Oct. 1834, l. 25 Feb. 1840. BURMAH 1824, qtrmt. and intpt. 2nd Batt. 1837, capture of Aden 1839, Ordce. 1840.   ret. 28 Feb. 1842.   d. 20 Feb. 1886.

325   **David Erskine,** b. 16 Feb. 1812.   Addis. 1828-30, 2 l. Army 11 June 1830, Regt. 21 Nov. 1834, l. 9 Aug. 1840. SIND 1840-43; five months besieged in Kahun 12 May to 28 Sept. 1840, highly commended; brgd.-m. to Arty. Sind, Meanee, Hydrabad.   d. 27 May 1843 at Hydrabad.

326   **Edward John Baynes,** b. 17 Aug. 1811.   Addis. 1829-30, 2 l. Army 11 June 1830, Regt. 20 Aug. 1835.   SIND and AFGHANISTAN 1838-39.   d. 12 Aug. 1839 at Quetta.

327   **Charles Yorke,** b. 4 Nov. 1814.   Addis. 1828-30, a supernumerary.   d. at Hursole 12 July 1835 before being brought on the strength.

328   **George Prevost Baynes,** b. 1 Dec. 1813.   Addis. 1828-30, 2 l. Army 10 Dec. 1830, Regt. 19 May 1836.   res. 15 Oct. 1837.

329   **James Frederick Turner,** b. 1813.   Addis. 1828-30.   d. 19 Feb. 1835 at Fort St. George, Bombay.

330   **John Pottinger,** C.B., half brother of Eldred (308), father of Eldred Thomas (475), Brabazon Henry (476), grandfather of Eldred Charles (R.A. 4562) and Robert Southey (R.A. 4787), b. 7 May 1816.   Addis. 1829-31, 2 l. Army 9 June 1831, Regt. 28 Feb. 1837, l. 20 Feb. 1841, brev.-cap. 9 June 1846, cap. 4 Feb. 1850, brev.-m. 26 Apr. 1859, l.c. 13 May 1859, c. 27 June 1862. Qtrmt. and intpt. 2nd Batt. 1833, adjt. 1st Batt. 1 Mar. 1841-15 Oct. 1848, drctr. Depôt of Instruction 3 Jan. 1852-21 Dec. 1861, PERSIA 1856-57 as brgd.-m. of Arty. Reshire, Khooshab, M. 1 cl., Desp. *Lond. Gaz.* 30 Jan. 1857, MUTINY, Ahmednuggur Field Force 1858, M., brev.-m., C.B. 28 Feb. 1861, commissary-gen. Bombay Army 27 Dec. 1861.   ret. 1 Sept. 1863. m.g. 1 Sept. 1863.   d. 12 Apr. 1877 at Castle Pottinger, Carrickfergus on Shannon.

331   **George Prince Sealy,** son of Henry William (185), father of Charles William Henry (R.A. 3153), b. 12 Sept. 1812.   Addis. 1830-31, 2 l. Army 8 Dec. 1831, Regt. 8 Sept. 1837, brev.-cap. 8 Dec. 1846, cap. 15 Apr. 1850, brev.-m. 27 Sept. 1859, l.c. 30 Mar. 1860, c. 1 Sept. 1863, m.g. 6 Mar. 1868, c.'s allowances 21 July 1874, col. commdt. 1 Sept. 1876, l.g. 1 Oct. 1877, g. 8 Dec. 1879, ret. list 1 July 1881. AFGHANISTAN 1838-39, Ghuznee 23 July 1839, M., qtrmt. and intpt. Goldze. 1844, adjt. Goldze. 5 Aug. 1845, afterwards of 3rd Batt. to 16 Oct. 1847, PERSIA 1857, M. 1 cl., o.c. Arty. Karrack 1857, MUTINY 1858, relief of Kolapoor, attack on insurgent Bheels, actions at Durba, Bowry, and Ambapawnee Apr. 1858, Desp. *Lond. Gaz.* 11 June 1858, operations in the Satpoora Hills in command of left column, M., comg. 4th

Batt. and Goldze. 1860–62, comg. 18th Brgd. R.A. 1862–67, brgd.-g. comg. at Nuseerabad 1867–72, o.c. R.A. Poona Division 1872, [R] 1 Jan. 1874. d. 11 Nov. 1892 at Ealing.

332 **William Curteis Say,** b. 3 Dec. 1813. Addis. 1830–31, 2 l. Army 8 Dec. 1831, Regt. 20 Oct. 1837. Intpt. H.B. 1838. d. 27 June 1841 at Ashford, Kent.

333 **George Keith Bell,** b. 15 Aug. 1814. Addis. 1830–32, 2 l. Army 14 June 1832, Regt. 19 Oct. 1837, l. 17 Aug. 1841, brev.-cap. 14 June 1847, cap. 17 Sept. 1850. Transferred to Invalid Establishment 25 June 1852. d. 29 July 1853 at Plymouth.

334 **William Hodgson,** b. 25 Mar. 1816. Addis. 1831–32, 2 l. Army 11 June 1833, Regt. 21 Oct. 1837, l. 17 Dec. 1840. Transferred to Native Veteran Batt. 6 Apr. 1846. d. 29 Sept. 1847 off Hurnee, Harbour of Bombay.

335 **Edward Deacon,** b. 14 Nov. 1815. Addis. 1832–33. Arrived at Bombay 21 June 1834. Promoted to 2 l., rank to be adjusted hereafter. d. 28 Apr. 1836 at Poona.

336 **Charles James Baker,** b. 2 Mar. 1814. Addis. 1832–33. Arrived at Bombay 3 June 1834. Promoted to 2 l., rank to be adjusted hereafter. d. 8 June 1834 at Bombay.

337 **Walter Scott Terry,** b. 2 May 1816. Addis. 1832–34, 2 l. Army 30 Dec. 1834, Regt. 30 Mar. 1838, l. 17 Aug. 1841. Comg. detachment of Arty. operations Mahee Kanta 1837, SIND and AFGHANISTAN 1840–42, rode alone through the enemy's country from Killa Abdoola to Khandahar to join his battery and 3rd Company 1st Batt. Battle of Urghundaub 12 Jan. 1842, action 8 Feb., Gohain 28 and 30 Aug., Ghuznee 5 Sept. comg. 2 guns, Beni-badan and Maidan 14 and 15 Sept., Istalaf 30 Sept. comg. 2 guns, on rearguard in Khyber pass, mortally wounded at Ali Musjid on the last day of the campaign. d. at Peshawur 7 Nov. 1842.

338 **Sir Arnold Burrowes Kemball,** K.C.B., K.C.S.I., b. 18 Nov. 1820. Addis. 1836–39, 2 l. Army 11 Dec. 1837, Regt. 4 June 1838, l. 17 Aug. 1841, cap. 28 Feb. 1851, brev.-m. 19 Jan. 1858, l.c. 11 Apr. 1860, c. 1 Sept. 1863, m.g. 6 Mar. 1868, c.'s allowances 21 Oct. 1875, l.g. 1 Oct. 1877, col. commdt. 30 June 1878, g. 28 Feb. 1880, u.s.l. 31 Mar. 1883. AFGHANISTAN 1838–39, Ghuznee 23 July 1839, M., Political employ Persian Gulf 1842, Acting Political Agent Turkish Arabia 1846, Resident Persian Gulf 1847–48, Political Agent and Consul Gen. Turkish Arabia 1856–68, PERSIA 1856–57, Political Asst. to Gen. Sir J. Outram, comg. Persian Expeditionary Force to Ahwuz. The Gov.-Gen. of India stated in his notification of the 18 June 1857, that "the valuable assistance afforded on every occasion of difficulty and danger, and especially in the brilliant expedition against Ahwuz by Cap. Kemball, has been highly commended by Sir James Outram, and merited the unqualified approbation and the hearty thanks of the Governor-Gen. in Council." Mohumra, M. 1 cl., Desp. *Lond. Gaz.* 15 May 1857, brev.-m., C.B. 21 Jan. 1858, K.C.S.I. 24 May 1866, British delegate to Joint Commission for delimitation of Turco-Persian Frontier 1875–76. Turco-Servian and Russo-Turkish wars as Military Commissioner at the Head Quarters of the Turkish Army, Turkish war medal, K.C.B. 29 July 1878.

339 **Thomas Gordon McDonnell,** b. 10 Sept. 1819. Addis. 1836–37, 2 l. Army 11 Dec. 1837, Regt. 20 Jan. 1839, l. 17 Aug. 1841. AFGHANISTAN 1838–39. d. 9 May 1842 at sea on passage home.

340 **William Cunliffe Outhwaite,** b. 25 Feb. 1820. Addis. 1837–38, 2 l. Army 11 Dec. 1838, Regt. 8 July 1839, l. 17 Aug. 1841. Adjt. and qtrmt. Arty. Northern Division 1845. d. 6 Nov. 1847 on board *Malabar* off Vingorla on passage home.

341 **Charles James Bruce,** b. 17 July 1819. Addis. 1837–38, 2 l. Army 11 Dec. 1838, Regt. 12 Aug. 1839, l. 17 Aug. 1841, cap. 28 Apr. 1851. Road and Tank Dept. 1845–47. ret. 23 Oct. 1854. d. 31 May 1872 at Ipswich.

342 **Reginald Best Brett,** b. 12 July 1820. Addis. 1838–39, 2 l. Army 11 Dec.

1839, Regt. 12* Aug. 1839, 1. 19 Dec. 1841, cap. 17 Aug. 1851, brev.-m. 6 June 1856. Line adjt. with Gen. Nott's force 6 Jan. 1842, SIND 1840–41, Hydrabad, M., adjt. and qtrmt. 2nd Batt. 3 July 1845–17 June 1846, Nizam's Arty. 1847. Expedition to Roree against Ali Morad 1852. Employed in the Ottoman Dominions with local rank of major 1853. Resident Agent at Constantinople for the Turkish Contingent, brevet rank confirmed on disbandment of Turkish Contingent. d. 13 Feb. 1859 on board *Eastern Monarch.*

343 **Robert Gordon,** b. 18 Dec. 1821. Addis. 1838–39, 2 l. Army 11 Dec. 1839, Regt. 30* Sept. 1839. d. 13 May 1840 at Cairo on passage out.

344 **John Richard Hawkins,** b. 14 Oct. 1821. Addis. 1838–39, 2 l. Army 11 Dec. 1839, Regt. 13 Dec. 1839, 1. 9 May 1842, cap. 17 Feb. 1852, l.c. 18 Feb. 1861. Adjt. Arty. entrenched camp Hydrabad 1844, Ordce. 1852–61. d. 2 Aug. 1865 at Ghizree, Kurrachee.

345 **James Hamilton,** b. 14 June 1841. Addis. 1838–40, 2 l. 11 June 1840, l. 27 May 1842, cap. 23 Feb. 1852. Line adjt. Ahmednuggur 1842, Southern Mahratta Country, capture of Punella Dec. 1844, qtrmt. and intpt. Goldze. 1845, PUNJAUB 1848–49, Mooltan, Goojerat, Desp. *Lond. Gaz.* 19 Apr. 1849, adjt. Arty. Division at Peshawur 1849. ret. 17 June 1855. d. 15 Dec. 1892 at Bakewell.

346 **William David Aitken,** b. 10 Dec. 1822. Addis. 1839–40, 2 l. 11 Dec. 1840, l. 27 June 1842, cap. 25 June 1852, brev.-m. 20 July 1858, l.c. 18 Feb. 1861, c. 3 Aug. 1865, m.g. 28 Oct. 1868, c.'s allowances 1 Sept. 1876, l.g. 1 Oct. 1877, g. 31 Mar. 1883, u.s.l. 1 July 1881, col. commdt. 27 Nov. 1885. Adjt. Arty. Hydrabad 1844, comg. 2nd Batt. 1857, PERSIA 1856–57, Mohumra, M. 1 cl., Desp. *Lond. Gaz.* 11 Aug. 1858, MUTINY 1857–58, throughout Rajpootana and Central India, Rewah, Awah, o.c. Arty., Desp., Kotah Desp., and subsequent operations in Central India, *Lond. Gaz.* 11 June 1858, brev.-m., M. 1 cl., A.A.G. R.A. Bombay 24 Feb. 1863–26 July 1864, I.G.O. 26 July 1864–26 July 1873, C.R.A. Northern Division 1874, [R] 21 July 1874, o.c. Field Arty. Woolwich 1875–76. d. 18 Nov. 1897 at Brighton.

347 **Charles Boudler Fuller,** b. 5 Nov. 1822. Addis. 1839–40, 2 l. 11 Dec. 1840, l. 28 June 1842, cap. 18 July 1852, l.c. 18 Feb. 1861, c. 3 Aug. 1865, m.g. 9 Nov. 1868, l.g. 1 Oct. 1877, c.'s allowances 30 June 1878, u.s.l. 27 Feb. 1882, g. 31 Mar. 1883, col. commdt. 12 Nov. 1892. SIND 1843, destruction of town of Malwassee. Adjt. 4th Batt. 14 Aug. 1846, exchanged on 22 Feb. 1850 to adjt. and qtrmt. Arty. Sind Division, Ordce. 1852–56, MUTINY 1858–59, Kota-ke-Serai, Morar, and recapture of Gwalior, M. 1 cl., o.c. R.A. Belgaum 1864, comg. E Brgd. R.H.A. 1868, Acting Inspector-Gen. of Arty. Bombay 1869, C.R.A. Mhow Division 1871, comg. C Brgd. R.H.A. 1873, exchanged to command of D Brgd. R.H.A. 1874, c. on Staff C.R.A. Ireland 24 May 1874–25 Feb. 1877.

348 **John Worgan,** b. 6 Aug. 1822. Addis. 1839–40, 2 l. Army 11 Dec. 1840, Regt. 20 Dec. 1840, l. 25 Aug. 1842, cap. 15 Aug. 1852, brev.-m. 19 Jan. 1858, l.c. 18 Feb. 1861, c. 26 Apr. 1866, m.g. 1 Oct. 1877. Adjt. 3rd Batt. 16 Oct. 1847–23 May 1851, PERSIA 1856–57, Mohumra in command of the Mortar Raft, about three miles from the main Army, and under fire of the forts for nearly two hours without support. Desp., specially mentioned by Sir James Outram as evincing much coolness and great gallantry. M. 1 cl., brev.-m. *Lond. Gaz.* 15 May 1857. G.C.F. 27 Aug. 1858–10 Mar. 1863, Ordce. 13 Mar. 1863–1 Dec. 1863, D.I.G.O. 1 Dec. 1863–26 July 1873, I.G.O. 26 July 1873–26 July 1878. ret. 31 Dec. 1878. Hon. l.g. 31 Dec. 1878.

349 **Edward Wray,** C.B., father of Edward St. Clair (R.A. 3297), b. 27 Nov. 1823. Addis. 1839–40, 2 l. Army 11 Dec. 1840, Regt. 17 Aug. 1841, l. 9 Nov. 1842, cap. 20 Jan. 1853, brev.-m. 6 June 1858, l.c. 18 Feb. 1861, brev.-c.

---

* These dates supported by G.O.

18 Feb. 1866, c. 26 Apr. 1866, m.g. 1 Oct. 1877. Adjt. H.B. 16 Jan. 1849-17 Dec. 1852. Employed in the Ottoman Dominions with local rank of major 27 Mar. 1855, CRIMEA 1855-56, with Turkish Contingent in command of a battery of H.A. at Kertch, brev.-m., 2nd class Medjidie Turkish medal, Ordce. 1856-60, MUTINY, commanded Siege Train with Rajpootana Field Force, Awah Desp., Kotah Desp., pursuit of Tantia Topee, *Lond. Gaz.* 11 June 1858, M. 1 cl., C.B. 28 Feb. 1861, G.P. 6 July 1860-20 Oct. 1862, I.G.O. 10 Mar. 1863-26 July 1864, Ordce. Select Committee England Oct. 1865-16 Dec. 1868, Staff of Drctr. of Arty. and adviser to the Sec. of State for India 16 Dec. 1868-31 Dec. 1878. ret. 31 Dec. 1878. Hon. l.g. 31 Dec. 1878. d. 27 July 1892 in London. Memorial tablet Garrison Church, Woolwich, by brother officers.

350 **John Granville Lightfoot**, C.B., b. 14 Nov. 1823. Addis. 1839-40, 2 l. Army 11 Dec. 1840, Regt. 17 Aug. 1841, l. 27 Dec. 1842, cap. 28 Mar. 1853, brev.-m. 20 July 1858, l.c. 18 Feb. 1861. PUNJAUB 1848-49, Mooltan, Goojerat, and pursuit of the Sikh Army, M. 2 cl., subaltern officer Recruiting Depôt Warley 1852-53,* MUTINY 1857-58, Barodea, Sangor, Garrakotah, Ratghur, where volunteered and led storming-party, which took one of the towers; Jhansi, battle of the Betwa wounded, Calpee, action at Morar, recapture of Gwalior, specially mentioned, Jowra Alipore, *Lond. Gaz.* 11 May, 12 Apr., 17 July 1858, 18 Apr. 1859, brev.-m., C.B. 22 Mar. 1861. ret. 1 Oct. 1861. Hon. c. 11 Feb. 1862. d. 15 Mar. 1878 at Mauritius. Name selected for inscription in list of distinguished Artillerymen on panels of Cadets' Library R.M.A. 1902.

351 **John Gordon Petrie**, C.B., b. 16 Oct. 1822. Addis. 1840-41, 2 l. Army 11 June 1844, Regt. 17 Aug. 1841, l. 28 Feb. 1843, cap. 31 Dec. 1853, brev.-m. 20 July 1858, l.c. 18 Feb. 1861, brev.-c. 18 Feb. 1866, c. 26 Apr. 1866, m.g. 1 Oct. 1877. SIND 1842-43, Meanee, Hydrabad, expedition against Shere Mahomed June 1843, M., adjt. and qtrmt. Arty. Sind 1844, brgd.-m. Arty. Indus Field Force 1846, adjt. and qtrmt. 1st Batt. 15 Oct. 1848-6 Jan. 1853, MUTINY 1857-58, Ahwah Kotah, battle of Bunnass, Desp. brev.-m., M. 1 cl., *Lond. Gaz.* 11 June 1858, 31 Jan. 1859. Comg. Golzde. Batt. 1862-64, comg. 21st Brgd. R.A. 1864, brgd.-g. comg. at Neemuch 1867, ABYSSINIA 1867-68, brgd.-g. comg. R.A. Arogee, Magdala, Desp. *Lond. Gaz.* 31 June 1868 ,C.B. 14 Aug. 1868, comg. 21st Brgd. R.A. 1868-72, c. on the Staff, C.R.A. Southern District Portsmouth 19 Feb. 1872-17 Apr. 1877, [R] 1 Sept. 1876. ret. 31 Dec. 1878. Hon. m.g. 31 Dec. 1878. d. 31 Dec. 1890 at Southampton.

352 **John Dobree Woollcombe**, C.B., son of Robert (R.A. 1325), b. 16 Nov. 1822. Addis. 1840-41, 2 l. Army 11 June 1841, Regt. 17 Aug. 1841, l. 27 May 1843, cap. 25 Feb. 1854, brev.-m. 24 Mar. 1858, l.c. 18 Feb. 1861, brev.-c. 18 Feb. 1866, c. 25 Mar. 1867. 2nd in command Poona Irregular Horse May 1848-Aug. 1850, MUTINY 1857-58, capture of Dhar, battle of Mundesore, capture of Jhansi and Chandaree, battle of Betwa, capture of Calpee, Desp. *Lond. Gaz.*, 11 Mar., 17 July 1858, brev.-m., M. 1 cl., C.B. 2 May 1859, comg. Arty. Aden 1865, Arabia 1865-66 against Foodlee Arabs, Birsaid, comg. 18th Brgd. R.A. 1868, o.c. R.A. Poona Division 1871, brgd.-g. comg. at Nusseerabad 6 Apr. 1872 to death on 28 Mar. 1875 at Nusseerabad.

353 **William Davidson**, b. 1 Feb. 1823. Addis. 1840-41, 2 l. Army 11 June 1841, Regt. 17 Aug. 1841, l. 11 Sept. 1843. ret. 3 May 1359. d. 13 Nov. 1852 in England.

354 **John Crawford Smith**, b. 25 Feb. 1822. Addis. 1840-41, 2 l. Army 11 June 1841, Regt. 17 Aug. 1841. SIND 1843, Hydrabad, Desp. *Lond. Gaz.* 6 June 1843. Killed at battle of Hydrabad 24 Mar. 1843.

355 **Thomas Biggs**, b. 22 Apr. 1822. Addis. 1840-41, 2 l. 10 Dec. 1841, l. 15 Nov. 1843, cap. 27 Feb. 1854, l.c. 18 Feb. 1861. Revenue Survey 1843-44, field service Surat to suppress salt riots 1844, field service Southern Mahratta Country, capture of Forts Munohur and Munsuntosh, Revenue Survey 1845-55, appointed by Court of Directors to copy

* PERSIA 1856-57.

inscriptions, sculptures, etc., by photography in Western India 1855, Ordce. 1856–61, special duty Ahnudabad 1864, sent to England by Gov. of Bombay to superintend publication of photographs 1865. ret. 14 Sept. 1865. Hon. c. 14 Sept. 1865.

356 **William Sparkes Hatch,** b. 11 Dec. 1824. Addis. 1840–41, 2 l. 10 Dec. 1841, ll. 7 Jan. 1844, cap. 29 Aug. 1854, brev.-m. 19 Jan. 1858, l.c. 18 Feb. 1861, brev.-c. 18 Feb. 1866, c. 6 Mar. 1868, m.g. 1 Oct. 1877, l.g. 26 Feb. 1880. SIND 1843, Khandeish capture of Wurkheira 31 Oct. 1844, Desp., adjt. and qtrmt. Arty. Sind Division 1851, expedition against Shere Mahomed June 1843, surrender of Fort Yawul 1844, expedition to Roree against Ali Murad 1852, PERSIA 1856–57, Reshiré, Bushire, Khooshab, Desp., M. 1 cl., brev.-m., *Lond. Gaz.* 30 Jan. 1857 and 11 Aug. 1858, MUTINY 1857–58, affair of Oononia, pursuit of Tantia Topee. Drctr. Depôt of Instruction 12 Dec. 1861, G.P. 20 Oct. 1862–10 Mar. 1863, G.C. 10 Mar. 1863–26 July 1878, member of Special Ordnance Commission 1874 and 1875, I.G.O. 26 July 1878–2 Mar. 1881, [R] 1 Apr. 1880. ret. 12 May 1882. Hon. g. 12 May 1882.

357 **Henry Lee Gibbard,** brother of Thomas Bayly (393), b. 16 Mar. 1825. Addis. 1840–41, 2 l. 10 Dec. 1841, l. 20 Sept. 1844, cap. 29 Aug. 1854, brev.-m. 19 Jan. 1858, l.c. 29 May 1861. PERSIA 1856–57, Reshire, Bushire, Khooshab, M. 1 cl., Desp. *Lond. Gaz.* 30 Jan. 1857 and 11 Aug. 1858. d. 17 May 1863 at Paris on way home.

358 **James Thomas Keir,** b. 14 Nov. 1821. Addis. 1839–40, res. Addis. 1840, 2 l. 11 Dec. 1841, l. 1 June 1845. PUNJAUB 1848, Mooltan, Desp. *Lond. Gaz.* 7 Mar. 1849. d. 20 Oct. 1849 at Kurrachee.

359 **Archibald Crawfurd,** son of Archibald (Madras Arty. 293), b. 1 Feb. 1822. 2 l. 11 Dec. 1841, l. 25 June 1845. res. 1 July 1852. Capture of fortress of Punella 1 Dec. 1844, Desp., PUNJAUB 1848–49, Mooltan. Drowned between Panwell and Bombay on way home 29 July 1852.

360 **George Robertson Douglas,** b. 16 Nov. 1823. R.M.C. 1838, res. 30 July 1841, 2 l. 11 Dec. 1841, l. 3 July 1845, cap. 29 Aug. 1854. d. 28 Apr. 1856 at St. Helena passage home.

361 **Duncan McDougall,** b. 1825. 2 l. 11 Dec. 1841, l. 3 July 1845. PUNJAUB 1848–49, Mooltan. d. 20 Feb. 1849 at Kurrachee.

362 **Douglas Gaye,** b. 9 Jan. 1825. 2 l. 11 Dec. 1841, l. 3 July 1845, cap. 29 Aug. 1854, l.c. 2 Oct. 1861, brev.-c. 2 Oct. 1866, c. 14 Sept. 1869. SIND 1843, command of 2 guns at night attack on British camp near Shadadpore, when the forces of Meer Shah Mahomed were defeated and all his guns taken 16 June 1843. Adjt. Arty. Southern Division 1849–52, comg. E Brgd. R.H.A. 21 Nov. 1869–72, comg. F Brgd. R.H.A. 1872, Inspector-General of Arty. India 19 Aug. 1873–13 Sept. 1878. ret. 31 Dec. 1878. Hon. m.g. 31 Dec. 1878.

363 **William Stevenson,** son of Thomas (210), brother of Walter James Hodgson (410), Russell Alexander (445), b. 18 Dec. 1825. 2 l. Army 18 Dec. 1841, Regt. 19 Dec. 1841, l. 3 July 1845. Adjt. and qtrmt. Arty. Sind Division 1847, exchanged to adjt. 4th Batt. 22 Feb. 1850–2 Feb. 1853, PUNJAUB 1848 as brgd.-m. of Bombay Arty. Mooltan, Goojerat, and pursuit of Sikh Army, Desp. *Lond. Gaz.* 19 Apr. 1849. d. 3 Nov. 1853 at Mandavie.

364 **Anthony Charles Romer,** son of Robert Franck (R.A. 1237), b. 1823. 2 l. Army 2 Feb. 1842, Regt. 19 May 1842, l. 3 July 1845. d. 7 Sept. 1845 at Bombay on way home.

365 **Thomas Blizard Stanley,** b. 11 May 1824. Addis. 1840–42, 2 l. Army 10 June 1842, l. 3 July 1845. d. 24 Nov. 1846 at Kurrachee.

366 **Hugh Maxwell Douglas,** b. 3 June 1824. Addis. 1840–42, 2 l. Army 10 June 1842, Regt. 27 June 1842, l. 3 July 1845, cap. 29 Aug. 1854. Field service Southern Mahratta Country 1844–45, adjt. and qtrmt.

Arty. Northern Division 1847-48, PERSIA 1856-57, brgd.-m. to 2nd Division Arty., M., MUTINY Southern Mahratta Country. d. 23 July 1862 at Edinburgh.

367 **Vero Seymour Kemball,** b. 19 Aug. 1825. Addis. 1840-42, 2 l. Army 10 June 1842, Regt. 25 Aug. 1842, l. 3 July 1845, cap. 23 Oct. 1854. Field service Southern Mahratta Country 1844-45, Revenue Survey 1844. d. 18 Oct. 1859 at Bombay.

368 **Anthony Maxstone Murray,** b. 22 Mar. 1824. Addis. 1840-42, 2 l. Army 10 June 1842, Regt. 9 Nov. 1842, l. 3 July 1845, cap. 10 Oct. 1854, l.c. 24 July 1862, brev.-c. 24 July 1867. Adjt. 2nd Batt. 16 Oct. 1847-6 Feb. 1850, Ordce. 1850-53, Ordce. 1856, MUTINY 1857-58, M., Ordce. 1860-63. ret. 1 Aug. 1872. Hon. m.g. 1 Aug. 1872.

369 **Benjamin Kington Finnimore,** b. 1823. Addis. 1840-42, 2 l. Army 10 June 1842, Regt. 27 Dec. 1842, l. 3 July 1845, cap. 17 June 1855, brev.-m. 19 Jan. 1858. Ordce. 1846-53, o.c. Arty. Aden 1855, Ordce. 1856-58, PERSIA 1856-57, brev.-m., Desp. *Lond. Gaz.* 30 Jan. 1857, G.P. 27 Aug. 1859-24 June 1860. d. 24 June 1860 at Bombay.

370 **Hugh Stacey Osborne,** b. 1825. 2 l. Army 11 June 1842, Regt. 27 Dec. 1842, l. 3 July 1845, cap. 12 Sept. 1855. Transferred to Invalid Establishment 13 Aug. 1859. d. 26 Dec. 1879 at the Neilgherries.

371 **Hibernicus Scott,** b. 26 Jan. 1824. 2 l. Army 11 June 1842, Regt. 24 Mar. 1843, l. 3 July 1845. d. 7 Apr. 1847 on board *Troubadour* passage home.

372 **George Hossack,** b. 2 Apr. 1826. 2 l. Army 11 June 1842, Regt. 26 May 1843, l. 3 July 1845, cap. 28 Apr. 1856, l.c. 21 Oct. 1862. Adjt. and qtrmt. Arty. Southern Division 1852. ret. 1 Jan. 1863. Hon. c. 1 Jan. 1863. d. 27 May 1895 at Hampstead.

373 **Richard Harte Keatinge,** V.C., C.S.I., b. 17 June 1825. 2 l. 11 June 1842, l. 3 July 1845, cap. 3 Jan. 1857, brev.-m. 20 July 1858. Asst. Political Supdt. Nimar 1847, Political Agent Western Malwa 1857, MUTINY 1857-58, siege of Dhar, battle of Mundesoor, siege of Chandaree, severely wounded, operations in Satpoorie Hills in pursuit of Tantia Topee. M. 1 cl., Desp. brev.-m V.C., *London. Gaz.* 18 Apr. 1859. Political Agent Nimar 1860-Apr. 1862. Transferred to Bombay Staff Corps 18 Feb. 1861. m. 11 June 1862, brev.-l.c. 13 Nov. 1866, l.c. 12 June 1868, c. Army 11 June 1873, c.'s allowances 11 June 1880, u.s.l. 1 Jan. 1884, m.g 1 Apr. 1884, l.g. 1 July 1887, g. 1 Apr. 1894. Political Agent Gwalior Apr. 1862-Feb.1863, Political Agent Kattywar Feb. 1863-Nov. 1867, commanded Field Detachments against rebel Wagheers in Kattywar 1865-66, commended in General Orders 28 Jan. 1866, C.S.I. 28 Mar. 1866, Gov.-Gen.'s Agent Rajpootana Nov. 1867-Feb. 1874, Chief Commissioner Assam Feb. 1874-81.

374 **Joseph McKenna,** b. 17 Oct. 1820. 2 l. 11 June 1842, l. 3 July 1845, cap. 12 Jan. 1857. d. 8 Feb. 1859 at Dublin.

375 **Thomas Richard Teschemaker,** b. 1826. Addis. 1841-42, 2 l. Army 9 Dec. 1842, Regt. 20 Sept. 1844, l. 3 July 1845, brev.-cap. 9 Dec. 1857, cap. 4 Apr. 1858. Qtrmt. and intpt. 4th Batt. 1845, Sind Survey 1847, Ordce. 1853-55. ret. 18 Dec. 1860. d. 14 May 1892 at Dawlish.

376 **William Cameron,** b. 3 June 1823. Addis. 1841-42, 2 l. Army 9 Dec. 1842, Regt. 20 Sept. 1844, l. 3 July 1845. Adjt. and qtrmt. 2nd Batt. 17 June 1846-16 Oct. 1847, qtrmt. and intpt. 3rd Batt. 1847, adjt. 2nd Batt. 6 Feb. 1850-1 June 1854. d. 25 June 1854 at Sholapoor.

377 **Andrew Aytoun,** b. 7 Dec. 1824. Addis. 1841-43, 2 l. Army 9 June 1843, Regt. 1 June 1845, l. 3 July 1845, cap. 27 Apr. 1858, l.c. 18 May 1863. Special duty to Madras under I.G.O. to report on Madras system of artificers and supply of Arty. harness 1840, thanks of Govt.; field service Southern Mahratta Country 1844-45, adjt. of Bombay Arty., capture of Forts Punella, Pownghur, Munohur, and Munsuntosh; special duty under

H

Political Agent Southern Mahratta Country to report on geology and minerals of the district, thanks of Govt. ; senior officer of Arty. at siege of Dwarka and pursuit of Wagheers in Okamundel 1860-61. ret. 27 May 1864.

378 **Hill Wallace,** C.B., b. 13 Aug. 1825. Addis. 1841-43, 2 l. Army 9 June 1843, Regt. 25 June 1845, l. 7 Sept. 1845, cap. 27 Apr. 1858, l.c. 1 Sept. 1863, brev.-c. 1 Sept. 1868, c. 10 May 1874. Adjt. H.B. 17 Dec. 1852-29 Apr. 1857, brgd.-m. of Arty. 29 Apr. 1857-22 Oct. 1861, Town-m. and Remount Agent Bombay 23 July 1859-12 Sept. 1860, A.A.G. R.A. Bombay 26 July 1864-4 Aug. 1869, ABYSSINIA 1867-68, o.c. R.A. 1st Division, Magdala, M., Desp. *Lond. Gaz.* 31 June 1868, C.B. 14 Aug. 1868, o.c. R.A. Mhow Division May 1873-May 1875, o.c. R.A. Mysore Division 12 Nov. 1877-31 Dec. 1878. ret. 31 Dec. 1878. Hon. m.g. 31 Dec. 1878. d. 4 June 1899 near Stourport, Worcestershire.

379 **George Rennie,** b. 13 May 1825. Addis. 1842-43, 2 l. Army 19 June 1843, Regt. 3 July 1845, l. 6 Mar. 1846. Southern Mahratta Country 1844-45. ret. 1 June 1849. d. between July 1876 and March 1877.

380 **Henry Peter Brassie Berthon,** brother of Thomas Porter (451), b. 19 Nov. 1825. Addis. 1841-43, 2 l. Army 9 June 1843, Regt. 3 July 1845, l. 1 May 1846, cap. 27 Apr. 1858. PUNJAUB 1848-49, Bombay Sappers and Miners, Asst. Field Engineer Bombay Force 1 May 1848, Mooltan, M. 1 cl., Desp. d. 30 Sept. 1858 on board *Ghenghis Khan.*

381 **George Gleig Brown,** b. 14 Nov. 1825. Addis. 1842-44, 2 l. Army 7 June 1844, Regt. 3 July 1845, l. 1 Aug. 1846, cap. 27 Apr. 1858, l.c. 1 Sept. 1863, brev.-c. 1 Sept. 1868, c. 1 Sept. 1876. Adjt. and qtrmt. Arty. Southern Division 1853, MUTINY 1857-58, Awah Kotah, action of Sango-neer, M. 1 cl., brev.-m., Desp. *Lond. Gaz.* 11 June 1858. ret. 31 Dec. 1878. Hon. m.g. 31 Dec. 1878. d. 26 Nov. 1891 at Clifton.

382 **Frederick Conybeare,** b. 13 Apr. 1825. Addis. 1843-44, 2 l. Army 9 Dec. 1844, Regt. 3 July 1845, l. 24 Nov. 1846, cap. 27 Apr. 1858, l.c. 29 Feb. 1864, brev.-c. 1 Mar. 1869. Adjt. 3rd Batt. 21 Feb. 1853-10 May 1855, o.c. R.A. Sind and 18th Brgd. R.A. 1867-68, o.c. R.A. Poona Division 1872. ret. 1 Aug. 1872. Hon. m.g. 1 Aug. 1872. d. 31 Dec. 1892 at Beckenham.

383 **David James Kinloch,** b. 16 Oct. 1826. Addis. 1843-44, 2 l. Army 9 Dec 1844, Regt. 3 July 1845, l. 6 Jan. 1847, cap. 4 July 1858, l.c. 27 May 1864. Ordce. 1860-64. ret. 1 May 1869. Hon. c. 1 May 1869. d. 10 Nov. 1873 at Edinburgh.

384 **Sir Herbert Bruce Sandford,** K.C.M.G., b. 13 Aug. 1826. Addis. 1843-44, 2 l. Army 9 Dec. 1844, Regt. 3 July 1845, l. 15 Jan. 1847, 2 cap. 27 Aug. 1858, 1 cap. 14 Feb. 1859, l.c. 24 Mar. 1865. Civil employ 1849, Asst. Commissioner Saltara 1851. ret. 3 Aug. 1865. Hon. c. 3 Aug. 1865. *Official Delegate and Executive Commissioner for England at the Philadelphia Exhibition 1875-76, Acting Asst. Director of South Kensington Museum 1877-79, Official Representative of the Royal Commission at the Melbourne Exhibition 1880-81, Sec. in Australia of the Royal Commission for the Adelaide Jubilee International Exhibition 1887-88, K.C.M.G. 2 Jan.* 1889. d. 31 Jan. 1892 at St. Leonards.

385 **Arthur Riddell Mark,** b. 5 Feb. 1829. Addis. 1843-45, 2 l. Army 13 June 1845, Regt. 3 July 1845, l. 17 Apr. 1847. Qtrmt. and intpt. 3rd Batt. 1850, adjt. 3rd Batt. 23 May 1851-22 Feb. 1853, adjt. 4th Batt. 22 Feb. 1853-26 July 1858. d. 26 July 1858 at Ahmednuggur.

386 **John Clement Hailes,** b. 8 Jan. 1826. Addis. 1843-45, 2 l. Army 13 June 1845, Regt. 3 July 1845, l. 1 Sept. 1848, 2 cap. 27 Aug. 1858, 1 cap. 8 May 1859, l.c. 3 Aug. 1865, brev.-c. 3 Aug. 1870, c. 27 Feb. 1877. Adjt. Arty. Sind Division Oct. 1854-May 1859, in charge Remount Depôt Kurrachee May 1858-May 1859, o.c. R.A. Aden 1867-71, o.c. R.A. Sind District 1875, o.c. R.A. Mhow Division 1875-77, comg. at Ahmednuggur May to Nov.

1877, o.c. R.A. Bombay District Nov. 1877-Dec. 1878. ret. 31 Dec. 1878. Hon. m.g. 31 Dec. 1878.

387 **Thomas Trenchard Haggard,** father of John (R.A. 4170), b. 11 July 1827. 2 l. Army 14 June 1845, Regt. 3 July 1845, l. 8 Jan. 1849, 2 cap. 27 Aug. 1858, brev.-m. 27 Aug. 1858, 1 cap. 13 May 1859, l.c. 3 Aug. 1865, brev.-c. 3 Aug. 1870. Qtrmt. and intpt. 4th Batt. 1847, Orderly officer Addis. 1852, adjt. and qtrmt. 2nd Batt. 1 June 1854-24 June 1857, Ordce. 1855-53, MUTINY 1857-58, in charge of Siege Train throughout Central India, Garrakhota, Jhansi, Gwalior, wounded, Jowrah, Alipore, M. 1 cl., brev.-m., Desp. *Lond. Gaz.* 11 May, 17 July 1858, 18 Apr. 1859, G.P. 10 Mar. 1863-23 July 1877. d. 23 July 1877 in London.

388 **Robert Alexander Morse,** b. 1827. 2 l. Army 14 June 1845, Regt. 3 July 1845, l. 20 Feb. 1849, 2 cap. 27 Aug. 1858, 1 cap. 14 Aug. 1859, l.c. 3 Aug. 1865, brev.-c. 3 Aug. 1870. A.d.c. to G.O. Southern Division 1847, MUTINY with Sir H. Rose Feb.-Apr. 1859. ret. 1 Aug. 1872. Hon. m.g. 1 Aug. 1872. d. 11 Apr. 1893 at Clifton.

389 **David Greenhill Anderson,** father of E. Bullar (R.A. 3775), b. 5 Mar. 1828. 2 l. Army 14 June 1845, Regt. 3 July 1845, l. 31 Mar. 1849, 2 cap. 27 Aug. 1858, 1 cap. 19 Oct. 1859, l.c. 14 Sept. 1865, brev.-c. 14 Aug. 1870. PUNJAUB 1848-49, Mooltan, Goojerat, surrender of Sikh Army at Rawal Pindi, M. 2 cl., Ordce. 1856-57, adjt. and qtrmt. 2nd Batt. 24 June 1857-11 July 1859, A.A.G. R.A. Bombay 4 Aug. 1869-1 Aug. 1872. ret. 1 Aug. 1872. Hon. m.g. 1 Aug. 1872. d. 12 July 1897 in London.

390 **Joseph Shekleton,** b. 7 Oct. 1823. 2 l. Army 14 June 1845, Regt. 3 July 1845, l. 16 Apr. 1849, 2 cap. 27 Aug. 1858, 1 cap. 30 Mar. 1860, l.c. 16 Mar. 1866, brev.-c. 16 Mar. 1871. PUNJAUB 1848-49, Mooltan, Goojerat, and pursuit of Sikh Army, M. 2 cl., PERSIA 1856-57, M. 1 cl., MUTINY 1858, Rajpootana, pursuit of Tantia Topee, M., adjt. Reserve Batt. 1857. ret. 1 Aug. 1872. Hon. m.g. 1 Aug. 1872. d. 4 July 1888 at Ryde, Isle of Wight.

391 **Charles James Barton,** son of James (214), father of ~~Richard Lionel~~ ~~(R.A. 5466),~~ b. 22 Apr. 1827. Addis. 1844-45, 2 l. 12 Dec. 1845, l. 1 June 1849, 2 cap. 27 Aug. 1858, 1 cap. 11 Apr. 1860, l.c. 26 Apr. 1866, brev.-c. 26 Apr. 1871. Qtrmt. and intpt. 4th Batt. 1850, adjt. 1st Batt. 6 Jan. 1853-26 Aug. 1859, o.c. R.A. Pegu Division 1870-71. ret. 1 Aug. 1872. Hon. m.g. 1 Aug. 1872. d. 19 Nov. 1879 at Richmond, Virginia.

392 **George Brown Mellersh,** b. 8 Dec. 1827. Addis. 1844-45, 2 l. 12 Dec. 1845, l. 25 June 1849, 2 cap. 27 Aug. 1858, 1 cap. 25 June 1860, l.c. 25 Mar. 1867, brev.-c. 25 Mar. 1872. Ordce. 1853-72, PERSIA 1856-57, M. ret. 1 Aug. 1872. Hon. m.g. 1 Aug. 1872.

393 **Thomas Bayly Gibbard,** brother of Henry Lee (357), b. 8 Aug. 1827. Addis. 1844-45, 2 l. 12 Dec. 1845, l. 4 Oct. 1849, 2 cap. 27 Aug. 1858, 1 cap. 19 Dec. 1860, l.c. 25 Mar. 1867, brev.-c. 25 Mar. 1872. PERSIA 1856-57, Reshire, Bushire, Khooshab, Mohumra, M., adjt. H.B. 29 Apr. 1857-13 May 1859, C.R.A. Mhow Division 1857. d. 10 May 1873 at Bombay.

394 **Samuel William Dewe,** b. 3 May 1826. Addis. 1844-45, 2 l. 12 Dec. 1845. d. 13 Aug. 1846 at Ahmednuggur.

395 **William Henry Anderson,** b. 18 Feb. 1829. 2 l. 13 Dec. 1845. PUNJAUB 1845-49, Mooltan. d. 22 June 1849 at Mooltan.

396 **Peter Daniel Marett,** b. 25 Mar. 1825. 2 l. 13 Dec. 1845, l. 20 Oct. 1849, 2 cap. 27 Aug. 1858, 1 cap. 18 Feb. 1861, l.c. 1 May 1869. PUNJAUB 1848-49, Mooltan, M. 1 cl., adjt. and qtrmt. Arty. Southern Division 1858, ABYSSINIA 1867-68 with Pioneer Force Magdala, M., Desp. *Lond. Gaz.* 31 June 1868. ret. 1 Aug. 1872. Hon. c. 1 Aug. 1872.

397 Charles Nasmyth, b. 22 Sept. 1825. Addis. 1843-44, 2 l. 13 Dec. 1845,
l. 4 Feb. 1850. 2nd Asst. Bombay Trigonometrical Survey 1851. Defence of
Silistria 1854, CRIMEA, Alma, Inkerman, Gold Medal from Turkish Govt.
4th class Medjidie, M. 2 cl. Transferred to H.M. Army as cap. unattached 15 Sept. 1854, allowed by Court of Directors half-pay as l.
brev.-m. 15 Sept. 1854, m. *unattached* 12 Dec. 1854, *A.A.G. Kilkenny,*
brgd.-m. Curragh, D.A.G. Dublin, brgd.-m. New South Wales Aug. 1858–*Feb.*
1860, *m. 4th Foot 25 May* 1860. *ret. by sale of commission 25 May* 1860.
d. 2 June 1861 at Pau.

398 William Henry Saulez, b. 6 Oct. 1823. 2 l. 13 Dec. 1845, l. 15 Apr. 1850,
2 cap. 27 Aug. 1858, 1 cap. 18 Feb. 1861, l.c. 14 Sept. 1869. Adjt. 4th
Batt. 26 July 1858–7 Dec. 1859. d. 21 Mar. 1871 on board H.M.S. *Jumna*
passage home.

399 Arthur Blunt, brother of Charles Harris (Bengal 742), b. 1 Jan. 1829.
R.M.C. 1843–45, 2 l. 13 Dec. 1845, l. 17 Sept. 1850, 2 cap. 27 Aug. 1858,
1 cap. 18 Feb. 1861, l.c. 22 Mar. 1871. PUNJAUB 1848–49, Mooltan,
Goojerat, and pursuit of Sikh Army, M. 2 cl. ret. 1 Aug. 1872. Hon. c.
1 Aug. 1872. *m. 1st Bristol Corps Gloucestershire Arty. Volunteers* 15 *Jan.*
1873, *m. comg. Administrative Brgd. Bristol* 19 *Feb.* 1873, *l.c.* 9 *Aug.* 1873–
17 *Aug.* 1879.

400 Harry William Gibb, son of Harry William Scott (R.A. 1591), b. 1824.
2 l. 13 Dec. 1845. d. 3 Sept. 1847 at Kurrachee.

401 Robert Charles Battiscombe, brother of Edmund George (481), b. 25
Sept. 1824. 2 l. 13 Dec. 1845, l. 28 Feb. 1851, 2 cap. 27 Aug. 1858, 1 cap.
18 Feb. 1861. Employed in the Ottoman Dominions with local rank of
cap. 27 Mar. 1855, CRIMEA with Turkish contingent, adjt. and qtrmt.
Reserve Arty. 8 July 1858, afterwards of 3rd European Batt. ret. 5 Jan.
1869. Hon. m. 5 Jan. 1859. d. 29 Mar. 1899 in London.

402 Abingdon Augustus Bayly, father of Abingdon Robert (R.A. 4839),
b. 15 Jan. 1825. 2 l. 13 Dec. 1845, l. 28 Apr. 1851, 2 cap. 27 Aug. 1858,
1 cap. 18 Feb. 1861, m. 5 July 1872, l.c. 1 Aug. 1872, brev.-c. 1 Aug. 1877,
m.g. 1 Sept. 1881, l.g. 7 Sept. 1885, c.'s allowances 27 Nov. 1885, u.s.l.
5 Apr. 1891, g. 25 May 1895, col. commdt. 19 Nov. 1897. PUNJAUB 1848–
49, Staff officer Bombay Arty. Mooltan, M. 1 cl., asst. to Military Auditor-g.
1857, Ordce. 17 Feb. 1863–9 Sept. 1877, G.P. 9 Sept. 1877–2 Mar. 1881,
I.G.O. 2 Mar. 1881–5 Apr. 1886. d. 11 Aug. 1900 at Interlaken.

403 James Renny Henderson, b. 25 July 1824. 2 l. 13 Dec. 1845, l. 28 Apr.
1851, 2 cap. 27 Aug. 1858, 1 cap. 18 Feb. 1861. Arabia, expedition to
Sheikh Othman 1858, adjt. 3rd Batt. 29 Oct. 1859–60, adjt. 4th Batt.
1860–61. ret. 1 July 1870. d. 28 Mar. 1873 in Bayswater, London.

404 Edward Spread Beamish, b. 17 Nov. 1825. 2 l. Army 13 Dec. 1845,
Regt. 6 March 1846, l. 17 Feb. 1852, 2 cap. 27 Aug. 1858, 1 cap. 18 Feb.
1861, m. 5 July 1872. Adjt. 3rd Batt. 10 May 1855–29 Oct. 1859. ret.
1 Aug. 1872. Hon. l.c. 1 Aug. 1872. d. 17 Apr. 1892 at Bexley, Kent.

405 William Hugh Jamieson Henderson, b. 1 Dec. 1826. Addis. 1844–
46, 2 l. 12 June 1846, l. 23 Feb. 1852, 2 cap. 27 Aug. 1858. PUNJAUB
1848–49, Mooltan, Goojerat (wounded), M. 2 cl., Desp. *Lond. Gaz.* 3 Apr.
1849, adjt. and qtrmt. Arty. Aden 1857, Ordce. 1858–60. d. 17 Jan. 1860
at Bombay.

406 Charles Clarke, b. 25 Apr. 1829. Addis. 1844–46, 2 l. Army 12 June
1846, Regt. 1 Aug. 1846, l. 3 May 1852, 2 cap. 27 Aug. 1858, 1 cap.
18 Feb. 1861, m. 5 July 1872, l.c. 1 Aug. 1872, brev.-c. 1 Aug. 1877,
c. 1 Oct. 1877, m.g. 21 July 1882. Ordce. 25 Apr. 1860–27 Oct. 1873,
Deputy I.G.O. 27 Oct. 1873–26 June 1879. ret. 1 Oct. 1882. Hon. l.g. 1
Oct. 1882. d. 7 Aug. 1893 at Brighton.

407 Charles Edward Henry Cotes, b. 29 Dec. 1826. Addis. 1844-46, 2 l. Army 12 June 1846, Regt. 13 Aug. 1846, l. 25 June 1852, 2 cap. 27 Aug. 1858, 1 cap. 18 Feb. 1861. Punjaub 1848-49, Mooltan, Goojerat, M. 2 cl., adjt. 4th Batt. 7 Dec. 1859-60. ret. 1 Jan. 1867. Hon. m. 1 Jan. 1867. d. 18 Feb. 1892 at Acton.

408 Charles Edwin Allom, b. 24 Aug. 1827. Addis. 1844-46, 2 l. Army 12 June 1846, Regt. 24 Nov. 1846. Punjaub 1848-49, Mooltan, Goojerat, and pursuit of Sikh Army; on survey duty at Peshawur Sept. 1849. d. 22 Nov. 1849 at Peshawur.

409 James Henry Reid, b. 9 Jan. 1829. Addis. 1845-46, 2 l. Army 11 Dec. 1846, Regt. 6 Jan. 1847, l. 1 July 1852, 2 cap. 27 Aug. 1858, 1 cap. 2 Dec. 1861, m. 5 July 1872, l.c. 1 Aug. 1872, brev.-c. 1 Aug. 1877, c. 1 Oct. 1877. Punjaub 1848-49, Mooltan, M. 1 cl., o.c. R.A. Northern Division 1878. ret. 1 Aug. 1872. Hon. m.g. 1 Aug. 1872. d. 24 Aug. 1890 at Llandrindod, Radnorshire.

410 Walter James Hodgson Stevenson, son of Thomas (210), brother of William (363), Russell Alexander (445), b. 29 July 1829. Addis. 1845-46, 2 l. Army 11 Dec. 1846, Regt. 5 Jan. 1847, l. 18 July 1852, 2 cap. 27 Aug. 1858, 1 cap. 27 June 1862, m. 5 July 1872. ret. 1 Aug. 1872. Hon. l.c. 1 Aug. 1872. d. 24 July 1892 in London.

411 Thomas Marshall Harris, b. 8 Nov. 1828. Addis. 1846-47, 2 l. Army 11 June 1847, Regt. 8 Sept. ante-d. 11 June 1847, l. 15 Aug. 1852, 2 cap. 27 Aug. 1858, 1 cap. 21 Oct. 1862, m. 5 July 1872, l.c. 1 Aug. 1872, brev.-c. 1 Aug. 1877, c. 1 Oct. 1877. Qtrmt. and intpt. 3rd Batt. 1851, again 1855, Persia 1856-57, Reshire, Bushire, Mohumia, M. 1 cl., Mutiny 1857-58, Central India, capture of Kotah and Chandaree, action at Kotah-ke-Serai, recapture of Gwalior, actions at Powree, Sindwala, and Kurai, pursuit to Koondrai (severely wounded), Desp. *Lond. Gaz.* 31 Jan. and 18 Apr. 1859, M. 1 cl., brgd.-m. of Arty. 22 Oct. 1861-19 Oct. 1862, brgd.-m. to I.G.A. Bombay 19 Oct. 1862-Nov. 1863, A.A.G. R.A. Bombay 7 Sept. 1872-7 Nov. 1877, comg. Field Arty. Dublin District 1 July 1878-25 Jan. 1879, consulting officer in Ordce. to Sec. of State for India 4 Mar. 1879-31 Oct. 1879, c. on the Staff C.R.A. Gibraltar 9 Dec. 1879-20 Sept. 1882. ret. 1 Oct. 1882.

412 George Napier, b. 17 Sept. 1829. Addis. 1845-47, 2 l. Army 11 June 1847, Regt. 3 Sept. 1847, l. 20 Jan. 1853, 2 cap. 27 Aug. 1858, 1 cap. 2 Jan. 1863, m. 5 July 1872. Adjt. and qtrmt. Arty. Sind 1861, Ordce. 1866-72. ret. 1 Oct. 1872. Hon. l.c. 1 Aug. 1872. d. 19 July 1886 at Eastbourne.

413 Thomas James Maclachlan, b. 21 Apr. 1828. Addis. 1846-47, 2 l. Army 11 June 1847, Regt. 1 Sept. 1848, l. 28 Mar. 1853, 2 cap. 27 Aug. 1858, brev.-m. 28 Aug. 1858, 1 cap. 18 Feb. 1863, brev.-l.c. 14 June 1869, l.c. 1 Aug. 1872, brev.-c. 1 Oct. 1877. Adjt. and qtrmt. Arty. Mhow Division 1858, adjt. Central India Field Force 1858-59, Mutiny 1857-58, Central India, Ratghur, Barodea, Garrakhota, siege of Jhansi, battles of the Betwa, Koonch, Gallowlee, Calpee, action at Morar, recapture of Gwalior, battle of Jowra Alipore, capture of Powree, Desp. *Lond. Gaz.* 18 Apr. 1859, M. 1 cl., brev.-m., adjt. H.B. 13 May 1859 and of 4th Brgd. R.H.A. to 18 Feb. 1863, A.A.G. R.A. Bombay 7 Nov. 1877-18 Jan. 1879. ret. 31 Dec. 1878. Hon. m.g. 31 Dec. 1878. d. 8 Feb. 1881 at Ramsgate.

414 Thomas William Grahame, b. 19 Aug. 1828. Addis. 1846-47, 2 l. Army 10 Dec. 1847, Regt. 8 Jan. 1849. Punjaub 1848-49, Mooltan, qtrmt. and intpt. 4th Batt. 1853. d. 4 Oct. 1853 at Colaba, Bombay.

415 Lidwell Heathorn, brother of Thomas Bridges (431), b. 23 Apr. 1829. Addis. 1846-47, 2 l. Army 10 Dec. 1847, Regt. 20 Feb. 1848. Punjaub 1848-49, Mooltan, M. 1 cl., Asst. Field Engineer Punjaub Division Bombay Army 1849. d. 22 Aug. 1851 in London.

416 Richard Pittman, b. 26 May 1831. Addis. 1846-47, 2 l. Army 10 Dec. 1847, Regt. 31 Mar. 1849, l. 3 Oct. 1853, 2 cap. 27 Aug. 1858, brev.-m. 29 Aug. 1858. Employed in the Ottoman Dominions with local rank of

cap. 20 July 1855, CRIMEA, Turkish Contingent with Bashi Bazooks, 5th class Medjidie, MUTINY, Central India, Barodea (severely wounded), Ratghur, Gallowlee, capture of Calpee, relief of Sangor, forcing Muddenpore pass, siege and capture of Jhansi, battle of the Betwa, Desp. *Lond. Gaz.* 11 May and 17 July 1858, brev.-m.   d. 13 Jan. 1867 at Belgaum.

417   **Thomas Carlisle Crowe,** father of Mordaunt Abingdon (R.A. 4365), b. 15 Sept. 1830. Addis. 1846–47, 2 l. Army 10 Dec. 1847, Regt. 16 Apr. 1849, l. 31 Dec. 1853, 2 cap. 27 Aug. 1858, 1 cap. 18 May 1863, m. 5 July 1872, l.c. 1 Aug. 1872, brev.-c. 1 Aug. 1877.   PUNJAUB 1849–50, Staff officer Arty. Mooltan 1849–50, PERSIA 1856–57, Bushire, M. 1 cl., MUTINY 1857–58, Ratghur, relief of Sangor, capture of Garrakhota, pursuit to Betwa, forcing of the Muddenpore pass, siege of Jhansi, battle of Betwa (specially mentioned by Sir H. Rose), battles of Koonch and Gallowlee, Calpee, pursuit to Surceela, battle of Morar, pursuit and defeat of the rebels at Jowra Alipore, operations in Bendelcund, capture of Garotha, pursuit of Shazada Ferozeshah, M. 1 cl., adjt. of Arty. Gwalior District 1858–59. Served in suppression of Fenian raid on Canada 1866, Canadian General Service, M. 1 cl. ret. 31 Dec. 1878. Hon. m.g. 31 Dec. 1878.

418   **Henry Forbes Manson,** son of Alexander (209), b. 25 Apr. 1829. Addis. 1846–47, 2 l. Army 10 Dec. 1847.   d. 23 Dec. 1848 at Bombay.

419   **Charles Shaw de Neufville Lucas,** son of Charles (266), brother of George Doyle Albert (422), James Cock de Neufville (463), b. 21 Feb. 1830. Addis. 1846–48, 2 l. Army 9 June 1848, Regt. 1 June 1849, l. 25 Feb. 1854, 2 cap. 27 Aug. 1858, 1 cap. 1 Sept. 1863, m. 5 July 1872, l.c. 11 May 1873, brev.-c. 11 May 1878, c. 31 Dec. 1878, m.g. 31 Dec. 1883.   MUTINY 1857–59, Ahmednuggur Field Force, action with insurgent Bheels Feb. 1858, Central India Field Force, Okamundel and Kattywar Field Force, capture of Ubhpoora Fort, Burda Hills Dec. 1859.   d. 16 Feb. 1887 in London.

420   **Thomas Graham,** b. 8 Sept. 1831. Addis. 1846–48, 2 l. Army 9 June 1848, Regt. 22 June 1849, l. 27 Feb. 1854. Qtrmt. and intpt. 4th Batt. 1853.   d. 5 June 1855 at Alexandria.

421   **Adam Gordon Newall,** brother of David John Falconer (Bengal 759), Marius Charles (490), b. 4 May 1829. Addis. 1847–48, 2 l. Army 8 Dec. 1848, Regt. 4 Oct. 1849.   d. 21 May 1853 at Nusseerabad.

422   **George Doyle Albert Lucas,** son of Charles (266), brother of Charles Shaw de Neufville (419), James Cock de Neufville (463), b. 14 Sept. 1832. Addis. 1847–49, 2 l. Army 8 June 1849, Regt. 4 Oct. 1849, l. 25 June 1854. d. 10 Aug. 1856 at Poona.

423   **James Henry Porter Malcolmson,** C.B., b. 20 Oct. 1832. Addis. 1847– 48, 2 l. Army 8 June 1849, Regt. 23 Oct. 1849, l. 29 Aug. 1854, 2 cap. 27 Aug. 1858, 1 cap. 1 Sept. 1863. MUTINY 1857–58, brgd.-m. of Arty. Kotah Field Force, Kotah, battle of Bunnass and pursuit of rebels under Tantia Topee, cavalry affair at Khooshana (horse wounded), Desp. *Lond. Gaz.* 5 May 1859, M. 1 cl. Transferred to the Bombay Staff Corps 7 Oct. 1863. *brev.-m.* 9 *Apr.* 1868, m. 8 *June* 1869, *l.c.* 8 *June* 1875, *c. Army* 8 *June* 1879, *Public Works Dept. Oct.* 1863–*Sept.* 1868, 3*rd Sind Horse* 18 *May* 1870, *Poona Horse* 19 *Aug.* 1871, 3*rd Sind Horse* 22 *Jan.* 1873, *commdt.* 3*rd Sind Horse* 12 *Apr.* 1873, AFGHANISTAN 1878–80, *actions Atta Karez. Khuskhi-Nakhud* (*wounded*), *Girishk, Maiwand, defence of Khandahar, sortie from Khandahar* (*severely wounded*), *Desp.* "*Lond. Gaz.*" 7 *Nov.* 1879, 15 *Oct.*, 10 *Nov.,* 3 *Dec.* 1880, *C.B.* 19 *July* 1879, *comg. Sind H.B.* 1880–82. *ret.* 1 *Oct.* 1882. *Hon. m.g.* 1 *Oct.* 1882.

424   **John Braithwaite Hardy,** son of Edmund (194), b. 22 Mar. 1832. Addis. 1847–49, 2 l. Army 8 June 1849, Regt. 22 Nov. 1849, l. 29 Aug. 1854, 2 cap. 27 Aug. 1858, cap. 29 Feb. 1864, m. 5 July 1872. PERSIA 1856–57, M. Detached by Sir James Outram on a political mission to

Herat during the Indian Mutiny with local rank of cap. 28 Aug. 1857, MUTINY 1858–59, Ahmednuggur flying column in pursuit of Tantia Topee, adjt. 18th Brgd. R.A. 9 Dec. 1861–10 Oct. 1864, Arabia 1865–66, expedition against Foodlee Arabs, present at Beer Said, Jowalla, and Ahmooda. ret. 1 Aug. 1872. Hon. l.c. 1 Aug. 1872. *Secretary English Church Union* 1876–1903.

425 **William de Vitre,** resumed old name of **Denis de Vitre** 1859, b. 18 Mar. 1831. Addis. 1848–49, 2 l. Army 11 Dec. 1849, Regt. 4 Feb. 1850, l. 29 Aug. 1854, 2 cap. 27 Aug. 1858, 1 cap. 24 Mar. 1865, m. 5 July 1872, l.c. 10 May 1874, c. 31 Dec. 1878. PERSIA 1857, M. 1 cl. Returning from Persia in command of detachment 4th Troop was wrecked in the *Julia* at Kurrachee; thanked in General Orders 17 July 1857, intpt. Arty. Head Quarters 1862, adjt. 4th Brgd. R.H.A. 18 Feb. 1863, afterwards of E. Brgd. R.H.A. to 15 May 1864, D.A.Q.M.G. Bombay Special Survey duty 1866–67, C.R.A. Rawul Pindi 1878, C.R.A. Meerut 1884, brigadier-g. C.R.A. Southern Afghanistan 1880, till evacuation of Khandahar Apr. 1881. ret. 4 Feb. 1885. Hon. m.g. 4 Feb. 1885.

426 **Godfrey Twiss,** father of Frank Arthur (R.A. 4941), brother of Arthur William (R.A. 2154), b. 20 Feb. 1832. Addis. 1848–49, 2 l. Army 11 Dec. 1849, Regt. 15 Apr. 1850, l. 29 Aug. 1854, ante-d. to 11 Dec. 1849, 2 cap. 14 Feb. 1859, 1 cap. 24 Mar. 1865, brev.-m. 15 Aug. 1868, m. 5 July 1872. PERSIA 1856–57, M. 1 cl., MUTINY 1858–59, brgd.-m. of Cavalry under Sir H. Rose in pursuit of Tantia Topee, adjt. and qtimt. 1st Batt. 26 Aug. 1859, afterwards of 18th Brgd. R.A. to 15 Nov. 1861, ABYSSINIA 1867–68, Magdala, M., brev.-m., Desp. *Lond. Gaz.* 16 and 30 June 1868. ret. 1 Aug. 1872. Hon. l.c. 1 Aug. 1872. *l.c. comg. Hants Arty. Volunteers 1 Nov. 1881–31 Oct. 1882, c. comg. 2nd Hants Volunteer Arty. 1 Nov. 1882–1 Feb. 1899.*

427 **George Henry Stone,** b. 1 May 1831. Addis. 1848–49, 2 l. Army 11 Dec. 1849, Regt. 17 Sept. 1850, l. 29 Aug. 1854, ante-d. to 11 Dec. 1849, 2 cap. 8 May 1859, 1 cap. 3 Aug. 1865, m. 5 July 1872, l.c. 16 Jan. 1875, c. Army 16 Jan. 1880. PERSIA 1856–57, Mohumra, M. 1 cl., served in the affairs of Beyt and Dwarka 1860–61. ret. 17 Aug. 1880. Hon. m.g. 17 Aug. 1880.

428 **Francis Swanson,** b. 20 June 1832. Addis. 1848–49, 2 l. Army 11 Dec. 1849, Regt. 28 Feb. 1851, l. 15 Sept. 1854, ante-d. to 11 Dec. 1849, 2 cap. 13 May 1859, 1 cap. 3 Aug. 1865, m. 5 July 1872, l.c. 16 Jan. 1875. MUTINY 1857–58, Ahwah Kotah, pursuit and action of Kotarea, M. 1 cl., Ordce. 1861–62, Ordce. 1863–77, ABYSSINIA 1867–68, M. d. 1 Dec. 1877 at Poona.

429 **Frederick Lloyd,** b. 20 Aug. 1831. Addis. 1848–50, 2 l. Army 14 June 1850, Regt. 28 Apr. 1851, l. 23 Oct. 1854, ante-d. 14 June 1850, 2 cap. 14 Aug. 1859. ret. 10 July 1861. d. 21 June 1864 at St. Pancras, London.

430 **Edward John Wrench,** b. 25 July 1831. Addis. 1849–50, 2 l. Army 9 Dec. 1850, Regt. 17 Aug. 1851. d. 22 Sept. 1854 at Sholapoor.

431 **Thomas Bridges Heathorn,** brother of Lidwell (415), b. 6 Sept. 1830. Addis. 1848–50, 2 l. Army 9 Dec. 1850, Regt. 22 Aug. 1851, l. 10 Nov. 1854, ante-d. 9 Dec. 1850, 2 cap. 19 Oct. 1859, 1 cap. 14 Sept. 1865. Employed in the Ottoman Dominions with local rank of cap. 27 Mar. 1855, CRIMEA 1854–55, with Turkish contingent in QM.G.'s dept. at Kertch, Turkish medal, 4th class, Medjidie, MUTINY 1858, Kotah, flying column at Oodepore, M. 1 cl., Desp. *Lond. Gaz.* 24 Mar. 1859, Orderly Officer Addis. 1860, Armament Committee War Office 1865. ret. 17 Aug. 1866.

432 John Ashmead Billamore, b. 6 July 1831. Addis. 1849–50, 2 l. Army
9 Dec. 1850, Regt. 17 Feb. 1852, l. 5 June 1855, ante-d. 9 Dec. 1850.
Arabia 1858, expedition against Sheikh Othman. d. 3 Dec. 1858 at
Bombay.

433 Francis Hemming, b. 2 Sept. 1831. Addis. 1849–50, 2 l. Army 9 Dec.
1850, Regt. 23 Feb. 1852, l. 17 June 1855, ante-d. 9 Dec. 1850. MUTINY
1857–58, Awah, battle of Bunnass. d. 29 Mar. 1860 at Bombay.

434 William Herbert Malden, b. 5 Jan. 1832. Addis. 1849–51, 2 l. Army
13 June 1851, Regt. 3 May 1852, l. 10 Aug. 1855, ante-d. 13 June 1851.
Employed in the Ottoman Dominions with local rank of 1st l. 27 Mar.
1855, CRIMEA with Turkish contingent, Turkish medal. d. 29 July 1859 at
Ahmednuggur.

435 Hubert le Cocq, b. 14 Apr. 1833. Addis. 1849–51, 2 l. Army 13 June
1851, Regt. 25 June 1852, l. 12 Sept. 1855, ante-d. 13 June 1851, 2 cap.
30 Mar. 1860, 1 cap. 14 Sept. 1865, m. 5 July 1872, l.c. 1 Sept. 1876, c. Army
1 July 1881, c. 1 Oct. 1882, m.g. 12 May 1887, l.g. 15 Nov. 1890, u.s.l. 1 July
1892, c.'s allowances 12 Nov. 1892, g. 25 May 1895, col. commdt. 12 Aug.
1900. PERSIA 1856–57, Reshire, Bushire, Khooshab, Mohumra, M.
1 cl. Returning from Persia was wrecked in the *Julia* June 1857 at
Kurrachee ; awarded Fisherman's and Mariner's Royal Benevolent Society's
silver medal for gallant conduct on that occasion. MUTINY 1857–58,
Kotah, recapture of Chandaree, Kotah-ke-Serai, Gwalior, pursuit of
Tantia Topee, Koonrai, M. 1 cl., Desp. *Lond. Gaz.* 2 Sept. 1859, adjt. E
Brgd. R.H.A. 15 May 1864–16 Mar. 1866, C.R.A. British North America
1882–84, c. on Staff C.R.A. Dublin District 1884–87, brigadier-g. C.R.A.
Ireland 1890–91.

436 Arthur Reginald Hoskins, b. 28 Jan. 1832. Addis. 1849–51, 2 l. Army
13 June 1851, Regt. 1 July 1852, l. 28 Apr. 1856, ante-d. 13 June 1851,
2 cap. 30 Mar. 1860, 1 cap. 16 Mar. 1866, m. 5 July 1872, l.c. 27 Feb. 1877.
PERSIA 1856–57, Reshire, Bushire, Khooshab, Mohumra., M. 1 cl., MUTINY
1857–58, Kotah, recapture of Chandaree, Kotah-ke-Serai, Gwalior,
Powree, and actions of Beejapore, Sindwala, Kurai, pursuit at Koondrai,
M. 1 cl., adjt. and qrtmt. Arty. Aden 1861, Ordce. 24 Nov. 1866–
22 Mar. 1871, officiating Deputy Sec. to Govt. of Bombay Military Dept.
1866 and Aug. 1870–Mar. 1871. ret. 28 Feb. 1877. Hon. c. 28 Feb. 1877.
d. 16 Mar. 1902 at King Ina's Palace, South Petherton, Somerset.

437 James Henry Murray Martin, son of James Henry Murray (253), b. 9
Jan. 1833. Addis. 1850–51, 2 l. Army 12 Dec. 1851, Regt. 18 July 1852.
d. 8 Sept. 1855 at Aden.

438 Francis Faulkner Sheppee, b. 24 June 1833. Addis. 1850–51, 2 l. Army
12 Dec. 1851, Regt. 15 Aug. 1852, l. 3 Jan. 1857, ante-d. 12 Dec. 1851,
2 cap. 11 Apr. 1860, 1 cap. 26 Apr. 1866, m. 5 July 1872. Adjt. and qrtmt.
Arty. Aden 1861–67. ret. 1 Aug. 1872. Hon. c. 1 Aug. 1872.

439 William Ferrie Stevenson, b. 14 June 1832. Addis. 1850–51, 2 l.
Army 12 Dec. 1851, Regt. 20 Jan. 1853, l. 12 Jan. 1857, ante-d. 12 Dec.
1851. d. 10 Apr. 1859 at Bombay.

440 Charles Pasley Roberts, b. 4 Nov. 1833. Addis. 1850–51, 2 l. Army
12 Dec. 1851, Regt. 28 Mar. 1853, l. 4 Apr. 1858, ante-d. 12 Dec. 1851,
2 cap. 25 June 1860, 1 cap. 17 Aug. 1866, m. 5 July 1872, l.c. 28 Feb.
1877. MUTINY 1857–58, Central India, Ratghur, Garrakhota, Jhansi,
Calpee, surrender of Gwalior, actions at Barodea, Mundespore, Koonch,
Gallowlee, Morar, Jourah Alipore, M. 1 cl., adjt. R.A. Belgaum 1866.
ret. 24 Aug. 1877. Hon. c. 24 Aug. 1877. d. 8 Sept. 1884 at Southsea.

441 Thomas Nelson Holberton, b. 21 Feb. 1833. Addis. 1850–52, 2 l.
Army 12 June 1852, Regt. 21 May 1853, l. 27 Apr. 1858, ante-d. 12 June
1852, 2 cap. 19 Dec. 1860, 1 cap. 24 Nov. 1866, m. 5 July 1872, l.c. 24 Aug.
1877, c. Army 24 Aug. 1881, Regt. 31 Dec. 1883. PERSIA 1856–57,
Reshire, Bushire, Khooshab, M. 1 cl., MUTINY 1857–58, capture of

Please substitute for No. 435 on page 104.

435 **Hubert le Cocq,** b. 14 Apr. 1833. Addis. 1849–51, 2 l. Army 13 June
1851, Regt. 25 June 1852, l. 12 Sept. 1855, ante-d. 13 June 1851, 2 cap.
30 Mar. 1860, 1 cap. 14 Sept. 1865, m. 5 July 1872, l.c. 1 Sept. 1876, c. Army
1 July 1881, c. 1 Oct. 1882, m.g. 12 May 1887, l.g. 15 Nov. 1890, u.s.l. 1 July
1892, c.'s allowances 12 Nov. 1892, g. 25 May 1895, col. commdt. 12 Aug.
1900. PERSIA 1856–57, Reshire, Bushire, Khooshab, Mohumra, M.
1 cl. Was awarded Fisherman's and Mariner's Royal Benevolent Society's
silver medal for gallant conduct on occasion of the wreck of the *Julia* at
Kurrachee June 1857. MUTINY 1857–58, Kotah, recapture of Chandaree,
Kotah-ke-Serai, Gwalior, pursuit of Tantia Topee, Koonrai, M. 1 cl., Desp.
Lond. Gaz. 2 Sept. 1859, adjt. E Brgd. R.H.A. 15 May 1864–16 Mar. 1866,
C.R.A. British North America 1882–84, c. on Staff C.R.A. Dublin District
1884–87, brigadier-g. C.R.A. Ireland 1890–91.

Kolapoor, pursuit of Tantia Topee, brgd.-m. to I.G.A. Bombay 13 Dec.
1863–13 Dec. 1868, A.A.G. R.A. Bombay 18 Jan. 1879–17 Jan. 1884, c.
on the Staff C.R.A. Poona Division and Kirkee station command 5 Mar.
1884–31 Dec. 1888. ret. 1 Apr. 1889.

442 **Octavius Sturges,** b. 19 Aug. 1833. Addis. 1850–52, 2 l. Army 12 June
1852, Regt. 4 Oct. 1853. res. 20 Aug. 1858. *B.A. and M.B. Cambridge
1862, M.A. 1867, F.R.C.P. London 1863, Physician and Lecturer on Medicine
Westminster Hospital.* d. 3 Nov. 1894 in London.

443 **Thomas Hawkins Turner,** brother of Samuel George Drury (516), b.
1 May 1834. Addis. 1850–52, 2 l. Army 12 June 1852, Regt. 3 Nov.
1853, l. 27 Apr. 1858, ante-d. 12 June 1852, 2 cap. 18 Feb. 1861. PERSIA
1856–57, brgd.-m. Arty. June–Sept. 1857, Reshire, Bushire, Khooshab
(charger killed), Mohumra on mortar raft, M. 1 cl., Ordce. 1858–60,
Examiner Ordce. accounts 21 Sept. 1860. Transferred to Bombay Staff
Corps 19 Feb. 1861. *m.* 12 *June* 1872. d. 18 June 1878 at Poona.

444 **Frederick Alexander Whish,** son of Richard (190), nephew of William
Sampson (Bengal 333), b. 27 July 1833. Addis. 1851–52, 2 l. Army
9 Dec. 1852, Regt. 31 Dec. 1853, l. 27 Apr. 1858, ante-d. 9 Dec. 1852, 2 cap.
18 Feb. 1861. res. 1 July 1863. *Supdt. of Panchganni.* d. 16 Sept.
1872 at Panchganni.

445 **Russell Alexander Stevenson,** son of Thomas (210), brother of William
(363), Walter James Hodgson (410), b. 25 Feb. 1834. Addis. 1851–52,
2 l. Army 9 Dec. 1852, Regt. 25 Feb. 1854, l. 27 Apr. 1858, ante-d. 9 Dec.
1852, 2 cap. 18 Feb. 1861, 1 cap. 24 Nov. 1866, m. 5 July 1872, l.c. 1 Oct.
1877. MUTINY 1857–58, pursuit of rebels in Rajpootana, actions of San-
gaueer and Bunnass, skirmish near Koosanah in command of Camel Corps,
M., C.R.A. Sind District 1878, C.R.A. Northern Division 1879. d. 17
June 1879 at Ahmedabad.

446 **Maitland Warren Bouverie Sabine Pasley,** father of Montague
Wynyard S. (R.A. 4222), b. 17 July 1834. R.M.A. 1848–50, Addis.
1851–52, 2 l. Army 9 Dec. 1852, Regt. 27 Feb. 1854, l. 27 Apr. 1858,
ante-d. 9 Dec. 1852, 2 cap. 18 Feb. 1861. Arabia 1858, expedition against
Sheikh Othman. ret. 25 Feb. 1865. *Adjt. Forfar and Kincardine Arty.
Militia* 1865. d. 6 June 1881 at Eastbourne.

447 **Walter William Woodward,** b. 6 May 1834. Addis. 1851–52, 2 l.
Army 9 Dec. 1852, Regt. 25 June 1854, l. 27 Apr. 1858, ante-d. 9 Dec.
1852, 2 cap. 18 Feb. 1861, 1 cap. 1 Jan. 1867, m. 5 July 1872, l.c. Oct.
1877, c. Army 1 Oct. 1881. PERSIA 1856–57, Khooshab, M., special
duty Cape of Good Hope 1857, MUTINY 1858–59, action of Myhee Kanta
in Guzerat, adjt. E Brgd. R.H.A. 16 Mar. 1866–1 Jan. 1867, C.R.A.
Bangalore 1880–81, C.R.A. Hydrabad Subsidiary Force 1881–82, C.R.A.
Eastern District Madras 1882–83, c. R.A. on the Staff Sirhind Division
1885, c. R.A. on the Staff Eastern District Colchester 1886–89. ret.
17 May 1889.

448 **George Francis Worsley,** b. 25 Sept. 1833. Addis. 1851–53, 2 l. Army
11 June 1853, Regt. 22 Aug. 1854, l. 27 Apr. 1858, ante-d. 11 June 1853,
2 cap. 18 Feb. 1861, 1 cap. 14 Jan. 1867, m. 5 July 1872, l.c. 17 Apr. 1878,
c. Army 17 Apr. 1882. PERSIA 1856–57, M. 1 cl., adjt. and qtrmt. 2nd
Batt. 11 July 1859–31 Mar. 1861, adjt. 21st Brgd. R.A. 31 Mar. 1861–14
Jan. 1867, Deputy I.G.O. 27 June 1879–27 Dec. 1884. ret. 22 Jan. 1887.
Hon. m.g. 22 Jan. 1887.

449 **John Ritchie,** father of John Robert (R.A. 4246), b. 31 Jan. 1834. Addis.
1851–53, 2 l. Army 11 June 1853, Regt. 29 Aug. 1854, l. 27 Apr. 1858,
ante-d. 11 June 1853, 2 cap. 18 Feb. 1861, 1 cap. 25 Mar. 1867, m. 5 July

1872, l.c. 31 Dec. 1878, c. Army 31 Dec. 1882. Asst. Supdt. Jawud Neemuch 1856–58, MUTINY 1857–58, actions of Numbhera and Jeerun, defence of Neemuch, capture of Kotah. Reported by Gen. Lawrence comg. in Rajpootana to have rendered valuable services at a critical period. Brought to notice of commdt. of Arty. by C.I.C.: thanks of Govt. of India and N.W. Provinces, M. 1 cl. ret. 22 Nov. 1886. Hon. m.g. 22 Nov. 1886.

450 **Charles Henry Strutt,** b. 8 Sept. 1833. Addis. 1851–53, 2 l. Army 11 June 1853, Regt. 29 Aug. 1854, l. 27 Apr. 1858, ante-d. 11 June 1853, 2 cap. 27 June 1862, brev.-m. 19 Jan. 1864. MUTINY 1857–58, Dhar (mentioned), action of Mundesore, battle of Goraria, Ratghur, action of Barodea, Garakhota (Desp.), Jhansi (Desp.), Koonch, Calpee, Gallowlee, Kotah-ke-Serai, capture of Gwalior (Desp.), Powree, Beejapore, specially mentioned by Sir H. Rose, *Lond. Gaz.* 17 July 1858, 18 Apr. 1859, M. 1 cl., Hyderabad Contingent 1858, a.d.c. to Governor of Bombay 1859, a.d.c. to C.I.C. India 1859–62, Dept. of Woods and Forests Bengal 1863–66. res. 1 May 1866. *Military Knight of Windsor* 10 Oct. 1901.

451 **Thomas Porter Berthon,** brother of Henry Peter Brassey (380), b. 1 Oct. 1835. Addis. 1851–53, 2 l. Army 9 Dec. 1853, Regt. 29 Aug. 1854, l. 4 July 1858, ante-d. 9 Dec. 1853, 2 cap. 24 Dec. 1861, 1 cap. 5 Jan. 1869, m. 5 July 1872, l.c. 31 Dec. 1878, c. Army 31 Dec. 1882, m.g. 30 Mar. 1890. PERSIA 1856–57, Mohumra, M. 1 cl., MUTINY 1857–58, M., lieut. Cadet Company R.M.A. 1861–63, adjt. 18th Brgd. R.A. 10 Oct. 1864–16 Nov. 1868, c. on Staff C.R.A. Chatham District 1 July 1884–30 June 1889. ret. 5 June 1890.

452 **Henry Marshall Davies,** b. 21 Jan. 1835. Addis. 1852–53, 2 l. Army 9 Dec. 1853. d. 17 June 1854 at Ahmednuggur.

453 **John Tasker,** b. 1 Aug. 1834. Addis. 1852–53, 2 l. Army 9 Dec. 1853, Regt. 29 Aug. 1854, l. 27 Aug. 1858, ante-d. 9 Dec. 1853, 2 cap. 27 June 1862. PERSIA 1856–57, Khooshab, M. 1 cl. res. 15 Feb. 1866.

454 **Philip Hanmer Harcourt,** b. 30 Jan. 1836. Addis. 1852–53, 2 l. Army 9 Dec. 1853, Regt. 15 Sept. 1854, l. 27 Aug. 1858, ante-d. 9 Dec. 1853, 2 cap. 21 Oct. 1862, 1 cap. 1 May 1869, m. 5 July 1872, l.c. 31 Dec. 1878, c. Army 31 Dec. 1882. MUTINY 1857–58, Central India, Ratghur, Barodea (horse shot), Garrakhota, Jhansi, Betwa, Muddenpoor Pass, Koonch, Gallowlee, Calpee, Morar, Gwalior (Desp.), specially mentioned by Sir H. Rose, *Lond. Gaz.* 18 Apr. 1859, commdt. Dalhousie Depot 1879–81, R.A. adviser Defence Committee Simla 1879, C.R.A. Quetta 1883. ret. 3 June 1884. Hon. m.g. 3 June 1884.

455 **Henry Charles Baskerville Tanner,** b. 30 June 1835. Addis 1852–54, 2 l. Army 8 June 1854, Regt. 22 Sept. 1854, ante-d. 8 June 1854, 2 cap. 2 Jan. 1863. PERSIA 1856–57, Reshire, Bushire, Khooshab, M. 1 cl. Transferred to Bombay Staff Corps 3 Jan. 1863. *m.* 8 *June* 1874, *brev.-l.c.* 22 *Nov.* 1879, *l.c.* 8 *June* 1880, *c. Army* 8 *June* 1884, *u.s.l.* 30 *June* 1892, *c.'s allowances* 8 *June* 1892. *Revenue Survey* 1 *July* 1865, *Deputy Supdt. Deccan Topographical Survey* 1 *Apr.* 1870, *Deputy Supdt. 2nd Grade Survey of India in charge Himalayan Survey party* 1 *Oct.* 1884, *Officiating Supdt.* 1st *Grade* 1889, *Lushai Expedition* 1871–72, *M.* 1 *cl.,* AFGHANISTAN 1878–79, *expedition to the Lughman Valley, M.* 1 *cl., Desp., brev. of l.c.* d. 16 Mar. 1898 at Bath.

456 **Arthur Carey,** brother of William (R.A. 2310), b. 8 Jan. 1836. Addis. 1852–54, 2 l. Army 8 June 1854, Regt. 23 Oct. 1854, l. 27 Aug. 1858, ante-d.

8 June 1854, 2 cap. 18 May 1863. Persia 1856-57, M. 1 cl. d. 30 July 1868 at Kirkee.

457 **Horace Seymour Kerr Pechell,** b. 13 Aug. 1834. Addis. 1852-54, 2 l. Army 8 June 1854, Regt. 10 Oct. 1854, l. 27 Aug. 1858, ante-d. 8 June 1854, 2 cap. 18 May 1863. Mutiny, Central India, Kotah (wounded), *Lond. Gaz.* 11 June 1858. res. 15 Dec. 1863. d. 20 Dec. 1867 at Bombay.

458 **William Home Brydon,** b. 18 Jan. 1835. Addis. 1852-54, 2 l. Army 8 June 1854, Regt. 5 June 1855, l. 27 Aug. 1858, ante-d. 8 June 1854. Persia 1856-57, M. res. 24 Aug. 1860. d. 4 Nov. 1880 at Dinard, France.

459 **Christopher Edward Newport,** b. 9 Aug. 1834. Addis. 1852-54, 2 l. Army 9 Dec. 1854, Regt. 17 June 1855, l. 27 Aug. 1858, ante-d. 9 Dec. 1854, 2 cap. 1 July 1863, 1 cap. 14 Sept. 1869, m. 5 July 1872, l.c. 31 Dec. 1878, c. Army 31 Dec. 1882. Persia 1856-57, Bushire, Khooshab, M. 1 cl., Mutiny 1858, pursuit of Tantia Topee, adjt. 4th Native afterwards Goldze. Batt. 19 Oct. 1861-63, adjt. R.A. Belgaum 15 Dec. 1863-18 Feb. 1865, C.R.A. Bermuda 1881. ret. 19 Apr. 1888. d. 6 Nov. 1895 at Cockpen, Edinburgh.

460 **John Vibart,** b. 11 Mar. 1835. Addis. 1853-54, 2 l. Army 9 Dec. 1854, Regt. 10 Aug. 1855, l. 27 Aug. 1858, ante-d. 9 Dec. 1854, 2 cap. 1 Sept. 1863. Persia 1856-57, Reshire, Bushire, Mohumra on mortar raft, M. 1 cl., Mutiny 1857-59, Central India, Kotah, battle of Sanganeer (mentioned), battle of Bunnass, pursuit of rebels through Bikanir desert, M. 1 cl. ret. 21 July 1864. d. 6 Feb. 1902 at Bideford, Devon.

461 **Henry Tanfield Vachell,** b. 26 Mar. 1835. Addis. 1853-54, 2 l. Army 9 Dec. 1854, Regt. 8 Sept. 1855, l. 27 Aug. 1858, ante-d. 9 Dec. 1854, 2 cap. 1 Sept. 1863, 1 cap. 1 July 1870, m. 5 July 1872, l.c. 18 June 1879, c. Army 18 June 1883. Persia 1856-57, Mutiny 1858, capture of Shorapore and surrender of Jhumkhundee. ret. 10 June 1885. Hon. m.g. 10 June 1885. d. 5 June 1902 at Hove, Brighton.

462 **Edward Henry Baker,** b. 24 Sept. 1836. Addis. 1853-54, 2 l. Army 9 Dec. 1854, Regt. 12 Sept. 1855, l. 27 Aug. 1858, ante-d. 9 Dec. 1854, 2 cap. 15 Dec. 1863, 1 cap. 22 Mar. 1871, m. 5 July 1872, l.c. 27 Sept. 1879. Abyssinia 1867-68, Arogee, Magdala, Desp. *Lond. Gaz.* 10 July 1868, M. ret. 21 Dec. 1881. Hon. c. 21 Dec. 1881.

463 **James Cock de Neufville Lucas,** son of Charles (266), brother of Charles Shaw de Neufville (419), George Doyle Albert (422), b. 3 Feb. 1836. Addis. 1853-54, 2 l. Army 9 Dec. 1854, Regt. 28 Apr. 1856. d. 11 Sept. 1858 at Howrah, Calcutta.

464 **John Thomas Leishman,** b. 16 Dec. 1835. Addis. 1853-55, 2 l. Army 8 June 1855, Regt. 12 Jan. 1857, l. 27 Aug. 1858, ante-d. 8 June 1855, 2 cap. 29 Feb. 1864, cap. 5 July 1872, m. 1 Aug. 1872, l.c. 17 Aug. 1880, c. Army 17 Aug. 1884. Mutiny 1859, with Sir H. Rose's Field Force in Nizam's country, Gunnery Instructor 18th Brgd. R.A. Sept. 1868-Sept. 1870. ret. 1 Dec. 1888. Hon. m.g. 1 Dec. 1888.

465 **Charles Percy Theobald,** b. 21 Oct. 1836. Addis. 1853-55, 2 l. Army 8 June 1855, Regt. 12 Jan. 1857, l. 27 Aug. 1858, ante-d. 8 June 1855, 2 cap. 21 July 1864, cap. 5 July 1872, m. 1 Aug. 1872. Brgd.-m. to I.G.A. Bombay 25 Jan. 1869-12 Apr. 1870. ret. 14 July 1875. Hon. l.c. 14 July 1875.

466 **Charles Edward Basevi,** b. 24 Sept. 1836. Addis. 1853-55, 2 l. Army 8 June 1855, Regt. 4 Apr. 1858, l. 27 Aug. 1858, ante-d. 8 June 1855, 2 cap. 11 Nov. 1864, cap. 5 July 1872, m. 1 Aug. 1872. Persia 1857, M. 1 cl., Mutiny 1858, Khandeish, action at Ambapawnee (distinguished himself by

attacking in single combat and securing one of the enemy, a leader of importance, being severely wounded with three sword cuts), Desp. *Lond. Gaz.* 11 June 1858, M. Passed Arty. College 1878. ret. 21 Dec. 1881. Hon. c. 21 Dec. 1881.

467 Henry Watts Stockley, b. 23 July 1836. Addis. 1854-55, 2 l. Army 7 Dec. 1855, Regt. 27 Apr. 1858, l. 27 Aug. 1858, ante-d. 7 Dec. 1855, 2 cap. 25 Feb. 1865, cap. 5 July 1872, m. 23 Nov. 1872, brev.-l.c. 1 July 1881, l.c. 21 Dec. 1881, c. Army 1 July 1885. PERSIA 1857, Mohumra, M. 1 cl., Station Staff Officer Kirkee 24 Aug. 1866-1 Oct. 1868, adjt. E Brgd. R.H.A. 1 Jan. 1867-12 May 1871, Station Staff Officer Kirkee 19 Sept. 1872-6 Jan. 1873, G.C. 1 Oct. 1878-1 Nov. 1888. ret. 3 June 1889.

468 Benjamin Christie, b. 3 Dec. 1836. Addis. 1854-56, 2 l. Army 13 June 1856, Regt. 27 Apr. 1858, l. 27 Aug. 1858, ante-d. 13 June 1856. MUTINY 1857-58, Dhar, severely wounded, Desp. d. 4 Mar. 1860 at Sehore from wounds inflicted by a tiger.

469 Townsend Henry Moore, b. 25 June 1835. Addis. 1855-56, 2 l. Army 12 Dec. 1856, Regt. 27 Apr. 1858, l. 27 Aug. 1858, ante-d. 12 Dec. 1856. d. 25 Oct. 1859 at Ahmednuggur.

470 Wallace William Benson, b. 29 Oct. 1838. Addis. 1855-57, 2 l. Army 12 June 1857, Regt. 27 Apr. 1858, l. 27 Aug. 1858, ante-d. 12 June 1857, 2 cap. 24 Mar. 1865. Drowned on voyage to Abyssinia 21 Jan. 1868.

471 Thomas Carr Fletcher, b. 20 Mar. 1838. Addis. 1855-57, 2 l. Army 12 June 1857, Regt. 27 Apr. 1858, l. 27 Aug. 1858, ante-d. 12 June 1857, 2 cap. 24 Mar. 1865, cap. 5 July 1872, m. 10 May 1874. Adjt. R.A. Aden 1867, adjt. 18th Brgd. R.A. 16 Nov. 1868-Nov. 1870. Cashiered 27 Nov. 1876. d. 3 Feb. 1896 at Durban, Natal.

472 Horace Cowley Brown, b. 8 Jan. 1839. Addis. 1855-57, 2 l. Army 12 June 1857, Regt. 27 Apr. 1858, l. 27 Aug. 1858, ante-d. 12 June 1857, 2 cap. 24 Mar. 1865, cap. 5 July 1872. Killed in an explosion on Sind Frontier 24 Mar. 1873.

473 Walter John Finch, b. 28 Mar. 1838. Addis. 1856-57, 2 l. Army 11 Dec. 1857, Regt. 27 Apr. 1858, l. 27 Aug. 1858, ante-d. 11 Dec. 1857, 2 cap. 24 Mar. 1865, cap. 5 July 1872, m. 16 Jan. 1875, l.c. 21 Dec. 1881, c. Army 21 Dec. 1885. C.R.A. London Division (for Auxiliary Arty.) 28 Feb. 1883-Dec. 1886. ret. 21 Dec. 1886. Hon. m.g. 21 Dec. 1886.

474 George William Borrodaile, C.B., b. 13 June 1838. Addis. 1856-57, 2 l. Army 11 Dec. 1857, Regt. 27 Apr. 1858, l. 27 Aug. 1858, ante-d. 11 Dec. 1857, 2 cap. 3 Aug. 1865, cap. 5 July 1872, m. 14 July 1875, brev.-l.c. 14 July 1882, l.c. 1 Oct. 1882, c. 14 July 1886. EGYPT 1882, Tel-el-Kebir, Desp. *Lond. Gaz.* 2 Nov. 1882, M. 1 cl., bronze star, 3rd class Medjidie, C.B. 18 Nov. 1882. A.A.G. R.A. Bombay 18 Jan. 1884-17 Jan. 1889. ret. 12 July 1894.

475 Eldred Thomas Pottinger, C.M.G., son of John (330), nephew of Eldred (308), twin brother of Brabazon Henry (476), uncle of Thomas Eldred (R.A. 4562), Robert Southey (R.A. 4787), b. 18 Sept. 1840. Addis. 1857, res. 21 Oct. 1857, but time allowed to count for pension, 2 l. Army 12 Dec. 1857, Regt. 27 Apr. 1858, l. 27 Aug. 1858, ante-d. 12 Dec. 1857, 2 cap. 3 Aug. 1865. Attack on the Burda Hills 19 Dec. 1859. res. 28 May 1870. cap. *Antrim Rifle Regt. of Militia* 30 July 1873, *l.c. Antrim Arty. Militia* 11 Oct. 1890, hon. c. 6 Nov. 1900, SOUTH AFRICA 1900-01 *in command*

Antrim and Donegal Arty. Militia, Desp. Lond. Gaz. 4 Sept. 1901, M., C.M.G. 28 Sept. 1901, ret. from Militia 1 Nov. 1901.

476 **Brabazon Henry Pottinger,** son of John (330), nephew of Eldred (308), twin brother of Eldred Thomas (475), father of Eldred Charles (R.A. 4562), Robert Southey (R.A. 4787), b. 18 Sept. 1840. Addis. 1857, res. 21 Oct. 1857, but time allowed to count for pension, 2 l. Army 12 Dec. 1857, Regt. 27 Apr. 1858, l. 27 Aug. 1858, ante-d. 12 Dec. 1857, 2 cap. 14 Sept. 1865, brev.-m. 15 Aug. 1868, cap. 5 July 1872, m. 1 Apr. 1876, brev.-l.c. 11 July 1877, c. Army 11 July 1881, l.c. 31 Dec. 1878, m.g. 31 Dec. 1888, l.g. 5 Apr. 1891. ABYSSINIA 1867–68 with Pioneer Force, D.A.QM.G. Sept. 1867– June 1868, Arogee, Magdala, Desp. Lond. Gaz. 3 June 1868, M., brev.-m., D.A.QM.G. Bombay 1873–75, A.QM.G. 1875–79, D.QM.G. 1879–84, C.R.A. Aden 1885, C.R.A. Northern Division 1885, C.R.A. Bombay District 1887, brgd.-g. comg. Nusseerabad 1887, Sec. to Govt. Bombay Military Dept. 9 June 1887–21 Dec. 1892, [R] 13 Dec. 1889. ret. 13 Dec. 1892.

477 **John Grierson,** b. 24 Aug. 1839. Addis. 1857, res. 21 Oct. 1857, but time allowed to count for pension, 2 l. Army 12 Dec. 1857, Regt. 4 May 1858, l. 27 Aug. 1858, ante-d. 12 Dec. 1857. Transferred to Bombay Staff Corps 10 Feb. 1864. cap. 12 Dec. 1869, m. 12 Dec. 1877, l.c. 12 Dec. 1883, c. Army 12 Dec. 1887, c.'s allowances 12 Dec. 1895, u.s.l. 24 Aug. 1896. Public Works Dept. Jan. 1871–Aug. 1894.

478 **John Henry Lloyd,** son of John (246), b. 12 Jan. 1841, 2 l. 12 Dec. 1857, l. 27 Aug. 1858, ante-d. 12 Dec. 1857, 2 cap. 15 Feb. 1866, cap. 5 July 1872, m. 1 Apr. 1876. Adjt. 2nd Northumberland Arty. Volunteers 15 May 1875–31 Mar. 1876. d. 25 July 1881 at Sheerness.

479 **Alexander Thomas Wallace,** b. 5 Jan. 1839, 2 l. 12 Dec. 1857, l. 27 Aug. 1858, ante-d. 12 Dec. 1857. d. 9 Apr. 1866 at Lough Eske Castle, Donegal.

480 **Arthur Thomas Briscoe Stevenson,** b. 26 Mar. 1841. Addis. 1857, res. 3 Feb. 1857, but time allowed to count for pension, 2 l. 12 Dec. 1857, l. 17 Aug. 1858, ante-d. 12 Dec. 1857, 2 cap. 1 May 1866. d. 5 Dec. 1866 at Cheltenham.

481 **Edmund George Battiscombe,** brother of Robert Charles (401), b. 23 Mar. 1839. Addis. 1857, res. 18 Nov. 1857, but time allowed to count for pension, 2 l. 12 Dec. 1857, l. 27 Aug. 1858, ante-d. 12 Dec. 1857, 2 cap. 26 Apr. 1866, cap. 5 July 1872, m. 1 Sept. 1876, brev.-l.c. 1 Sept. 1883, l.c. 31 Dec. 1883, c. Army 1 Sept. 1887. MUTINY 1858, Central India, Public Works Dept. Bombay 1866–68, adjt. 18th Brgd. R.A. 28 Jan. 1871–13 July 1875, C.R.A. Ferozepore 1885, C.R.A. Northern Division Bombay 1885–86, C.R.A. Presidency Division Calcutta 1886–88, comg. at Barrackpore 1886–89. ret. 11 Apr. 1892.

482 **Thomas Heathcote Ouchterlony,** b. 8 Apr. 1841. Addis. 1856–57 res. but time allowed to count for pension, 2 l. 12 Dec. 1857, l. 27 Aug. 1858, ante-d. 12 Dec. 1857, 2 cap. 1 May 1866, cap. 5 July 1872, m. 25 Jan. 1877. a.d.c. to C.I.C. 1860, intpt. Arty. Head Quarters 1862, a.d.c. to Governor 1863, a.d.c. to G.O. Mhow Division 1862–65, a.d.c. to G.O. Northern Division 1866–67, adjt. 21st Brgd. R.A. 14 Jan. 1867–21 Jan. 1877. ret. 9 Sept. 1880. Hon. l.c. 9 Sept. 1880.

483 Henry Francis Gibb, b. 3 Apr. 1837. 2 l. 12 Dec. 1857, l. 27 Aug. 1858, ante-d. 12 Dec. 1857, 2 cap. 17 Aug. 1866, cap. 5 July 1872. Siege and capture of Dwarka Okamundel and action on Burda Hills Dec. 1859. res. 25 Sept. 1872. d. 18 Mar. 1884.

484 Frederick Boyd Roberts, b. 17 July 1841. Addis. 1857, res. 1 Aug. 1857, but time allowed to count for pension, 2 l. 12 Dec. 1857, l. 27 Aug. 1858, ante-d. 12 Dec. 1857, 2 cap. 24 Nov. 1866, cap. 5 July 1872, m. 27 Feb. 1877. a.d.c. to G.O. comg. Northern Division 1858. d. 17 Feb. 1882 in London.

485 Philip Henry Greig, b. 27 Sept. 1841. 2 l. 12 Dec. 1857, l. 27 Aug. 1858, ante-d. 12 Dec. 1857, 2 cap. 24 Nov. 1866, cap. 5 July 1872, m. 28 Feb. 1877, l.c. 1 Jan. 1884, c. Army 1 Jan. 1888. Station Staff Officer Kirkee 22 Dec. 1875-30 May 1877, AFGHANISTAN 1879-80, defence of Khandahar, battle of 1 Sept., Desp. *Lond. Gaz.* 3 and 31 Dec. 1880, M. 1 cl., C.R.A. Mhow Division 1887, A.A.G. R.A. Bombay 18 Jan. 1889-22 Apr. 1894. rct. 1 June 1894.

486 Willoughby Hammond Sandham, brother of Robert (R.A. 2486), nephew of Charles Freeman (R.A. 1021), great nephew of Robert (R.A. 206), b. 8 Apr. 1839. 2 l. 12 Dec. 1857, l. 27 Aug. 1858, ante-d. 12 Dec. 1857, 2 cap. 6 Dec. 1866, cap. 5 July 1872, m. 24 Aug. 1877, l.c. 1 Jan. 1884, c. Army 1 Jan. 1888. Instructor Gunnery 1st Division Depôt Brgd. 5 Feb. 1872-3 Feb. 1874, adjt. 12th Brgd. R.A. 4 Feb. 1874-30 June 1877, SOUTH AFRICA 1879, Zulu War, M. 1 cl. ret. 12 Feb. 1890. d. 19 Oct. 1899 at Hastings.

487 George Henry Candy, b. 23 May 1839. Addis. 1856-58, 2 l. 11 June 1858, l. 27 Aug. 1858, ante-d. 11 June 1858, 2 cap. 1 Jan. 1867, cap. 5 July 1872, m. 1 Oct. 1877. Station Staff Officer Kirkee 2 Apr. 1870-19 Sept. 1872. ret. 24 Aug. 1881. d. 28 Feb. 1883 at Brighton.

488 Christopher Charles Pemberton, b. 11 Jan. 1840. Addis. 1856-58, 2 l. 11 June 1858, l. 27 Aug. 1858, ante-d. 11 June 1858. Transferred to Bombay Staff Corps 9 Sept. 1864. *c.* 11 *June* 1870, m. 11 *June* 1878, *l.c.* 11 *June* 1884, *c. Army* 11 *June* 1888, *Asst. Supdt. Revenue Survey Khandeish* 14 *Sept.* 1864, *transferred to Berar Revenue Survey* 11 *Mar.* 1865-79, *reverted to Military Duty, command of Depôts of 3rd, 5th, and 19th N.I. Regts.* 9 *Jan.* 1880, *wing commander 24th N.I.* 1881, *acting commdt. 25th Bombay Light Infantry* 9 *Jan.* 1885, BURMAH 1885-87, *M.* 1 *cl., 2nd in command 8th Bombay N.I.* 16 *Sept.* 1887, *commdt. 21st Bombay N.I. Marine Batt.* 1 *Feb.* 1889. *ret.* 11 *June* 1890.

489 Percy Reid Lempriere, son of William Charles (R.A. 1205), b. 13 Nov. 1839. Addis. 1856-58, 2 l. 11 June 1858, l. 27 Aug. 1858, ante-d. 11 June 1858, 2 cap. 25 Mar. 1867. Lieut. of Cadet Company R.M.A. 1865-67. res. 8 June 1868. d. 24 Mar. 1880 at Manchester.

490 Marius Charles Newall, brother of David John Falconer (Bengal 759), Adam Gordon (421), b. 24 Sept. 1839. 2 l. Army 12 June 1858, l. 27 Aug. 1858, ante-d. 12 June 1858, 2 cap. 21 Dec. 1867, cap. 5 July 1872, m. 1 Oct. 1877, l.c. 1 Jan. 1884. Adjt. 1st Administrative Batt. East Riding Yorkshire Arty. Volunteers 29 Jan. 1872-30 Sept. 1877, l.c. comg. South Irish Division for Auxiliary Arty. 1884-85. ret. 4 Nov. 1884. Hon. c. 4 Nov. 1884.

491 Robert Le Mesurier, b. 22 Aug. 1838. Addis. 1856-57, res., but time allowed to count for pension, 2 l. 12 June 1858, l. 27 Aug. 1858, ante-d. 12 June 1858, 2 cap. 22 Jan. 1868. d. 5 June 1871 at Quebec.

492 William Ward, father of Bertram Sumner (R.A.   ), b. 25 Nov. 1838. 2 l. 12 June 1858, l. 27 Aug. 1858, ante-d. 12 June 1858, 2 cap. 9 June 1868, cap. 5 July 1872, m. 17 Apr. 1878, brev.-l.c. 18 Nov. 1882, l.c. 1 Jan. 1884.

Arabia 1865-66, expedition against Foodlee Arabs, EGYPT 1882, Tel-el-Kebir, Desp. *Lond. Gaz.* 2 Nov. 1882, M. 1 cl., 3rd class Medjidie, bronze star, brev. of l.c. ret. 18 June 1885. Hon. c. 18 June 1885.

493 **John Bridges Walker,** b. 12 Mar. 1840. 2 l. 12 June 1858, l. 27 Aug. 1858, ante-d. 12 June 1858, 2 cap. 31 July 1868, cap. 5 July 1872, m. 31 Dec. 1878. Arabia 1865-66, expedition against Foodlee Arabs, Ber Saaed. Adjt. Royal Sussex Artv. Militia 1875-79. ret. 18 Oct. 1882. Hon. l.c. 18 Oct. 1882. *Commdt. Gordon Boys' Home Mar. 1892-Mar. 1901.*

494 **James Graham Edwardes,** b. 17 July 1835. *Royal Marine Light Infantry,* 2 l. 17 *Aug.* 1855, *res.* 29 *Apr.* 1858. 2 l. 12 June 1858, l. 27 Aug. 1858, ante-d. 12 June 1858, 2 cap. 5 Jan. 1869, half pay 8 Jan. 1870. ret. 5 Nov. 1884. Hon. m. 5 Nov. 1884.

495 **Shakespear Campbell Crawford,** b. 1841. 2 l. 12 June 1858, l. 27 Aug. 1858, ante-d. 12 June 1858. d. 3 June 1861 at sea.

496 **Mark Algernon Chaldecott,** b. 8 Jan. 1837. 2 l. 12 June 1858, l. 27 Aug. 1858, ante-d. 12 June 1858, 2 cap. 1 May 1869, cap. 7 July 1872, m. 31 Dec. 1878, l.c. 1 Jan. 1884. d. 29 May 1886 at Dorking.

497 **Henry Stevenson,** b. 8 Sept. 1840. Addis. 1857-58, res. 16 June 1858, but time allowed to count for pension, 2 l. 12 June 1858, l. 27 Aug. 1858, ante-d. 12 June 1858, 2 cap. 14 Sept. 1869. d. 28 July 1870 at Glangwilly, Carmarthenshire.

498 **Cornwall Henry Campbell,** b. 11 Feb. 1840. Addis. 1858, res. 16 June 1858, but time allowed to count for pension, 2 l. 12 June 1858, l. 27 Aug. 1858, ante-d. 12 June 1858, 2 cap. 8 Jan. 1870, cap. 5 July 1872, half pay 23 Mar. 1871, full pay 29 Jan. 1872, m. 31 Dec. 1878, l.c. 18 June 1884. Instructor Gunnery E Brgd. R.H.A. 18 Aug. 1864-24 Dec. 1869, adjt. 11th Brgd. R.A. 12 Feb. 1873-30 June 1877, adjt. R.A. Barrackpore 1 July 1877-23 Nov. 1877. ret. 25 Jan. 1886. Hon. c. 25 Jan. 1886. d. 19 May 1894 at Hastings.

499 **Charles Edward Hanbury,** b. 22 Sept. 1840. Addis. 1858, res. 16 June 1858, but time allowed to count for pension, 2 l. 12 June 1858, l. 27 Aug. 1858, ante-d. 12 June 1858, 2 cap. 28 May 1870. d. 12 May 1872 in the districts near Secunderabad.

500 **Sir Samuel Swinton Jacob,** K.C.I.E., son of William (244), b. 14 Jan. 1841. Addis. 1857-58, l. 10 Dec. 1858. Transferred to Bombay Staff Corps 13 Nov. 1862. *cap.* 10 *Dec.* 1870, *m.* 10 *Dec.* 1878, *l.c.* 10 *Dec.* 1884, *c.* 10 *Dec.* 1888, *c.'s allowances* 10 *Dec.* 1896, *u.s.l.* 14 *Jan.* 1898. *With Bombay Sappers and Miners 1862, Asst. Engineer Public Works Dept. 1862. Arabia 1865-66 Asst. Field Engineer, expedition against Foodlee Arabs. Thanks of Sec. of State for services in connection with water-supply of Aden 1866; thanks of Govt. of India for exertions during famine in Rajpootana 1868-69. Services lent by Govt. of India to the Jaipur State, Rajpootana, as engineer 1867; retained by special request in that appointment until present time. Commended by Govt. of India for valuable services to the Jaipur State in 1872 and 1890. C.I.E. 21 May 1870, 1st Class Supdt. Engineer 1893. Awarded decoration " Palmes Acedemiques" and nominated Officier d'Academie by the French Govt. Feb. 1897. Kaiser-i-Hind gold medal of the 1st Class 9 Nov. 1901. Political officer with H.H. the Maharaja of Jaipur at the Coronation of H.M. King Edward VII. 1902. K.C.I.E. 26 June 1902.*

501 **Francis Ward Major,** b. 12 May 1840. Addis. 1857-58, l. 10 Dec. 1858. Transferred to Bombay Staff Corps 23 Apr. 1865. cap. 10 Dec. 1870, m. 10 Dec. 1878, l.c. 10 Dec. 1884, c. Army 10 Dec. 1888, c.'s allowances 10 Dec. 1896, u.s.l. 12 Aug. 1897. Revenue Survey 1865-79, Military Accounts Dept. 1879-12 Aug. 1892.

502 **Frederick William Mackenzie Spring.** b. 16 Oct. 1841. 'l. Army 11 Dec. 1858, Regt. 14 Feb. 1859, 2 cap. 1 July 1870, cap. 5 July 1872, m. 31 Dec. 1878, l.c. 18 June 1884, c. Army 18 June 1888. Ordce. 29 Oct. 1867-14 Apr. 1884, ABYSSINIA 1867-68, M., Deputy I.G.O. Bengal 15 Apr. 1884-5 Apr. 1886, I.G.O. Bombay 6 Apr. 1886-6 Oct. 1893. ret. 1 Feb. 1894.

503 **Charles Willis Godfrey,** b. 19 June 1840. l. Army 11 June 1858, Regt. 11 Apr. 1859. Transferred to Bombay Staff Corps 13 July 1864. cap. 11 Dec. 1870, m. 11 Dec. 1878, l.c. 11 Dec. 1884, c. Army 11 Dec. 1888, c.'s allowances 11 Dec. 1896, u.s.l. 19 June 1897. Revenue Survey, Asst. Supdt. 1864, Supdt. 1886.

504 **Thomas Henry Trafford,** b. 1839. l. Army 11 Dec. 1858, Regt. 8 May 1859. d. 16 July 1863 at Bombay.

505 **Francis James Mortimer,** b. 9 Dec. 1840. Addis. 1857-58, res. 21 July 1858, but time allowed to count for pension, l. Army 11 Dec. 1858, Regt. 13 May 1859, 2 cap. 29 July 1870, cap. 5 July 1872, m. 31 Dec. 1878, l.c. 4 Nov. 1884, c. Army 4 Nov. 1888, c.'s. allowances 19 Nov. 1897, u.s.l. 9 Dec. 1898. ABYSSINIA 1867-68 with reconnoitring party, Arogee, Magdala, Desp. Lond. Gaz. 16 and 20 June 1868, M., Ordce. 1886, Deputy Director-General of Ordce. in India 10 June 1895-15 Mar. 1896, I.G.O. Madras 15 Mar. 1896-9 Dec. 1898.

506 **Thomas Walker,** father of Edward William May (R.A. 4881), b. 11 Feb. 1841. Addis. 1857-59, l. Army 11 June 1859, Regt. 30 July 1859, 2 cap. 22 Mar. 1871, cap. 5 July 1872, m. 18 June 1879, l.c. 17 Aug. 1885, c. Army 17 Aug. 1889. Station Staff Officer Kirkee 1 Oct. 1864-5 May 1870, adjt. E Brgd. R.H.A. 12 May 1871-26 June 1871, adjt. R.A. Mhow Division 1870-72, a.d.c. to G.O. Mhow Division 1 Feb.-7 May 1872, brgd.-m. Delhi Camp Dec. 1875, Ordce. 1880-88, G.C. 1 Nov. 1888-11 Mar. 1891, I.G.O. Madras 14 Mar. 1891-14 Mar. 1896. ret. 15 Mar. 1896.

507 **George Edward Hancock,** b. 28 Jan. 1841. Addis. 1857-59, l. Army 10 June 1859, Regt. 14 Aug. 1859. Intpt. Arty. Head Quarters Kirkee May-Oct. 1863. Transferred to Bombay Staff Corps 12 Oct. 1863. cap. 10 June 1871, m. 10 June 1879, l.c. 10 June 1885, c. Army 10 June 1889, c.'s allowances 10 June 1897, u.s.l. 28 Jan. 1898. Revenue Survey Guzerat 1863-72, Asst. Political Agent Kattiawar 3 July 1872, Supdt. of Survey Kattiawar 2 Oct. 1878, President of the Rajasthanik Court Kattiawar 13 May 1885, Political Supdt. Kattiawar 6 Jan. 1894-15 Apr. 1896.

508 **Francis Coningsby Hannam Clarke,** C.M.G., b. 4 Feb. 1842. Addis. 1858-59, l. 9 Dec. 1859, 2 cap. 6 June 1871, cap. 5 July 1872, brev.-m. 30 Oct. 1878, m. 27 Sept. 1879, l.c. 17 Aug. 1885, c. Army 17 Aug. 1889. Passed Staff College 1868. D.A.QM.G. Intelligence Branch, Head

Quarters of the Army (employed on Asiatic Boundary Commission) 9 Apr. 1872-8 Apr. 1880, C.M.G. 12 Apr. 1880. Special service South Africa 6 Feb. 1881-18 Sept. 1881, Transvaal campaign as A.QM.G. lines of communication. Professor of Military Administration Staff College 29 Oct. 1881-30 Aug. 1884, Surveyor-General Ceylon 31 Aug. 1884, l.c. and commdt. Ceylon Volunteers 1886. ret. 24 May 1890. d. 27 Aug. 1893 at Hove, Brighton.

509 **Augustus Berkeley Portman,** b. 15 Mar. 1842. Addis. 1858-59, l. 9 Dec. 1859. Transferred to Bombay Staff Corps 18 Apr. 1866. *cap.* 9 Dec. 1871, m. 9 Dec. 1879, l.c. 9 Dec. 1885, c. Army 9 Dec. 1889. *Asst. Supdt. Police* 12 *May* 1868, *Supdt.* 1 *May* 1876. *ret.* 9 *Dec.* 1890.

510 **Theodore Methven Ward,** b. 28 Jan. 1842. Addis. 1858-59, l. Army 9 Dec. 1859, Regt. 10 Jan. 1860. Transferred to Bombay Staff Corps 9 Nov. 1864. *cap.* 9 Dec. 1871, m. 9 Dec. 1879, l.c. 9 Dec. 1885, c. Army 9 Dec. 1889. *Asst. Supdt. Revenue Survey* 26 *Nov.* 1864, *Supdt. Sind Revenue Survey* 13 *June* 1889. *ret.* 9 *Dec.* 1891.

511 **Charles Faulkner Glass,** b. 29 Apr. 1842. Addis. 1859-60, l. 8 June 1860, 2 cap. 13 May 1872, cap. 5 July 1872, m. 27 Sept. 1879. Adjt. 23rd Brgd. Division R.A. Sheerness 3 Apr. 1876-31 Dec. 1877. d. 30 Aug. 1883 at Agra.

512 **Francis James Caldecott,** C.B., b. 29 Apr. 1842. Addis. 1859-60, l. 8 June 1860, 2 cap. 15 May 1872, cap. 5 July 1872, m. 1 Apr. 1880, brev.-l.c. 2 Mar. 1881, l.c. 17 Aug. 1885, c. Army 2 Mar. 1885, m.g. 19 Mar. 1894. ABYSSINIA 1867-68 in the Transport Train, Desp. *Lond. Gaz.* 10 July 1868, M. Ordce. 1872-81, AFGHANISTAN 1879-80, defence of Khandahar, attack on Khairabad and Deh Khoja, battle of 1 Sept. 1880, Desp. *Lond. Gaz.* 3 Dec. 1880, M. 1 cl., brev.-l.c., G.P. 2 Mar. 1881-Nov. 1894. ret. 1 Oct. 1897.

513 **Alan Coulston Gardner,** b. 19 Nov. 1842. Addis. 1859-60, l. 8 June 1860. res. 27 July 1866. Cornet *11th Hussars* 27 *July* 1866, *l.* 15 Dec. 1869, cap. *14th Hussars* 21 *Aug.* 1872, *brev.-m.* 29 *Nov.* 1879. *Adjt. Auxiliary Forces* 24 *Feb.* 1876-31 Oct. 1878, special service South Africa 1 Nov. 1878-11 July 1879, Zulu Campaign 1879-81, battle of Isandhlwana, action of Kambula Hill (wounded), and assault and retreat of Inhlobana Mountain, Desp. " Lond. Gaz." 5, 15, and 21 Mar. and 7 May 1879, M. 1 cl., brev.-m. Transvaal Campaign. a.d.c. extra to Lord-Lieutenant of Ireland 17 Nov. 1880-28 Oct. 1881. ret. as cap. with hon. rank of l.c. 29 Oct. 1881, and became cap. Reserve of Officers, commuted retired pay 23 Mar. 1882.

514 **Frank Lodge,** b. 28 June 1841. Addis. 1859-60, l. 8 June 1860, cap. 1 Aug. 1872, m. 1 Apr. 1880. Adjt. 2nd Division Depôt Brgd. R.A. 1873-74, adjt. Depôt Brgd. R.A. 1874-76, adjt. Scarborough Arty. Militia 20 Sept. 1877-31 Apr. 1880, Deputy-Governor H.M. Prison Wakefield 3 June 1880-30 Apr. 1887. ret. 24 Nov. 1882. Hon. l.c. 24 Nov. 1882. *Deputy-Governor Holloway and Millbank Prison* 1 *May* 1887-30 *Sept.* 1889, *of Parkhurst Convict Prison* 1 *Oct.* 1889-23 *Mar.* 1897, *Governor of Winchester Prison* 28 *Aug.* 1900.

515 **Henry Cariston Seton,** b. 22 Jan. 1842. Addis. 1859-60, l. Army 8 June 1860, Regt. 25 June 1860, cap. 1 Aug. 1872. ABYSSINIA 1867-68, M.,

I

Hydrabad Contingent Arty. 1872-80. d. 11 Sept. 1880 on board *Pekin* passage home.

516   **Samuel George Drury Turner,** brother of Thomas Hawkins (443), b. 27 Nov. 1841. Addis. 1857-60, l. Army 8 June 1860, Regt. 25 Aug. 1860. Transferred to the Bombay Staff Corps 14 Sept. 1866. *cap. 8 June 1872, Asst. Engineer P.W.D. Sept. 1866-Dec. 1871. Placed on half-pay 17 Nov. 1877. ret. 17 Nov. 1883.*

517   **Emmanuel Monteflore,** b. 1 Mar. 1842. Addis. 1859-60, l. Army 8 June 1860, Regt. 19 Dec. 1860, cap. 1 Aug. 1872, m. 12 Sept. 1880. Asst. Inspector of Warlike Stores and Firemaster Barbadoes 11 May 1878-16 May 1879, adjt. Northumberland Arty. Militia 6 Aug. 1879-11 Sept. 1880. ret. 20 June 1881. Hon. l.c. 20 June 1881.

518   **Henry Elliott Yorke,** b. 4 July 1841. Addis. 1859-60, l. Army 8 June 1860, Regt. 18 Feb. 1861. d. 16 July 1864 at Sholapoor.

SUPPLEMENTARY LIST.

In 1809, in consequence of want of officers in the Battalion of Artillery, the Governor and Council transferred officers from the Infantry. Such action was disapproved of by the Court of Directors, and all commissions thus granted in the Artillery were cancelled 20 June 1810.

Officers temporarily Commissioned in Bombay Artillery.

1   H. W. Bond. From European Infantry, lfw. 28 Mar. 1809. Permitted to resign and accept cornetcy in H.M. 17th Light Dragoons.
2   F. Hickes. From 2nd Regt. N.I., lfw. 28 Mar. 1809.
3   F. Ivatts. From 4th Regt. N.I., lfw. 28 Mar. 1809.
4   W. Hammond. From 8th Regt. N.I., lfw. 27 Mar. 1809.
5   G. Sangster. From 9th Regt. N.I., lfw. 27 Mar. 1809.
6   W. D. Robertson. From 4th Regt. N.I., lfw. 27 Mar. 1809.
7   C. Ovans. From 3rd Regt. N.I., lfw. 25 June 1809.
8   David Powell. From European Regt., lfw. 12 Sept. 1809.
9   Holden Dunbabin. lfw. 24 Sept. 1809.
10   Stratford Powell. From 5th N.I., lfw. 24 Nov. 1809.

LISTS OF MEDICAL OFFICERS AND
VETERINARY SURGEONS OF THE
BOMBAY ARMY WHO SERVED WITH
THE BOMBAY ARTILLERY.

PART VII.

LISTS OF MEDICAL OFFICERS AND VETERINARY SURGEONS OF THE BOMBAY ARMY WHO SERVED WITH THE BOMBAY ARTILLERY.

LIST OF MEDICAL OFFICERS OF THE BOMBAY ARMY WHO SERVED WITH THE ARTILLERY.

Dates of Rank are those of posting to the Regiment. War services are those with Artillery only.

1 **Richard Penman,** Surgeon Feb. 1769.
2 **Peter Fraser,** Surgeon Mar. 1771.
3 **Charles Riley,** Surgeon Mar. 1772.
4 **John Blakeman,** Surgeon Mar. 1774.
5 **John Laplain,** Surgeon Oct. 1774.
6 **John Blackwell,** Surgeon June 1775. :
7 **Grant Alexander Clugston,** Surgeon Nov. 1777.
8 **William Durham,** Surgeon May 1778.
9 **Helenus Scott,** Apothecary Jan. 1783, Surgeon 1784. Agent for Gun-powder 1797–98.
10 **William Sandwith,** Surgeon Dec. 1783.
11 **William Lloyd,** Surgeon Nov. 1784.
12 **Joseph Buxton Carver,** Surgeon Nov. 1787.
13 **Ephraim Smith,** Surgeon 20 Aug. 1789.
14 **Walter Anderson,** Surgeon's Mate May 1791.   d. on service 1791.
15 **David Carnegie,** Asst. Surgeon 1792.
16 **John Carmichael,** Surgeon's Mate Apr. 1792.
17 **George Keir,** Surgeon's Mate Dec. 1793.
18 **C. M. Kehn,** Surgeon's Mate Feb. 1794.   d. 6 Oct. 1802 at Bombay.
19 **John Macneelance,** Surgeon Dec. 1795.   Capture of Colombo Dec. 1796. ret. 25 May 1808.
20 **William Boag,** Surgeon's Mate Dec. 1795, Surgeon 30 Oct. 1801.   d. 1 Apr. 1806.
21 **Robert Stewart,** Surgeon 2 Feb. 1796.
22 **Archibald H. Bogle,** Asst. Surgeon 6 Feb. 1799.   MYSORE WAR 1799.
23 **Benjamin Phillips,** Asst. Surgeon 7 Feb. 1799.   MYSORE WAR 1799.
24 **Dougall Christie,** Asst. Surgeon 2 Dec. 1799, Surgeon 4 Sept. 1811. Agent for Gunpowder 1818–21. ret. 1 June 1826. d. 15 Aug. 1837 at Freshwater, Isle of Wight.

25 **William Gourlay,** Asst. Surgeon 5 Dec. **1799.** ret. 17 June **1817.** d. 6
    Jan. **1843.**
26 **Robert Hoyes,** Asst. Surgeon 7 Nov. **1800.** Service in the Red Sea **1801.**
    d. 12 Apr. **1818.**
27 **Peter C. Baird,** Asst. Surgeon 24 Apr. **1801.** d. 5 Nov. **1821** at Bombay.
28 **David White,** M.D., Surgeon 8 Apr. **1806.** d. 6 Jan. **1818** at Bombay.
29 **Sutherland Meek,** M.D., Surgeon 26 Mar. **1807.** d. 12 Feb. **1823** in India.
30 **John Strachan,** Surgeon 28 July **1807.** d. 18 July **1824** at Surat.
31 **Samuel Sproule,** Surgeon 9 Oct. **1808.** d. 16 June **1828** in England.
32 **Alexander Paton,** Asst. Surgeon **1808.** d. 25 June **1829.**
33 **Robert B. Perrin,** Surgeon 9 Feb. **1809.** d. 18 Oct. **1816** at Bombay.
34 **James Dow,** Asst. Surgeon **1809.** d. 13 Apr. **1836.**
35 **John Heatherley,** Asst. Surgeon 9 Jan. **1810.** d. 5 Apr. **1811** on board
    Providence passage home.
36 **John Taylor,** Asst. Surgeon 24 Sept. **1811.** d. 6 Dec. **1821** at Sheras in
    Persia.
37 **David Craw,** Asst. Surgeon 1st Troop on formation **1811.** MAHRATTA
    WAR **1817-19.** Surgeon 2nd Batt. 1 May **1821.** d. 26 Nov. **1839.**
38 **George Skene Keith,** Asst. Surgeon 8 Jan. **1811.** Field service Guzerat
    and Kattywar, on which he died 12 Sept. **1815.**
39 **Francis Sheppee,** Surgeon 25 Nov. **1814.** ret. 1 Mar. **1844.** d. 8 Aug.
    1863 at Lee, Kent.
40 **Andrew Pollock,** Asst. Surgeon 29 May **1816.** d. 21 Mar. **1821** at Kaira.
41 **John Grenfell Moyle,** Asst. Surgeon **1818,** H.B. ret. 3 Jan. **1836.** d.
    3 June **1860.**
42 **Robert Colegate,** Asst. Surgeon 19 Oct. **1818.** d. 26 May **1820.**
43 **William Hall,** Asst. Surgeon 12 Apr. **1820,** 2nd Batt. on formation. d. 15
    Aug. **1822** at Cape of Good Hope.
44 **William Fraser,** Asst. Surgeon 6 Apr. **1820,** H.B. ret. 5 Sept. **1827.** d. 27
    Dec. **1873.**
45 **Sir John McNeill,** G.C.B. (civil), K.L.S., Asst. Surgeon 6 Apr. **1820,** H.B.
    ret. 4 June **1836.** d. 17 May **1883** at Cannes.
46 **Robert Martin,** Surgeon 16 June **1819,** 1st Batt. d. 11 Nov. **1825** at Bhooj.
47 **Archibald Young,** M.D., Surgeon 5 Sept. **1820.** d. **1839.**
48 **Henry Michie,** Surgeon 15 Sept. **1820,** 2nd Batt. d. 10 May **1827** on board
    Fortune passage to England.
49 **James Fortnum,** Asst. Surgeon 29 May **1821,** 1st Batt. ret. 15 Sept. **1834.**
    d. 3 Oct. **1854** at Cheltenham.
50 **James Bird,** F.C.S., Asst. Surgeon 25 Feb. **1822,** 2nd Troop. At capture of
    Kittoor Dec. **1824.** ret. 1 Dec. **1847.** d. **1864** at Fernacre Lodge, Gerrards
    Cross, Bucks.
51 **George Smyttan,** Surgeon 13 Nov. **1821,** 1st Batt. ret. 31 Dec. **1838.** d.
    1863.
52 **William Fell Mercer Cockerill,** Asst. Surgeon 24 Dec. **1822,** 1st Troop,
    Surgeon 3 May **1829,** H.B. d. 24 Dec. **1835** in India.
53 **Robert Liddell,** Surgeon 21 Sept. **1822,** 1st Batt. d. 4 Jan. **1833** in England.
54 **John McMorris,** Asst. Surgeon 14 Oct. **1822,** 2nd Batt. d. 20 Nov. **1843.**
55 **Marten Thomas Kays,** Asst. Surgeon 5 Oct. **1824.** ret. 30 Oct. **1855.** d.
    21 Dec. **1867** in Kensington.
56 **Samuel Love,** Asst. Surgeon 6 Feb. **1824,** 2nd Troop. d. 24 Oct. **1828.**
57 **Alexander John Robertson,** Asst. Surgeon 5 Oct. **1824,** 1st Batt. d. 29
    May **1825** on board *Regalia* passage home.
58 **Richard Thomas Barra,** Asst. Surgeon 12 Jan. **1826,** Surgeon 11 May
    1836, 2nd Batt. ret. 1 Apr. **1839.** d. 23 July **1859.**
59 **Rupert Kirk,** Asst. Surgeon 22 Apr. **1826.** d. 31 May **1852** at Rajkote.

60 **James Brydon**, M.D., Surgeon 9 May 1826, 1st Batt. d. 12 May 1836.

61 **George Henry Davis**, Asst. Surgeon 9 May 1826, Surgeon 2 Dec. 1834. Drowned off Bombay 18 June 1840.

62 **John Doig**, Asst. Surgeon 3 Nov. 1826, H.B., Surgeon 2 Oct. 1848. ret. 17 Apr. 1852. d. 18 Apr. 1871.

63 **James Cunningham**, Asst. Surgeon 30 Nov. 1826, H.B. d. 9 Jan. 1843 at Bombay.

64 **Alexander Gibson**, Asst. Surgeon 28 Feb. 1827, 2nd Troop. ret. 8 May 1860. d. 16 Jan. 1867.

65 **Archibald Arnott**, Asst. Surgeon 2 Jan. 1828, 2nd Troop. d. 6 May 1846 at Kummes.

66 **James Anderson**, Asst. Surgeon 12 Jan. 1831, Surgeon 5 May 1834. Golundauze. ret. 1 May 1839. d. 3 July 1859 at Dalston.

67 **Andrew Montgomery**, Asst. Surgeon 30 Mar. 1831, Surgeon 3 Apr. 1839. ret. 3 Oct. 1849. d. 6 Feb. 1863 at Bath.

68 **Lechmere Hathway**, Surgeon 26 Apr. 1833. ret. 30 Jan. 1839. d. 1 Feb. 1839.

69 **Mark Alexander Raucland**, Asst. Surgeon 11 Apr. 1834, 1st Troop. d. 11 May 1846 at Ahmednuggur.

70 **John Bates·Daly**, Asst. Surgeon 14 Apr. 1834, 3rd Troop. d. 22 June 1834 at Deesa.

71 **Robert Brown**, M.D., Asst. Surgeon 27 July 1834. ret. 1 Oct. 1846. d. 22 Mar. 1878 at Milford, Hants.

72 **William Leggett**, Asst. Surgeon 22 Oct. 1834. d. 16 May 1854 on board *Calcutta.*

73 **Francis Wilmer Watkins**, Asst. Surgeon 28 Mar. 1836, 2nd Troop and 3rd Troop. SIND and AFGHANISTAN 1838-41. d. 2 Apr. 1853 at Bombay.

74 **Andrew Henderson Leith**, Asst. Surgeon 17 Dec. 1838, 1st Troop. SIND and AFGHANISTAN 1840-41, Kujjuck Feb. 1841. ret. 3 Aug. 1867. d. 28 Nov. 1875 at Tonbridge.

75 **William Gray**, Asst. Surgeon 30 Mar. 1839. ret. 20 May 1846. d. 9 July 1848.

76 **William Parsons**, Asst. Surgeon 21 Sept. 1839, 2nd Troop. d. 11 May 1842 at Poona.

77 **John Cramond**, Asst. Surgeon 3 Feb. 1840, 1st Troop. SIND and AFGHANISTAN, afterwards 4th Troop. d. 9 Mar. 1850 on board *John Gray.*

78 **Charles Frederick Collier**, Asst. Surgeon 14 Apr. 1840, 3rd Troop. ret. 11 June 1862. d. 9 Nov. 1866 at Bridport, Devon.

79 **Thomas Robson**, Surgeon 2 Feb. 1841, 2nd Batt. d. 5 Jan. 1847 at Bombay

80 **John James Atkinson**, Asst. Surgeon 8 Mar. 1841, 1st Troop, Surgeon 27 Oct. 1856. ret. 1 July 1857. d. 29 Mar. 1860 at St. Thomas', Devon.

81 **Robert Thomas Cook Baxter**, Asst. Surgeon 15 May 1841, 1st and 4th Troops. SIND and AFGHANISTAN 1840-41. d. 19 May 1843 at Mhow.

82 **Elijah Impey**, Asst. Surgeon 18 Nov. 1841, 3rd Troop. d. 19 Nov. 1868 at Southampton.

83 **Jeffery Amherst Sinclair**, Surgeon 15 Mar. 1842, 1st Batt. ret. 3 Jan. 1852. d. 15 July 1859.

84 **William Loch Cameron**, Asst. Surgeon 21 May 1842, 1st and 4th Troops, Surgeon 27 Oct. 1856, 1st. Batt., Surgeon-Major 23 Mar. 1861, 4th Brgd. R.H.A. d. 24 June 1865 in London.

85 **Robert James Russell**, Asst. Surgeon 30 Dec. 1843, 2nd and 3rd Troops. d. 20 Nov. 1855 at Bombay.

86 **Henry John Carter**, Asst. Surgeon 1843. SIND, Meanee. ret. 31 Mar. 1864. d. 4 May 1895 at Budleigh Salterton.

87 **John Young Smith**, Asst. Surgeon 1845. ret. 21 Feb. 1876. d. 30 Oct. 1887 at Edinburgh.

88   **Francis Manisty**, Asst. Surgeon 23 May 1845, 1st Batt.   ret. 1 Apr. 1864. d. 5 Jan. 1890 at Gresford, Wrexham.

89   **John Turner**, Asst. Surgeon 11 Jan. 1846, 1st and 2nd Troops, Surgeon 9 June 1860, Head Quarters H.B., Surgeon-Major 17 May 1862, 21st Brgd. R.A.   ret. 31 Oct. 1874.   d. 23 Nov. 1889 at Bath.

90   **Joseph Furlonge Shekleton**, A.B., M.D., Asst. Surgeon 29 Jan. 1847, 3rd Troop. PUNJAUB 1848–49, Mooltan, Goojerat, and pursuit of Dost Mahomed, and occupation of Peshawur.   ret. 7 Jan. 1873.

91   **John Frederick Steinhauser**, Asst. Surgeon 1848.   PUNJAUB 1848–49, Mooltan.   d. 29 July 1866 at Berne.

92   **William Barker Taylor**, Asst. Surgeon 1847.   ret. 17 Jan. 1855.   d. 29 Mar. 1864 at Marseilles.

93   **William French Clay**, Asst. Surgeon 1848.   PUNJAUB 1848–49, Mooltan, Goojerat, pursuit of Shere Singh, and occupation of Peshawur.   ret. 12 May 1858.   d. 9 Nov. 1889 at Clapham, the Rev. W. F. Clay, M.A., M.D.

94   **Thomas Mackenzie**, C.B., Surgeon 17 May 1848, 1st Batt.   ret. 13 Feb. 1864.   d. 17 Mar. 1864 at Cheltenham.

95   **Alexander Burn**, M.D., Surgeon 9 Nov. 1849, 2nd Batt.   ret. 7 Oct. 1861. d. 3 Mar. 1877 in Kensington.

96   **John Henry Wilmot**, M.D., Asst. Surgeon 25 Nov. 1850, 2nd, 3rd, and 4th Troops.   PUNJAUB 1848–49, Mooltan, PERSIA 1856–57, MUTINY, Central India.   d. 7 Apr. 1865 at Ahmedabad.

97   **Peter Gray**, Surgeon 19 Apr. 1851, 2nd Batt.   d. 11 Nov. 1852.

98   **George Nayler**, Asst. Surgeon 26 Nov. 1852.   ret. 23 Nov. 1861.   d. 9 Mar. 1876 at Brighton.

99   **Adam Macdougall Rogers**, Asst. Surgeon 3 Dec. 1852.   d. 15 July 1878 at Bombay.

100   **Sir William James Moore**, K.C.I.E., Asst. Surgeon 5 Jan. 1853.   ret. 26 Feb. 1888.   d. 9 Sept. 1896 in London.

101   **Henry James Gane**, Asst. Surgeon 5 May 1853.   ret. 28 Apr. 1875.   d. 27 July 1886 at Barton Regis, Bristol.

102   **John Milford Barnett**, Asst. Surgeon 30 May 1853.   ret. 13 Aug. 1868.

103   **William Boxwell Barrington**, LL.D., Surgeon 6 Sept. 1854.   ret. 24 July 1855.   d. 24 Apr. 1880 at Bexley Heath, Kent.

104   **George Coates Bell**, M.D., Asst. Surgeon 1856.   PERSIA, MUTINY, 4th Troop, Kolapore.   d. 28 Oct. 1883.

105   **John Evan Freeman**, M.D., Asst. Surgeon 21 Feb. 1855.   d. 11 Nov. 1861 at Vingorla.

106   **Frederick Trestrail Bond**, Asst. Surgeon 28 Mar. 1855.   d. 11 Jan. 1862 at Truro.

107   **Horace Day**, Asst. Surgeon 31 Mar. 1855.   ret. 4 Mar. 1883.   d. 16 Jan. 1893 at Los Gatos, California, U.S.A.

108   **Thomas William Ward**, Surgeon 24 Aug. 1855, 2nd Batt.   ret. 20 Oct. 1871.

109   **William Crawford Brown**, M.D., Asst. Surgeon 1 Mar. 1856, 2nd Troop. MUTINY, Kotah, battle of the Bunnass, pursuit of the rebels.   d. 26 Aug. 1863 at Exeter.

110   **William Edward Wood**, Asst. Surgeon 1856.   PERSIA, Mohumra on mortar raft.   ret. 19 Apr. 1869.   d. 1 Mar. 1885 at South Norwood Hill.

111   **Robert Clarke McConnell**, Asst. Surgeon 1856.   With the 3rd Troop PERSIA.   d. 1 Apr. 1871.

112   **William Henry Pigou**, Surgeon 14 Mar. 1857.   d. 10 Sept. 1858 at Poona.

113   **Ebenezer Robert Butler**, M.D., Asst. Surgeon 1857, 4th Company 2nd Batt. MUTINY, attack on mutineers at Aurungabad and pursuit, siege and storm of Dhar (severely wounded), Mundesore, Gooraria, relief of Neemuch, siege and storm of Chandaree, battle of the Betwa, siege and storm of Jhansi, Koonch, Lohari, Muttra and Deopora, Gallowlee, Calpee,

Morar, Kotah-ke-Serai, capture of Gwalior, Jowrah Alipore. Three times mentioned in Desp., *Lond. Gaz.* 11 Mar. 1858. ret. 1 Apr. 1877.

114 **James Vaughan,** Asst. Surgeon 10 June 1857. ret. 14 Mar. 1864. d. 17 Dec. 1884 at Llanwar House, Builth.

115 **Henry Dunn Glasse,** Surgeon 21 Jan. 1858, 2nd Batt. ret. 31 Mar. 1867. d. 1 Apr. 1887 in Guernsey.

116 **John Cruickshank,** M.D., Asst. Surgeon 1857. H.B. Asst. Surgeon 25 May 1859, 2nd and 3rd Troops 4th Brgd. R.H.A. Asst. Surgeon 25 Sept. 1861. ret. 1 Apr. 1857. d. 11 June 1897.

117 **John Lumsdaine,** Asst. Surgeon 4 Feb. 1858. 1st Troop. MUTINY 1857-58, Ratghur, relief of Sangor, forcing of Muddenpore pass, siege, capture, and storm of Jhansi, Betwa, Koonch (wounded), Muttra, Deopore, Gallowlee, Calpee, pursuit to Surceela, advance on Gwalior, final pursuit of enemy, Jowrah Alipore, M. 1 cl., Desp., specially mentioned. ret. 1 May 1883.

118 **John Fortnom Straker,** Asst. Surgeon 1 Apr. 1861, 4th Troop and 4th Brgd. R.H.A. 25 Sept. 1861. d. 31 Jan. 1877 at Kirkee.

119 **Charles William Fettes,** M.D., Asst. Surgeon 1 Nov. 1861, 2nd Troop and 4th Brgd. R.H.A. d. 6 July 1866 at Plymouth.

120 **Peter S. Turnbull,** Asst. Surgeon 11 Mar. 1863, 18th Brgd. R.A. ret. 2 Mar. 1896.

121 **David Simpson,** Asst. Surgeon 13 Mar. 1863, 1st Troop. ret. 1 Jan. 1878.

122 **Abraham Nickson Hojel,** Asst. Surgeon 24 Mar. 1863, 18th Brgd. R.A. ret. 30 Apr. 1891. d. 1 Sept. 1901 at Birchington-on-Sea.

123 **Frederick William Harris,** Surgeon 29 Apr. 1863, 18th Brgd. R.A. ret. 25 Mar. 1873. d. 7 Aug. 1884 at Torquay.

LIST OF VETERINARY SURGEONS OF THE BOMBAY ARMY WHO SERVED WITH THE HORSE BRIGADE.

Dates of Rank are those of posting to the Brigade.

1 **Langdon MacMurdo Rogers,** Vet. Surgeon 2 Dec. 1828. ret. 28 May 1839. d. 17 Feb. 1878 at Bromley, Kent.

2 **Thomas Hilton,** Vet. Surgeon 29 Sept. 1831. d. 13 Sept. 1839 on board *Linton.*

3 **Henry Freake,** Vet. Surgeon 15 Sept. 1840. d. 6 Apr. 1843 at Mauritius.

4 **John Surtees Stockley,** Vet. Surgeon 26 Feb. 1841. Not in Army List 1854.

5 **Frederic McDowall,** Vet. Surgeon 29 Aug. 1846. d. 10 May 1852.

6 **Augustus John Poett,** Vet. Surgeon 8 Nov. 1850. ret. 14 Aug. 1874. d. 6 June 1882 in the Isle of Wight.

7 **Edward Battersbee,** Vet. Surgeon 24 Mar. 1852. ret. 30 May 1857. d. 29 Jan. 1876.

8 **James Herbert Brockencote Hallen,** C.I.E., Vet. Surgeon 1 July 1858. ret. 20 May 1894. d. 1 Aug. 1901 at Stratford-on-Avon.

9 **Francis Friend Smith Constant,** Vet. Surgeon 24 June 1859, 4th Brgd. R.H.A. 17 June 1863. d. 14 June 1889 in India.

10 **William Lamb,** Vet. Surgeon 31 July 1862, 4th Brgd. R.H.A. 9 Apr. 1863. ret. 4 July 1886. d. 6 Oct. 1888 at Coonoor Neilgherries.

LISTS OF RIDING-MASTERS AND QUAR-
TER-MASTERS AND MEN COMMIS-
SIONED FOR DUTY IN DEPARTMENTS.

PART VIII.

LISTS OF RIDING-MASTERS AND QUARTER-MASTERS AND MEN COMMISSIONED FOR DUTY IN DEPARTMENTS.

RIDING-MASTERS.

1 **James Randall.** From R.M. sergt. H.B. 30 March 1834, l. 4 Sept. 1848. d. 30 June 1851 at Poona. Memorial obelisk erected by Officers of Horse Brigade.

2 **James Tant.** From sergt.-m. 1st Light Cavalry, R.M. 1st Light Cavalry 30 Mar. 1834. d. 2 Oct. 1841.

3 **Thomas Heffernan.** From sergt.-m. 1st Troop, R.M. 2nd Light Cavalry 15 Apr. 1850–11 Jan. 1854, l. 4 Apr. 1851. d. 8 Apr. 1862 in England.

4 **Edward Morgan.** From sergt.-m. 4th Troop, R.M. H.B. 30 June 1851, l. 5 May 1859. ret. 14 Oct. 1861. d. 16 June 1871 at Poona.

5 **Michael Toole.** R.M. 1st Light Cavalry 30 Nov. 1859, ensign 24 Nov. 1859, R.M. H.B., afterwards of 4th and E Brgds. R.H.A. 26 Oct. 1861, hon. l. 11 Apr. 1865, hon. cap. 24 Nov. 1871. Qtrmt. Deolalee Depôt 1870, Pension Dept. Poona 1875. d. 5 Sept. 1877 at Poona.

6 **Arthur Steers.** From sergt.-m. 2nd Light Cavalry, R.M. 2nd Light Cavalry 11 Jan. 1854, ensign 24 Nov. 1859, hon. l. 11 Apr. 1865, hon. cap. 11 Apr. 1872, R.M. 18th Brgd. R.A. 10 Sept. 1863. Transferred to Invalid Establishment 18 Oct. 1876. d. 16 Nov. 1891 at Bombay.

QUARTER-MASTERS.

1 **Matthew Robinson.** From Conductor Unattached List, qtrmt. 18th Brgd. R.A. 1 May 1862. Tem. half pay 12 Feb. 1873–30 June 1874, ret. half pay 7 Jan. 1880. Hon. cap. 7 Jan. 1880. Commuted half pay 1 July 1880. d. 22 Aug. 1892 at Lahore.

2 **Harry Parkes.** From Conductor Ordce., qtrmt. 21st Brgd. R.A. 1 May 1862. ret. half pay 4 Aug. 1875. Hon. cap. 4 Aug. 1875. ret. 1 July 1881.

3 **Rowland Hill New.** From sergt.-m. 2nd Troop, qtrmt. 4th Brgd. R.H.A. 1 May 1862, afterwards E and D Brgd. R.H.A. MUTINY 1857–58, Awah. Kotah, battle of the Bunnass, pursuit of Tantia Topee. M. 1 cl. ret. half pay 12 Sept. 1874. *Inspector of Police in St. Kitt's, Leeward Islands, 2 Oct. 1874, until his death there on 6 Aug. 1877.*

4 **Alexander Walker.** From Brgd. qtrmt.-sergt. 21st Brgd. R.A., qtrmt. 2nd Brgd. Scottish Division R.A. 8 Sept. 1875. Hon. cap. 8 Sept. 1875. ret. 27 July 1892.

MEN COMMISSIONED FOR SERVICE IN DEPARTMENTS.

1 **John Bellew.** Ordce. l. 13 Dec. 1842. d. 24 July 1843 at sea.

2 **Thomas Hook.** Ordce. l. 11 Dec. 1843. d. 10 Dec. 1845 at Bombay.

3 **Christopher Kean.** Ordce. l. 12 Oct. 1844. d. 27 Sept. 1855 in London.

4 **Patrick Cowley.** Ordce. l. 4 June 1852, hon. cap. 18 Nov. 1864. MUTINY 1857–58. Pensioned 13 Oct. 1864. d. 8 Jan. 1868 at Agra.

5 **Jeremiah Coleman.** Ordce. l. 1 Jan. 1855, hon. cap. 18 Nov. 1861. Pensioned 25 Nov. 1868. d. 8 Feb. 1869 at Kurrachee.

6 **Charles Parsons.** Ordce. l. 21 Jan. 1855. Pensioned 30 Sept. 1861. d. about 1895.

7 **James Seater.** Ordce. l. 11 June 1858, hon. cap. 29 May 1866. Pensioned 25 Mar. 1859. d. 16 Mar. 1880 at Bombay.

8 **James Frederick Wilkins.** Ordce. l. 23 June 1858, hon. cap. 29 May 1866. Pensioned 1 Apr. 1870. d. 23 Apr. 1885 in England.

9 **Samuel Chetham.** Ordce. l. 13 Dec. 1858, hon. cap. 29 May 1866. Pensioned 17 Mar. 1868. d. 26 Mar. 1872 at Poona.

10 **George McKeon.** Ordce. l. 30 Mar. 1859. Pensioned 27 Aug. 1861. d. 12 Feb. 1901, Europe.

11 **Henry Purcell.** Ordce. l. 20 Sept. 1859. MUTINY, Central India, 1857–58. d. 3 Apr. 1878 at Panchganni.

12 **Thomas Bingham,** father of John (28). Ordce. hon. l. 17 Nov. 1863. d. 21 Dec. 1868 at Neemuch.

13 **Thomas Shore.** Ordce. hon. ensign 16 Nov. 1866. Pensioned 17 Nov. 1869. d. 10 Sept. 1877, Europe.

14 **John Osborne.** Ordce. hon. ensign 16 Nov. 1866.

15 **John Murray.** Adjutant-General's Office, hon. ensign 27 Nov. 1867, hon. l. 6 Aug. 1868, hon. cap. 12 Aug. 1870, hon. m. 19 Dec. 1888. Military Dept. Govt. of India 1882. Pensioned 7 Feb. 1890.

16 **George Patrick Hazelgrove.** Ordce. hon. ensign 7 Nov. 1868, hon. l. 11 Dec. 1868, hon. cap. 18 Feb. 1869. Pensioned 2 May 1877. d. 25 Sept. 1897, Europe.

17 **Daniel Connell.** Ordce. hon. ensign 7 Nov. 1868, hon. l. 7 Nov. 1868, hon. cap. 11 Dec. 1869. Pensioned 18 June 1870. d. 1877 at Poona.

18 **Francis Bunyer.** Ordce. hon. ensign 7 Nov. 1868, hon. l. 18 Feb. 1869, hon. cap. 19 June 1870. AFGHANISTAN 1838–39, Ghuznee, M., PUNJAUB 1849, Mooltan, Goojerat, M. 2 cl., MUTINY, Central India, 1857–58, M. 1 cl. Pensioned 13 Nov. 1870. d. 6 June 1882 at Poona.

19 **Patrick Walsh.** Ordce. hon. ensign 26 Nov. 1868, hon. l. 1 Apr. 1870, hon. cap. 2 May 1877. Pensioned 12 Dec. 1878. d. 7 Nov. 1893, Europe.

20 **John Blair.** Ordce. hon. ensign 18 Feb. 1869, hon. l. 11 Sept. 1874. d. 4 July 1876 at Ahmedabad.

21 **George Judd.** Ordce. hon. ensign 1 Apr. 1870, hon. l. 17 Dec. 1874. MUTINY 1858, Central India, M. 1 cl. d. 28 Nov. 1877 at Neemuch.

22 **David Sadler.** Ordce. hon. ensign 19 June 1870. Pensioned 15 June 1872. d. 6 July 1873 at Bombay.

23 **David Vint.** Ordce. hon. ensign 19 June 1870, hon. l. 28 Apr. 1875, hon. cap. 22 Nov. 1878. ABYSSINIA 1867–68, M. d. 18 June 1880 at Bombay.

24 **T. Glover.** Ordce. hon. ensign 27 Nov. 1867, hon. l. 26 Oct. 1874. d. 1 Jan. 1897 at Bombay.

25 **Henry Sutton.** Ordce. hon. l. 28 Apr. 1875. Pensioned 12 Dec. 1877.

26 **Henry Doyle Ford.** Ordce. hon. l. 25 June 1876. d. 8 Jan. 1878 at Kurrachee.

27 **Charles McMillan.** Ordce. hon. l. 2 May 1877, hon. cap. 19 Dec. 1878. Pensioned 16 Sept. 1882, and hon. m. same date. d. 30 Nov. 1892 at Poona.

28 **John Bingham,** son of Thomas (12). Ordce. hon. l. 29 Nov. 1877, hon. cap. 16 Sept. 1882. Pensioned 6 Dec. 1887, and hon. m. same date. d. 6 May 1895 at Mazagon, Bombay.

29 **Martin Corkery.** Ordce. hon. 1. 12 Dec. 1877. Pensioned 14 May 1884.

30 **Edward McKenzie.** Ordce. hon. 1. 12 Dec. 1877. Pensioned 16 Sept. 1882. d. 1883.

31 **William McDonald.** Ordce. hon. 1. 9 Jan. 1878. Pensioned 1 May 1881. d. 16 Sept. 1897 at Bombay.

32 **Thomas Courtenay.** Ordce. hon. 1. 29 Dec. 1879. Pensioned 29 Jan. 1883. d. 14 Feb. 1894, Europe.

33 **Giles Penstone.** Ordce. hon. 1. 1 May 1881, hon. cap. 1 May 1890. Pensioned 8 Oct. 1890.

34 **Maurice Hanley.** Ordce. hon. 1. 16 Sept. 1882, hon. cap. 8 Oct. 1890. ABYSSINIA 1867–68, M. Pensioned 20 Jan. 1895.

35 **James Hamilton.** Ordce. hon. 1. 16 Sept. 1882. Pensioned 26 July 1888.

36 **Charles Driver Wise.** Adjutant-General's Office, hon. 1. 10 Apr. 1885, hon. cap. 15 Sept. 1888. Pensioned 7 Dec. 1890. d. 27 July 1901 at Bombay.

37 **John Merriman.** Ordce. hon. 1. 31 Apr. 1888. Pensioned 28 Aug. 1889.

INDEX TO NAMES IN LISTS.

(tem.) *Supplementary List*, p. 114. (*med.*) *Medical.* (*vet.*) *Veterinary.* (*dep.*) *Departmental Officers.* R.M., *Riding-Masters.* Q.M., *Quarter-Masters.*

K

THE END.